COMPENSATION MECHANISMS FOR JOB RISKS

COMPENSATION MECHANISMS FOR JOB RISKS

WAGES, WORKERS' COMPENSATION, AND PRODUCT LIABILITY

Michael J. Moore and W. Kip Viscusi

PRINCETON UNIVERSITY PRESS   PRINCETON, NEW JERSEY

Library of Congress Cataloging-in-Publication Data

Moore, Michael J., 1953–
Compensation mechanisms for job risks :
wages, workers' compensation, and product liability /
Michael J. Moore and W. Kip Viscusi.
p.   cm.
Includes bibliographical references (p.)
ISBN 0-691-04247-0
1. Workers' compensation—United States.   2. Risk management—
United States.   3. Employers' liability—United States.
4. Products liability—United States.
I. Viscusi, W. Kip.   II. Title.
HD7103.65.U6M66   1990
331.2'1—dc20   89-28882

To Marian and Cate

Contents

List of Figures

List of Tables _____

Preface

THIS WORK integrates much of our recent research on labor market risks. By bringing together our past work and adding new results, we show the diverse nature of the labor market response to job risks and, in particular, the important role that is played by compensation mechanisms for these risks.

Our work cuts across a variety of areas, which hitherto have been of professional interest to fairly distinct groups. Thus, there is some but not complete overlap among the set of individuals concerned with the themes of this volume—wage-risk tradeoffs, workers' compensation effects on wages and risks, the role of unions, and the role of product liability suits for job-related injuries. By bringing together work that touches on these diverse topics, we hope to foster additional interaction among researchers in these areas, since the functions and responsibilities of these various mechanisms overlap.

The structure of the book provides a comprehensive and systematic treatment of these issues and enables the reader to isolate particular segments of the work that are of particular interest. Chapter 1 provides a nontechnical summary of the major conclusions of the book. Chapter 2 reviews the previous research literature on topics covered in the book. In addition, we relate our findings to this literature in that chapter.

The first chapters presenting new research results—Chapters 3 and 4—focus on the implications that can be drawn from the wage offset that workers accept in return for higher levels of workers' compensation benefits. Chapters 5 and 6 focus on a different tradeoff—that between wages and job risks. In those chapters we draw implications with respect to such issues as the labor market value of life and the choice of discount rate for long-term health risks. Chapter 7, which deals with the role of worker quitting, investigates the implications of worker learning for the results in Chapters 3 through 6. In particular, how do the tradeoff rates differ in situations in which workers have learned about adverse job information and are likely to quit? Similarly, the material in Chapter 8 on the role of unions examines how a different labor market institution—unions—influences both the wage–workers' compensation tradeoff discussed in Chapters 3 and 4 and the wage-risk tradeoff discussed in Chapters 5 and 6.

In Chapter 9 we turn our attention away from wage tradeoff issues to explore the implications of the compensation package for workplace

safety. In particular, how do higher levels of workers' compensation benefits affect fatality risks in the workplace? This issue relates to the earlier results in that the risk reductions created by these incentive effects also influence the wage compensation that workers receive. Finally, Chapter 10 addresses an increasingly important class of issues—the role of product liability suits in addressing on-the-job injuries. Although workers' compensation systems were created as a substitute for tort liability remedies, in recent years there has been a rash of tort liabilty suits for job-related injuries, with the result that these systems in effect operate in parallel. Chapter 10 explores the extent and nature of these interactions, using a large data set on product liability claims. The final chapter in the book, Chapter 11, offers concluding perspectives on the work and is also quite general in terms of its orientation.

Portions of this manuscript have appeared in abridged and somewhat different form elsewhere. We would like to thank the publishers of the following journals for permission to draw upon this work: *Review of Economics and Statistics, Journal of Policy Analysis and Management, Economic Inquiry, Journal of Law, Economics, and Organization,* and the *Rand Journal of Economics.*

We would also like to single out two individuals who have been most instrumental in making this manuscript a reality. At Princeton University Press, Jack Repcheck expedited the preparation and production of our manuscript so that a volume that pertained to a variety of current policy debates could be published before these debates were resolved. At Duke University, our efforts to turn this manuscript into a reality depended largely on the efforts of Ann Stringer, who did a superb job in both typing and supervising the production of the draft manuscript.

During the course of our research, a number of individuals provided helpful comments and suggestions. Our tally of these people produced a list of seventeen individuals and participants and seventeen university seminars and conferences where we presented various parts of the manuscript. Rather than provide what comes close to a complete roster of researchers in the field, we would like to offer our general thanks to the many people whose suggestions improved this work. We would, however, also like to extend our thanks to John Burton, Alan Krueger, John Ruser, and Paul Weiler, who provided detailed comments on the manuscript, and to Gary Zarkin, who provided helpful comments on many of the empirical analyses.

Abbreviations and Symbols _____

A	Expected court award
a	Insurance loading factor
b	Weekly workers' compensation benefits
c	Benefit ceiling
	or
	Cost
e	Worker reaction
G	Worker's expected utility
LC	Litigation costs
p	Injury/fatality rate
R	Weekly wage replacement rate
RL	Worker's remaining lifetime
s	Safety
SL	Spouse's remaining lifetime
t	Marginal tax rate
TP	Total workers' compensation premiums
U	Union status dummy variable
tt	Error in expectation
V	Expected lifetime utility
	or
	Expected payoff from going to court
v	Value of output
w	Hourly or weekly wage
Z	Expected lifetime utility of marginal worker at end of period 1
	or
	Vector of variables causing variation in benefit max.
z	Worker's marginal product
α	Coefficient vector for control variables in death risk equations
β	Coefficient vector for control variables in wage equations
β_q	Coeffecent vector for control variables in quit equations
β_u	Coefficient on union status in wage equation
γ_u	Coefficient on union status–death risk interaction in wage equation
γ_w	Coefficient on risk variable in wage equations
δ_b	Coefficient on benefit variables in risk equations
δ_{bs}	Coefficient on benefit–firm size interaction variables in risk equations
δ_{bb}	Coefficient on squared benefit variables in risk equations

δ_q Coefficient on workers' compensation variable in quit equations

δ_u Coefficient on union status–weighted weekly benefit interaction
        in wage equation

δ_w Coefficient on workers' compensation variable in wage equations

ϕ_q Coefficient on wage variable in quit equations

γ_q Coefficient on risk variable in quit equations

COMPENSATION MECHANISMS FOR JOB RISKS

One

Overview

EACH WEEK, 125 American workers are killed by on-the-job accidents. Although this performance record represents an improvement over earlier years, society's aspirations with respect to job safety have risen during this period as well, as increased wealth has created an increased demand for safety and a willingness to support government efforts to foster improvements in safety.

Discussions of such modes of intervention generally follow two themes. First, while many people feel that health and safety outcomes result from a random and capricious process, over the past decade, economists have established the importance of market responses to job risks, in terms of both compensating wage differentials and turnover responses. In this book we extend the economic analysis of these market responses. In particular, we present new evidence on both the wage and the quit effects of job risks, and we explore other aspects of the risk compensation package. Most notable is our emphasis on the role of workers' compensation insurance as it relates to the mix of the components of compensation for job risks.

Second, most safety policy discussions focus on direct intervention options. The Occupational Safety and Health Administration (OSHA) has been regulating health and safety conditions in the workplace for almost two decades. In addition, for most of this century, the workers' compensation system has provided income replacement for injured workers and their surviving families. Thus, direct regulations are the policy remedy for risk levels that are too high, and a social insurance effort provides the ex post remedy for any risks that remain.

There is a general sentiment that neither of these efforts has fulfilled its original promise. Policies of the Occupational Safety and Health Administration are generally viewed as ineffective, having but a small impact on workplace safety. Workers' compensation is viewed more favorably, though many claim that the benefit levels provided are inadequate from the standpoint of income replacement.

Our analysis suggests that matters cannot be isolated in as simple a fashion as this. For example, one cannot view workers' compensation as simply a social insurance effort. Viewed only as social insurance, the funding support of the program represents a lump sum cost to firms, which must then bear the burden of this effort with no corresponding safety incentives created for the firms. The workers' compensation system is not, however, a broadly based social insurance scheme. Rather, it constitutes an insurance program directed quite specifically at reducing the costs to workers of undesirable workplace characteristics. Since these characteristics vary across firms, hazardous firms will reap greater benefits from these efforts, because their workers are more likely to receive benefits. These greater benefits to workers in turn generate lower wage costs for more risky firms, since workers willingly accept a lower base wage in return for greater workers' compensation benefits. Similarly, to the extent that the funding mechanism for workers' compensation is linked to the risk performance of the firm, safety incentive effects lead firms to provide greater levels of safety, thereby reducing their premium levels. These safety incentives may be more effective than OSHA's direct regulations in terms of promoting safety, and the substantial levels of insurance provided make workers' compensation benefits an important compensation package component.

This book emphasizes the exploration of interactions such as these, and the refining of estimates of previously analyzed key relationships that constitute the compensation mechanism. In some cases, we raise new classes of issues. No previous study attempts to address through a formal test whether the level of social insurance provided by workers' compensation is optimal. Similarly, no previous empirical work analyzes the overlap between workers' compensation and the tort liability system. This latter omission is particularly serious, given the emerging product liability crisis of the 1980s.

In Chapter 2 we establish the research context for our work. We begin by summarizing the major details of the literature that address several of the key relationships that we examine. These relationships include the link between job risks and wages, the effect of workers' compensation benefits on safety, and the effect of workers' compensation benefits on wage levels. We then provide a capsule overview of how the structure of our study and the nature of the results that we report later in this volume differ from those in the literature. Chapter 2 does not set out to summarize the entire book. It does, however, provide a survey of the earlier work that has been done in the field and an indication of how our results relate to that work.

Our analysis begins in Chapter 3 by analyzing the relationship between wages and workers' compensation. The conceptual model that we develop relates workers' compensation and wages in a manner similar to the relationship between job risks and wages. Under the classic compensating differential model, workers demand wage premiums for jobs that pose extra risk. Insurance benefits for hazardous jobs, on the other hand, constitute a positive job attribute. In return for workers' compensation benefits for the risks they face, workers will be willing to work on risky jobs for a lower wage. We expect to observe a negative compensating differential for workers' compensation benefits, just as we expect a positive compensating differential for job safety. These differentials are related even further since the wage offset workers are willing to accept in return for more generous workers' compensation benefits is an increasing function of the risk.

The most novel insight produced by this model is that we develop an empirical procedure that makes it possible to test for the adequacy of workers' compensation benefits. Whereas the earlier literature both on workers' compensation and more generally on social insurance raised the benefit adequacy issue, until now there has been no available test to ascertain the validity of the claims of inadequacy. We use as our reference point for the appropriate benefit level the efficient level of benefits that workers would select either under conditions of actuarially fair insurance or under conditions that reflect current rates of insurance loading. We then develop an empirical test of benefit optimality based on observed wage responses to workers' compensation.

The results presented in Chapter 3 from 1977 survey data indicate that at that time benefit levels were underprovided. This result corroborates the general consensus in the field, including that of the National Commission on State Workers' Compensation Laws. In particular, the wage offsets that workers willingly accept, as revealed by the data, greatly exceed the actuarial value of the benefits.

The wage equation estimates also provide estimates of the implicit value that workers place on on-the-job injuries. For the lost workday injuries considered in Chapter 3, workers' wage-risk tradeoffs imply valuations per expected injury in the range of $30,000 to $40,000. The more distinctive aspect of these results is that we are able to break down this valuation into the valuation of health loss and the valuation of income loss, thus providing the first empirical estimates of the costs of pain and suffering and nonwork disability in the literature. The valuation of injuries consists in large part of the nonmonetary losses, as the pain and suffering component ranges from $17,000 to $26,000 per injury.

In Chapter 4 we present an update of the 1977 results in an attempt to capture the influence of the dramatic increases in workers' compensation benefit levels in the late 1970s and in the early 1980s. Although the presumed inadequacy of benefits in the early 1970s was a major factor in an expansion in benefit amounts, there has been no examination in the literature of whether the subsequent benefit increases were inadequate or excessive, judged from the standpoint of optimal social insurance. The results that we present in Chapter 4 indicate that the change in the structure of workers' compensation benefits closed the benefit inadequacy gap. By 1982, the wage offsets that a worker accepted corresponded closely with what one would expect if the benefit levels were adequate.

These substantial wage offsets suggest additional implications as well. As workers' compensation premium levels passed the $20 billion per year mark, observers viewed this escalation in employer costs with alarm. Our analysis suggests, however, that the premium level is not an appropriate measure of the true cost of workers' compensation to the employer. In assessing the net cost of benefits to the firm, one must include the wage offset resulting from the benefits. In doing so, we find that the workers' compensation system more than pays for itself, on average.

In Chapter 5 we shift our focus from nonfatal injuries to fatal job accidents. Much of the interest in the compensating differential literature derives from its use in policy debates on the value of life. In particular, what do individuals' risk–dollar tradeoffs with respect to risks of death tell us about the value of risk reduction? These statistics do not yield the value of a certain death, but they do tell us something more generally useful, which is how individuals react to small probabilities of death in terms of their willingness to bear the risk or their willingness to pay for reduction in those risks.

Value of life numbers are used throughout the federal government to provide a yardstick for the cost-effectiveness of government policies. To assess the stringency of risk regulations, it is often instructive to compare the cost per life saved with the value that the beneficiaries of these programs implicitly place on the lives saved through these governmental efforts. Since available survey data on the U.S. labor market are so extensive, most analysts focus on estimates of the wage-risk tradeoff as a source of these implicit valuations.

The death risk data previously utilized in such studies constitute the weak link in the valuation process. Until recently, death risk data series based on spotty fatality reports have been extrapolated to obtain national fatality risk projections. Because occupational fatalities are not a particularly frequent event, this procedure is fraught with error.

In 1987, the National Institute of Occupational Safety and Health (NIOSH) released a new set of fatality risk data based on a census of all occupational fatalities that occurred during 1980–1984. The results in Chapter 5 provide new estimates of the value of life based on these data and then compare the estimates with those obtained from a more traditional data source, the U.S. Bureau of Labor Statistics data.

We generate quite striking results. The shift to the new data set roughly doubles the estimated value of life, from a figure in the $3 million range to one in the $5–$6 million range. The comparison of the two data sets suggests that the main reason for the increase stems from greater measurement error in the Bureau of Labor Statistics data.

Since individual lifetimes are finite, risk reduction policies do not save lives permanently. Rather, they extend them. This distinction is of substantial consequence from a policy standpoint, where often the choices among policies involve risk reductions for people in different age groups. One expects the value per expected life saved to increase with the expected longevity of the individual, but there has never been a concerted attempt to make such distinctions on an empirical basis.

From a conceptual standpoint, a closely related issue concerns the rate of discount that individuals use when valuing deferred risks of death. If one's life expectancy is extended by five years, then the fifth year of the additional life expectancy may well be valued differently than are the more immediate years. If markets were perfect, then we could use capital market rates as an index of individual rates of time preference with respect to long-term health risks. However, because of potential financial market imperfections and, in particular, because of the inability to trade health resources across time, many observers question whether rates of time preference for health coincide with financial rates of interest. At one extreme, some observers suggest that individuals may be myopic with respect to long-term risks so that they act as if they have high implicit rates of interest when making personal safety decisions, such as whether to wear a seat belt. On the other hand, governmental agencies are reluctant to discount health benefits at all because doing so decreases the attractiveness of many of their health risk reduction efforts. Some agencies urge that a zero discount rate be used.

The findings in Chapter 6 address each of these concerns. First, the estimated value per life year extended equals $175,000. The estimated rates of time preference with respect to these death risks range between 10 and 12 percent, which is consistent with financial market interest rates at the time of the employment survey. Thus, evidence does not indicate that rates of time preference with respect to deferred health risks diverge substantially from rates of time preference with respect to deferred dollar amounts.

The empirical results in Chapters 3 through 6 represent average estimates across an employment population. Attitudes toward risk differ across individuals in the population, however, suggesting important differences in the way in which the compensation mechanism works across different components of the labor force. Compensating differentials successful in attracting the worker to a job initially may not prove sufficient to retain the worker if he or she acquires very adverse risk information while working on the job. In these situations, learning about job risks induces worker quitting.

Although the job hazard–quit relationship is well established, a variant of this relationship is also of interest. Workers on the quit–no quit margin will tend to have a higher perceived risk of an on-the-job accident or death than will workers overall at a particular firm. Those workers on the quit margin consequently should place a higher value on workers' compensation benefits than do members of the work force in general. By analyzing the wage–workers' compensation tradeoffs implied by a conventional wage equation as well as the wage–workers' compensation tradeoffs implied by workers' quit decisions, we can establish the different rates of tradeoff for each segment of the work force.

The results that we generate are consistent with theoretical predictions. Workers' compensation benefits reduce worker turnover significantly, a reduction in employment costs that should be taken into account when assessing the performance of this social insurance scheme. Furthermore, the results provide a new and more refined test of the role of worker learning and how it influences worker responses to the structure of the compensation package.

Labor unions represent another important institutional influence on the structure of compensation. Indeed, the high level of job accidents experienced earlier in this century provided the impetus for the initial unionization of many American workplaces. From a conceptual standpoint, labor unions provide the advantage to their workers of representing the preferences of the "inframarginal" workers, rather than those of new hires and the "marginal workers"—workers on the quit–no quit margin. Workers with substantial seniority rights and on-the-job experience are of less concern to the employer, because of these workers' limited mobility. In contrast, wages and job conditions must be made attractive to retain the marginal workers—new hires and those on the verge of quitting. Labor market evidence indicates that unions place a greater emphasis on the preferences of inframarginal workers than does the market, which leads to higher levels of fringe benefits and lower levels of job risks for union workers relative to nonunion workers.

The results in Chapter 8 corroborate the job risk–union influence as unions raise the premium that workers receive for the job risks that they face. These premiums in turn induce greater incentives for safety. In addition, in this chapter we present new results that relate the influence of unions to the wage–workers' compensation benefit tradeoff as well. Our results indicate that unions alter this tradeoff in a manner favorable to workers by reducing the wage offset that ordinarily occurs in response to higher workers' compensation benefits. Thus, in terms of compensation for job risks, unions have a twofold effect in that they raise the wage premiums workers receive for risk and they reduce the wage offset that workers experience in response to higher workers' compensation benefit levels. The net effect of this influence is that workers' compensation is not a self-financing proposition in unionized firms.

Although workers' compensation is designed primarily as a social insurance effort to provide income replacement for injured workers and their surviving families, such social insurance efforts create incentive effects as well. The main source of these incentive effects from the standpoint of the firm's provision of safety is the funding mechanism for the program. In particular, the experience-rating procedure that links workers' compensation premiums to higher risk levels at the firm provides strong incentives for the firm to reduce these premium amounts by improving workplace safety.

Past attempts to estimate this safety effect have largely been unsuccessful because the risk data used for such assessments measured risks for all injuries. Use of the new death risk data developed by the National Institute of Occupational Safety and Health enables us to focus on safety effects only, since moral hazard and reporting problems are minimized in the case of fatalities.

Chapter 9 reports dramatic effects. Workers' compensation is not a minor adjunct to the safety incentive process, but, rather, a driving force in reducing fatalities in the workplace. Our results indicate that in the absence of workers' compensation, fatality risks in American industries could rise by over 40 percent. By almost any standard, this considerable impact suggests that the incentives created by this program save the lives of almost 2,000 workers per year. With a value of life estimate of $5–$6 million per expected life saved, the value of the lives saved by this program accounts for almost half of the total premium cost to employers.

The effect of workers' compensation in reducing fatalities suggests the injury tax approach to promoting safety as an attractive policy alternative to pursue in lieu of direct social regulation. Based upon studies of past direct regulation efforts by the Occupational Safety and Health Administration, the impact of direct workplace controls appears far more modest than that of the safety incentive effects achieved through the workers' compensation system.

The risk reduction effects of workers' compensation imply further ramifications in terms of the compensation package. The compensating differential model indicates that as the workplace is made safer, workers will be willing to accept a lower wage. Chapter 9 explores these indirect compensation effects.

Perhaps the most important safety policy development in recent years has been the emergence of the tort liability system as a remedy for workers injured on the job. The workers' compensation system, established by the states in part to eliminate the litigation costs associated with handling accident claims, remains the exclusive remedy of workers against their employers in most states. Despite this, the courts have of late become increasingly active in dealing with job-related claims.

Two types of claims are typical. First, although the worker cannot generally sue his or her employer, he or she can sue a third party that produced equipment or provided services at the workplace that led to the accident. For example, a worker whose forklift turned over can sue the forklift manufacturer as well as seeking a recovery through the workers' compensation system. The wave of asbestos-related lawsuits fits this general pattern. Furthermore, the workers' compensation carrier can seek subrogation for the value of claims that it pays off. After a worker has obtained benefits from the workers' compensation carrier, the employer or the insurer can seek reimbursement for these benefits from a producer of products used in the workplace that were responsible for the injury.

Chapter 10 provides the first analysis of these linkages between workers' compensation and product liability, using a sample of almost 1,500 job-related product liability claims. The overlaps are quite substantial, as a variety of legal doctrines define the relationships that exist between these two programs, as well as the context in which such suits can arise. The results are generally consistent with rational economic models of the litigation process. Decisions to drop a claim or settle a claim and the settlement amount for the claims are governed by key variables in the expected manner. For example, claims involving large financial losses are likely to be settled for a larger amount, as are claims with characteristics that give the claim a higher probability of winning in court.

A noteworthy feature of the job-related claims is that they involve much larger stakes than do the typical liability claim, as the payments received for the injuries average over three times more than for nonjob claims. Job-related claims are also more likely to involve fatalities or serious injuries. The mix of such claims no doubt reflects the greater incentive for workers to rely on the workers' compensation remedy for small claims, rather than on tort liability remedies, which offer a lower prospect of a favorable payoff. Workers view product liability remedies as providing a potential source of compensation for large loss claims.

As the overview of these chapters indicates, complex and extensive linkages exist among the various institutional mechanisms involved in determining compensation for job risks. In Chapter 11 we offer concluding observations regarding the importance of these linkages in understanding the market for potentially hazardous jobs.

Two

The Research Context of the Analysis

INTEREST in the labor market effects of adverse working conditions dates from the beginnings of modern economics. Adam Smith ([1776] 1937), in the famous passage from Book 10 of *The Wealth of Nations*, was the first to note that wages must adjust to differences in the conditions of work.[1] More recently, labor economists have sought to verify this proposition in a variety of contexts. The standard approach, which involves the regression of some measure of compensation on a measure of the nonpecuniary characteristics associated with the worker's job, generally provides support for the classic model of compensating wage differentials for job hazards. In particular, if one controls properly for other aspects of the worker and the job, then the wages paid to workers increase with the probabilities of on-the-job fatalities. The evidence for nonfatal injuries is less clear.

Although this compensating differential model is fundamental in its character, it does not exhaust the range of market responses. Risk compensation includes not only higher ex ante wage compensation but also greater ex post compensation. The same type of reasoning that leads one to expect a positive wage increment for job risks predicts a negative wage offset for workers' compensation benefits.

A third component of the labor supply response pertains to changes in workers' risk perceptions over time. Sufficiently adverse information acquired by workers about their jobs will induce the workers to quit. This dynamic aspect of workers' labor supply implies a number of important interrelationships among the various compensation components. Many of the empirical results we present provide new evidence on the character of these relationships.

A fourth empirical issue found in the literature concerns the supply of safety by firms. Changes in the structure of workers' compensation induce important changes in the financial incentives for safety. The importance of the funding mechanism in promoting safety is of substantial policy interest, since one could structure an injury tax approach to the promotion of workplace safety.

Finally, the rapid emergence of product liability remedies as both a supplement and an alternative to workers' compensation requires consideration of the interrelationship between these compensation mechanisms. This issue has never been considered previously, but it cannot be ignored in the wake of the liability crisis of the 1980s.

The Role of Markets

Wage-Risk Tradeoffs

The fundamental compensation mechanism in implicit markets for job risks is the compensating risk differential, whereby workers receive higher wages for exposure to adverse working conditions. In efficiently functioning labor markets, workers will leave jobs in which the risks are too great unless they are rewarded sufficiently for remaining. Similarly, firms will pay for the exposure only if doing so is more profitable than eliminating the risk.

Wage-risk differentials, if they are found to exist, provide two useful pieces of information for policy purposes. First, the existence of such differentials satisfies a necessary condition for market efficiency, and their magnitude indicates the strength of market incentives for the allocation of risk. Second, wage-risk differentials provide the basis for valuing risks to health and safety in cost-benefit analyses of policies directed toward saving and extending lives.

Recent interest in estimates of the wage–job risk tradeoff dates from the paper by Thaler and Rosen (1976), who analyzed the response of wages to fatality risks, as measured by the Society of Actuaries data on occupational fatalities. Perhaps the most notable feature of the Thaler and Rosen study from a policy perspective was its focus on the labor market as a source of information on the implicit valuation of risks to life. Value of life issues have become major topics of policy debate in recent years, as both regulatory agencies and the courts have struggled with the question of valuing lives saved or lost and the costs of pain and suffering.

Table 2.1 summarizes the results of the major wage–death risk tradeoff studies in the literature. The study by Viscusi (1979) remains the most comprehensive treatment of the labor market implications of employment hazards. The principal findings of this research—that rational worker behavior in the form of learning about health and safety risks leads to both compensating wage differentials and self-sorting among jobs according to risk preferences—indicate that market mechanisms play a fundamental role in determining both the allocation of workers to jobs and their compensation in those jobs.

The implicit valuations that workers place on their health and safety were also shown by Viscusi to be substantial. These estimates of the value of life were larger than the earlier Thaler and Rosen estimates. This result, which appears to reflect the lower risk levels in the data used by Viscusi, yields two important implications for safety policy. First, workers exhibit considerable heterogeneity in their implicit valuations of life, with workers less concerned with risks exhibiting lower

TABLE 2.1
Summary of Selected Wage-Fatality Risk Tradeoff Studies

Author(s)	Sample	Risk Variable	Mean Risk	Implicit Value of Life (millions of dollars)[a]
Thaler and Rosen (1976)	Survey of Economic Opportunity	Society of Actuaries	0.001	$0.7
Smith (1976)	Current Population Survey (CPS)	Bureau of Labor Statistics (BLS)	0.0001	3.9
Viscusi (1979a)	Survey of Working Conditions	BLS	0.0001	3.5
Brown (1980)	National Longitudinal Survey of Young Men (NLSYM)	Society of Actuaries	0.002	1.3
Olson (1981)	CPS	BLS	0.0001	4.4
Viscusi (1981)	Panel Study of Income Dynamics (PSID)	BLS	0.0001	5.5
Arnould and Nichols (1983)	U.S. Census	Society of Actuaries	0.001	0.8
Dillingham (1985)	Quality of Employment Survey (QES)	Constructed by author	0.00014	2.1–4.5
Dillingham (1985)	QES	U.S. Department of Labor	0.00008	5.7
Gerking, de Hann, and Schulze (1988)	Mail survey conducted by authors	Perceived risk of death; based on Society of Actuaries variables	0.0007	2.9
Moore and Viscusi (see Chapter 5)	PSID	National Traumatic Occupational Fatality (NTOF)	0.00008	6.2
Moore and Viscusi (see Chapter 5)	PSID	BLS	0.00005	2.1
Moore and Viscusi (see Chapter 6)	QES	Discounted expected life years lost; based on BLS death rate	0.00006	6.2

[a] Expressed in 1987:4 dollars using the GNP deflator, as reported in the *Economic Report of the President, 1988*. U.S. Government Printing Office, Washington, D.C.

valuations. Second, the per worker compensation for exposure to fatality risks approached almost $1,000 per year in 1988 dollars.

If worker tastes for safety differ, as the heterogeneity result suggests, then worker self-sorting provides a potentially powerful market mechanism for promoting job safety. Workers more willing to bear risks will work on dangerous jobs, and employers will pay them a compensating wage increase for the risk. If conditions on a given job are so poor that no one will work there, the firm will have to eliminate the risk, increase wages, or shut down, whichever is most profitable.

Given the heterogeneity result, proof that this sorting operates in practice requires evidence that worker turnover is positively related to job risks. Table 2.2 summarizes the studies by Viscusi and the related work in this volume that provide the empirical basis for the sorting effect by showing that increases in the riskiness of a job consistently lead to higher turnover. This result holds for a number of measures of turnover at different levels of aggregation, such as quit rates, actual quits, and quit intentions, and for a number of different measures of the riskiness of the job.

The compensation required to keep workers on a risky job can also be substantial. In the Survey of Working Conditions blue-collar sample analyzed by Viscusi, for example, market-generated compensation for fatality risk averages almost $1,000 per worker annually. Thus, despite the evidence that many workers leave jobs that they consider too risky and that those who remain are more willing to incur the health and safety risks, workers who remain on risky jobs receive significant additional compensation.

The primary policy implication of the evidence on the turnover and wage effects of job risks is that they do not indicate a need for regulatory control of the workplace. It is only fair to note, however, that these results do not prove that risk is allocated efficiently by the labor market. Rather, they indicate that complete market failure does not necessarily exist. Any call for intervention must therefore be based on subjective judgments of the adequacy of the compensating differential and self-sorting market mechanisms. At face value, both of these mechanisms appear to have significant effects.

A useful classification scheme for evaluating the substantial literature on wage-risk differentials considers the two general issues of estimation and application. The principal econometric issues associated with estimation of these differentials relate to the quality of the available risk data, the size and significance of the estimates, and the appropriate estimation technique. On the application side, the main issues concern the appropriate estimates of the values of life, health, and safety. More refined issues in this area, which have only recently been addressed, include the estimation of the costs of pain and suffering net of earnings loss and the determination of the appropriate discount rate to apply to life years saved in some future period.

Early estimates of wage-risk tradeoffs in many cases yielded mixed results. These somewhat lackluster results led Smith (1979), in his review of the early compensating differential literature, to conclude that estimates of compensating wage differentials were of little use for policy purposes. Exceptions to the early problems of inconsistency with the theory were the papers by Thaler and Rosen (1976) and Viscusi (1978).

Explanations for the poor performance of the early estimates centered primarily around two problems—data quality and specification of the wage equation. Very few data sets at that time, and to this day for that matter, contain information about worker characteristics, wages, and adverse working conditions. The majority of studies in the area instead match working condition data from external sources to various popular microeconomic data sets using reported industry or occupation and, if relevant to the risk data, state of residence as matching variables. Risk data measured at the level of the industry or occupation do not capture the true risk level on the job of a given worker, thus introducing error into the job risk variable. The consequences of the standard errors in variables model—downward bias in the coefficients and inflated standard errors—provide one possible explanation for the lack of significance of these early results.[2] Furthermore, a positive income elasticity of demand for good health would render more affluent workers less willing to incur job risks. Any empirical study of wage-risk tradeoffs must, therefore, disentangle the income elasticity effect from the wage-risk tradeoff by controlling properly for those worker and job characteristics related to wealth.

The primary specification issue concerns the treatment of the risk variable in the wage equation. In the compensating differential model, wages and working conditions are jointly chosen, and many authors argue that this calls for the treatment of the risk variable as endogenous. In particular, Brown (1980) and Duncan and Holmlund (1984) apply the ability bias arguments common to the human capital literature to the wage-risk model. The implications of omitting ability from wage equations are obvious. If ability is positively correlated with both risk levels and wages, then estimates of the compensating differential will be biased upward. If, on the other hand, ability is negatively related to the risk level, downward bias results. The studies by Brown and by Duncan and Holmlund attempt to mitigate the ability bias by estimating fixed effect wage equations. Their results differ markedly, as Brown finds little or no compensating differentials in his wage change equations, while Duncan and Holmlund find the expected increase in the compensating differential. The major difference in these two studies, namely, that Duncan and Holmlund used individual-level risk data while Brown used industry level risk data, could explain this result. Based on Freeman's (1984) results, in fact, the measurement error bias caused by the industry risk measure could be exacerbated in the fixed effect regressions.

Rosen (1974) first pointed out that in the likely case in which tastes for safety among workers and safety production functions among firms exhibit substantial heterogeneity, the wage equation is merely a reduced form locus of tangencies of indifference and isoprofit curves and, as such, has no structural interpretation. Smith (1979) argues in his review article that this obviates the need for two-stage estimation of the wage equation. Despite Smith's criticism, interest in instrumental variable estimation of the wage locus continues to this day. This is most likely attributable to the problems of measurement error in the risk variable, which call for instrumental variable estimation independently of any issues of structural interpretation. Furthermore, despite this continued interest, the majority of studies continue to use simple regression techniques such as ordinary and weighted least squares to estimate the market locus. Notable exceptions are the studies by Butler (1983), Biddle and Zarkin (1988), and Garen (1988).

Given that estimation of wage-risk tradeoffs is possible, the important policy question attached to these estimates asks what, if any, information they give concerning individual risk valuations. Evidence that a typical worker will accept a marginal increase in risk for an increase in the market wage provides information on that worker's implicit willingness to pay for job safety. It is then possible to use the individual willingness to pay for a small reduction in risk as the basis for determining collective valuations of large risk changes. For example, suppose that a worker accepts a $500 annual wage premium for an extra 1/10,000 probability of death on the job. For small risk changes such as this, this worker also would be willing to accept a $500 reduction in annual earnings for a 1/10,000 decrease in the fatality risk; the buying and selling prices of risk should be the same. If we assume that this particular worker represents the entire population, then a simple extrapolation implies that 10,000 workers would collectively pay $5 million for 10,000 risk reductions of 1/10,000 each. In this exercise, one life has been saved on an expected value basis, and the group of workers valued this life collectively at $5 million.

Numerous empirical estimates of the value of life based on labor market data have been generated. Table 2.1 summarizes the results of a selection of these studies, beginning with Thaler and Rosen (1976) and ending with the papers by Moore and Viscusi (1988a, 1988b) discussed in detail in Chapters 5 and 6. These results represent a broad spectrum of estimates, based on a number of widely used data sets, including the Current Population Survey (CPS), the U.S. Census, the Quality of Employment Surveys (QES), and the University of Michigan Panel Study of Income Dynamics (PSID), among others. In each of the studies reported, fatality risk data are taken from an external source and matched to workers in each data set by reported industry. The lone exception is the Society of Actuaries occupational fatality data, which are matched by reported occupation.

As a rule, the Society of Actuaries and Bureau of Labor Statistics (BLS) fatality risk data are highly aggregated. These data are typically measured at the one- or two-digit national level, providing at most about thirty separate observations of the death risk. The National Traumatic Occupational Fatality (NTOF) data used in Chapter 5, on the other hand, vary by state and one-digit industry, providing over four hundred observations of the death risk. The precision of the results reported in Chapter 6 reflects the increased quality afforded by the NTOF data.

A common view of value of life estimates argues that these estimates vary so much that they are of little use for policy purposes. Indeed, taken at face value, the results shown in Table 2.1 tend to support this assertion. Upon closer inspection, however, much of the variation appears to be attributable to observable differences in the data, and the choice of the appropriate estimate thus becomes a question of which risk data are the most appropriate.

It is clear first of all that there is a broad dependence of the value of life estimate on the level of the fatality risk. Those studies that use the Society of Actuaries data, for example, which sampled high-risk occupations only, yield a much lower estimated value of life than do those that use more representative risk data, such as the BLS data on industrial fatality rates. This observed heterogeneity in the value of life is consistent with the sorting that underlies the compensating differential theory, as workers with low valuations are more likely to locate in high-risk jobs.

For a given set of risk data, the value of life estimate appears quite robust with respect to the individual data set used. For example, the three studies using the high-risk actuarial data all yield a value of life estimate of about $1 million. Similarly, the studies by Smith (1976), Olson (1981), and Viscusi (1981) imply a value of life in the range of $3.5–$5.5 million. Moreover, in the study by Viscusi (1981) that estimated the heterogeneity of the value of life explicitly, workers in high-risk jobs revealed values of life in the $1 million range or less, whereas workers in low-risk jobs revealed values of life as high as $7 million. It is also interesting to note that the remaining BLS-based estimate in Table 2.1, taken from Chapter 5, also reflects the heterogenity attributable to risk level seen in the comparison of the BLS and the Society of Actuaries data above.

Dillingham (1985) explores the dependence of the value of life estimate on the risk variable, using the 1977 QES and a number of different fatality risk measures. Table 2.1 illustrates his findings for two risk measures. These results provide an alternative explanation for differences in the estimates. In Dillingham's study, the estimated value of life is about $6 million at a risk level similar to those in the studies that used the BLS data. For the same sample of workers, however, a different risk variable, again matched by reported industry, yields a higher mean risk level and a lower estimated value of life. From this perspective, the lower estimate reflects nothing more than a scaling effect—that is, if the risk data are scaled by a factor of k, then the risk coefficient in the wage equation will be decreased by the same factor and, consequently, so will the estimated value of life.

One characteristic common to the risk variables discussed so far is that they are all constructed from random samples of firms within an industry or occupation. Thus, in addition to the errors associated with using aggregated risk measures as proxies for firm level risks in a wage equation, there is also a sampling error in the industry measures. Until recently, the effect of this component of the error in the risk variables on the estimated value of life could not be determined. This is no longer true, however, following the release of a new series of fatality risk data from the NTOF Project, an ongoing survey being conducted by NIOSH. Unlike their predecessors, these data represent an actual census of occupational fatalities for the years 1980–1984. Consequently, there is less sampling error in the data, and it is possible to use the NTOF data to determine the extent of the sampling error bias.

In Chapter 5, we compare estimates derived from the NTOF data to those derived from unpublished BLS data for a subsample of the PSID. These results indicate substantial bias due to sampling error, particularly given that BLS risk data indicate lower risk levels than do NTOF. As in the case of Dillingham's findings, if there were only a scale difference between the BLS and NTOF surveys the value of life estimate would be a decreasing function of the mean risk level, and should therefore be lower for the NTOF data, since the average NTOF risk level in the PSID sample used is about 60 percent higher than the comparable BLS risk. Despite this scale difference, the NTOF estimates are between two and three times larger than the BLS estimates, indicating a substantial downward bias due to the sampling.

The remaining result presented in Table 2.1 is based on our study analyzing the role of discounting in the life cycle job risk problem (Moore and Viscusi 1988a). This research, which is discussed in Chapter 6, represents the first attempt to estimate discount rates for risks to longevity.[3] Conceptually, this is the appropriate approach to valuing health and safety policy, since lives can only be extended, not permanently saved.

Consideration of the role of discounting raises a number of interesting issues. For instance, how do we value a one-year extension of life relative to a ten-year life extension? How do the answers to such questions change if there is a time lag before such life extensions occur? The two main discounting issues pertain to the timing and to the duration of the life extension. These generic issues are among the most salient controversies in governmental debates over the future direction of health and safety programs. Should our emphasis be on cancer reduction, which has modest and deferred life extension effects, or should we focus on more imminent hazards? Given a health and safety budget of $1 billion, for example, should we spend the money on an occupational safety improvement that will save 100 lives this year or on medical research that might save 200 lives in five years? Tradeoffs such as these arise as a matter of course, and governmental agencies must have some means for establishing these priorities. To make sensible decisions on such issues, it is imperative to establish the appropriate discount rate to apply to deferred health benefits.

A less extensive literature on the value of health and safety benefits seeks to ascertain the willingness to pay for reductions in nonfatal accident rates. Most empirical death risk studies ignore injury rates, largely because most injury rate data are only available at the industry level, and are thus highly collinear with the death risk data. However, some exceptions to this rule exist, including Viscusi (1981). Of those studies that have included nonfatal injury rates, most have found an annual willingness to pay about $20,000 for a reduction in injury frequency equivalent to one statistical accident.

Risk, Workers' Compensation, and Job Turnover

An essential element of the compensating differential model is the sorting of workers into jobs according to their tastes for safety. In a formal model of this behavior, Viscusi (1979a) establishes a number of theoretical results. Most important, optimal experimentation by workers implies that they will initially show a preference for jobs about which little is known. Following entry into jobs whose characteristics are only dimly understood, worker learning leads to quits if the initial employment experiences are sufficiently unfavorable. The potential for turnover in the face of unpleasant working conditions represents the dynamic counterpart of the compensating differential mechanism described above.

Table 2.2 summarizes Viscusi's early research on the risk-turnover relationship. As expected, increased risks lead to worker quitting and also to decreased job tenure. This result holds in both industry-level and individual-level data, for a variety of risk measures. Sex differences in quit rates are explored by Viscusi (1980d). Most important, increases in individually assessed hazard perceptions are shown

TABLE 2.2
Effects of Job Risks and Workers' Compensation on Turnover: Summary of Selected Results

Author	Sample	Risk Variable	Benefit Variable	Turnover Variable	Risk Effect	Benefit Effect
Viscusi (1979a)	Two-digit industries, 1970	BLS lost workday cases	—[a]	Industry quit rate	0.023[b]	—
Viscusi (1979a)	Three-digit industries, 1974	BLS total injury and illness rate, 1974	—	Industry quit rate	0.026[b]	—
Viscusi (1979a)	Three-digit industries, 1974	BLS lost workday cases, 1969	—	Industry quit rate, five-year average	0.012[b]	—
Viscusi (1979a)	Survey of Working Conditions	Hazard perceptions dummy variable	—	Strong quit intentions	0.886[b]	—
Viscusi (1979a)	PSID, 1975	BLS lost workday cases, 1974	—	Actual quits	0.035[b]	—
Viscusi (1979a)	NLSYM, 1969–1970	BLS lost workday cases, 1969	—	Actual quits	0.005	—
Viscusi (1979a)	NLSYM, 1969–1970	BLS lost workday cases, 1969	—	Quits due to working conditions	0.009	—
Viscusi (1979a)	NLSYM, 1969–1970	BLS lost workday cases, 1969	—	Quit intentions due to working conditions	0.018[b]	—
Viscusi (1979a)	NLSYM, 1969–1970	BLS lost workday cases, 1969	—	Job tenure	−0.077[b]	—
Viscusi (1979a)	National Longitudinal Survey of Mature Men (NLSMM)	BLS lost workday cases, 1969	—	Actual quits or quit intentions	0.017[b]	—
Viscusi (1979a)	NLSMM	BLS lost workday cases, 1969	—	Job tenure	−0.070[b]	—
Viscusi (1980d)	PSID, 1975–1976, women only	BLS lost workday cases, 1969	—	Actual quits	2.10[b]	—
Moore and Viscusi (see Chapter 7)	PSID, 1982	NTOF	Expected weekly benefits	Actual quits	−0.056	−1.57E − 4[b]
Moore and Viscusi (see Chapter 7)	PSID, 1982	NTOF	Expected weekly benefits	Quit intentions	−0.022	−4.48E − 4[b]

[a] Dash indicates not applicable.
[b] Statistically significant at the 0.05 confidence level, one-tailed test.

to increase quit intentions, as measured by the 1969 Survey of Working Conditions. Individual quits are also responsive to risks in the PSID, and in the two National Longitudinal Surveys (Young Men and Mature Men), where the risks are proxied by BLS industry-level risk measures.

Chapter 7 extends these results to include the effects of workers' compensation benefits on both actual quits and on quit intentions. Since increases in insurance benefits reduce the potential losses from an injury on any given job, it is expected that benefits should reduce job turnover. The results in Chapter 7 support this assertion.

The Role of Workers' Compensation

Effective market forces notwithstanding, a number of institutions operate today that alter the basic wage-risk and turnover-risk relationships. The most recent of these, the Occupational Safety and Health Administration, has been analyzed in detail elsewhere, and will not be discussed at length here.[4] The other major institutional forces include publicly provided insurance for on-the-job accidents, that is, workers' compensation insurance, judicial relief through the tort liability system, and trade unions.

Following the recommendations of the Report of the National Commission on State Workmen's Compensation Laws (1972), benefits for losses incurred because of accidents on the job grew rapidly. Similarly, coverage of the workers' compensation system has been extended to the point that some form of mandatory accident insurance now covers virtually every worker in the United States.

Research on the labor marker impact of the workers' compensation system has focused on five key issues. By far the most extensively researched of these are analyses of the effects of benefits on wages and on risk levels. Less frequent, yet by no means unimportant, are studies of the effects of benefits on the frequency and duration of claims, the incidence of premiums, and the adequacy of benefits from a societal perspective.

Wage-Benefit Tradeoffs

The compensating differential theory predicts that increases in a desirable aspect of the job, such as workers' compensation benefits, should result in an accompanying decrease in wages. Workers' compensation insurance provides ex post compensation to workers for industrial accidents. Consequently, one would expect workers to substitute the ex ante compensation embodied in compensating risk differentials for insurance benefits, up to the point that equates the marginal contributions of each to expected utility. Attempts to establish this relationship empirically, which typically consist of estimates of a wage equation with some measure of benefits as an explanatory variable, have been fairly successful, and illustrate the importance of workers' compensation as a component of the overall compensation package.

Table 2.3 summarizes the chief characteristics of the major papers in this area. Following Butler's original (1983) study using South Carolina industrial time series data, benefit increases have been shown to reduce wages in a number of data sets. This result holds regardless of both the risk and the benefit measure used.

The early wage equation studies (Butler 1983, Dorsey 1983, Dorsey and Walzer 1983, and Arnould and Nichols 1983) established two principal results. First, increases in workers' compensation benefits decrease wages in a manner consistent with the compensating differential model. Second, wage-risk differentials would be much higher in the absence of workers' compensation, as workers would demand more ex ante compensation for exposure to risk in the absence of ex post guarantees.

These results, while informative in their own right, give rise to three important questions about the role of the workers' compensation system. First, given that benefits appear empirically to have some value to workers, are benefit levels high enough? This question has been raised repeatedly in policy discussions of the efficacy of the system, particularly following the dramatic increases in benefits and premiums paid in the last decade.

At issue for the worker is whether benefits are worth the wages forgone in return. Conceptually, it is clear that workers will willingly accept benefit increases as long as the marginal contribution of the increase to their welfare exceeds their marginal valuation of the forgone wages. If we make the assumption that a dollar spent at a given wealth level is more valuable to a healthy worker than to an injured one, workers will not wish fully to insure their earnings losses, which is a standard result in the insurance literature. On the other hand, if other forms of wealth (such as physical capital) decrease because of injury, a dollar may take on greater value for an injured worker. These influences, which are discussed in the household production literature, are probably relatively minor, since workers rarely purchase supplementary insurance. Beyond these rather general conclusions, however, little quantitative evidence had been brought to bear on the issue of benefit adequacy.

TABLE 2.3
Summary of Selected Wage–Workers' Compensation Tradeoff Studies

Author(s)	Sample	Risk Variable	Benefit Variable	Dependent Variable	Wage-Benefit Tradeoff Elasticity
Butler (1983)	South Carolina Industrial Commission	Death claim rate	Benefit index	After-tax weekly wage	5162.4[a,b]
		Lost workdays	Benefit index	After-tax weekly wage	3.66[a,b]
		Risk index	Benefit index	After-tax weekly wage	62.32[a,b]
Dorsey (1983)	Employer's Expenditures for Employee Compensation Survey	Lost workdays, fatality rate, injury rate	Actual costs per $100 of payroll	*ln*(hourly wage)	−0.032[c]
Arnould and Nichols (1983)	U.S. Census, 1970	Society of Actuaries	Wage replacement rate	Weekly wage	−460.0[a,c]
Moore and Viscusi (see Chapter 3)	QES, 1977	BLS lost workday cases	After-tax wage replacement rate conditioned by risk level	*ln*(hourly after-tax wage)	−0.098[c]
Moore and Viscusi (see Chapter 4)	PSID, 1977	BLS lost workday cases	After-tax wage replacement rate conditioned by risk level	*ln*(hourly after-tax wage)	−0.033[c]
Moore and Viscusi (see Chapter 4)	PSID, 1982	BLS lost workday cases	After-tax wage replacement rate conditioned by risk level	*ln*(hourly after-tax wage)	−0.063[c]
Moore and Viscusi (see Chapter 5)	PSID, 1982	NTOF death rate	After-tax wage replacement rate conditioned by risk level	*ln*(hourly after-tax wage)	−0.035[c]
Moore and Viscusi (see Chapter 6)	QES, 1977	BLS death rate	Present value of survivor's benefits	*ln*(hourly after-tax wage)	−0.047[c]
Moore and Viscusi (see Chapter 7)	PSID, 1982	NTOF death rate	Weekly benefits conditioned by risk level	*ln*(hourly after-tax wage	−0.057[c]
Moore and Viscusi (see Chapter 7)	PSID, 1982	NTOF death rate	Weekly benefits conditioned by risk level	Quit intentions	−1.81
Moore and Viscusi (see Chapter 7)	PSID, 1982	NTOF death rate	Weekly benefits conditioned by risk level	Actual quits	−0.575[c]

TABLE 2.3, *cont.*

Author(s)	Sample	Risk Variable	Benefit Variable	Dependent Variable	Wage-Benefit Tradeoff Elasticity
Moore and Viscusi (see Chapter 9)	PSID, 1982	NTOF death rate	Weekly benefits conditioned by risk level	Weekly wage	Range between −0.046 and −0.130[c]

[a] Elasticity data unavailable.
[b] Significance level unavailable.
[c] Statistically significant at the 0.05 confidence level, one-tailed test.

Chapter 3 develops the framework in which Viscusi and Moore (1987) resolved the benefit adequacy issue by developing an empirical basis for evaluating the optimality of workers' compensation benefits. In this study, and in the follow-up study in Chapter 4, it is shown that benefits were too low in the mid-seventies but that, following the benefit increases in the latter part of that decade and beyond, workers' compensation benefits had increased to the point considered optimal at the average risk levels in the workplace.

The observed wage-benefit tradeoffs lead to a second question: What is the incidence of the workers' compensation tax? Under the structure of all state systems, premiums charged to participating firms are based, to a certain extent, on their safety records. Following the rise in premiums resulting from the rise in benefit payments documented in Figures 2.1 and 2.2, firms sought relief from the increasing burden of the system. However, it appears clear that wages fall when benefits (and therefore premiums) rise. If sufficiently large reductions in wages could offset the cost of the premiums, the system would be financed by workers, not by the firms on whom the tax is initially levied. This issue is the focal point of Chapter 4, where we apply microeconomic estimates of the wage-benefit tradeoffs to national data on workers' compensation premiums and benefits to evaluate the overall average incidence of the system.

The third issue that arises from the observation that workers tradeoff wages and benefits is how to value the residual risk compensation, given that earnings losses and medical expenses have been insured. Any excess of the compensating risk differential over the benefit differential reflects the implicit valuation by workers of the nonpecuniary losses associated with an accident, that is, the costs of "pain and suffering." In Chapter 3 these losses are shown to be substantial, with workers willing to pay between $17,000 and $26,000 to avoid a nonfatal in-

FIGURE 2.1
Trends in real and nominal benefits—indemnity payments

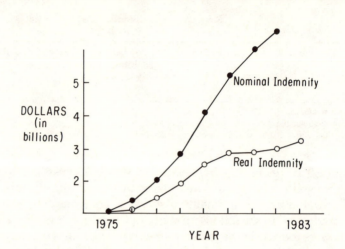

FIGURE 2.2
Trends in real and nominal benefits—medical payments

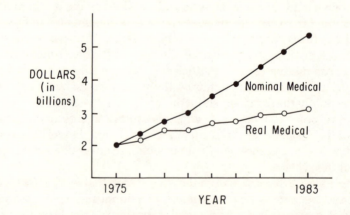

jury at full earnings replacement. To the extent that this valuation gives some perspective on the relative importance of earnings and health losses, the two appear to be roughly equal in magnitude for the typical injury.

The remaining studies reported in Table 2.3 explore some more sub-
tle aspects of wage-benefit tradeoffs. Chapter 7 represents the only research that does not use the wage equation framework to estimate
wage-benefit tradeoffs. In this chapter, the wage and benefit effects in
turnover equations are used to construct a measure of the wage-benefit
tradeoff. These estimates are then compared to a more conventional
estimate from a wage equation, which is estimated jointly with the
turnover equation. It is anticipated that workers on the quit-no quit
margin, whose preferences are represented in the turnover equations,
will value benefits more highly than do the marginal hire workers,
whose preferences are reflected in the wage equation. The results in
Chapter 7 bear this out, supporting the hypothesis that workers learn
about health risks on the job.

Most research on wage-benefit, wage-risk, and risk-benefit tradeoffs
has evaluated each of these effects in isolation. In particular, in estimating the effect of benefits on wages, any indirect effects that operate
through the compensating risk differential are ignored. If wages adjust
to risk changes, as has been established, and if benefits alter risk levels,
the total effect of benefits on wages will include this indirect effect.
Chapter 9 explores this influence in a two-equation model of wage and
risk determination. The primary focus of this chapter is the effect of
benefits on fatality risk levels. As a by-product of the risk equation
estimates, which indicate that risk levels decrease with benefits, it is
shown that the wage-benefit tradeoff is understated by ignoring the
indirect risk effect, which equals about 20 percent of the direct effect.

The remaining entry in Table 2.3 reflects the wage-benefit estimates
from the life cycle model of Chapter 6. The relevant insurance construct
in the life cycle model, the discounted value of survivor's benefits, is
entered as a regressor in a wage equation and has a significant negative
effect on wages.

The Role of Unions

Another institutional interface arises in unionized settings, where collective bargaining agreements may alter the market-determined wage-
risk and wage-benefit tradeoffs. The exact nature of the predictions of
union effects depends on the model of union behavior. Models of surplus maximization, such as Viscusi (1980e), and the median voter
model (Freeman and Medoff 1984; Farber 1986) imply higher wage-risk
differentials in unionized contexts. Similarly, ad hoc arguments about
the higher quality of job risk information in unionized firms and the
documented higher average tenure of unionized workers both support

the prediction that wage-risk tradeoffs will be greater in the presence of a trade union. An alternative view is that of Dickens (1984), who uses a Nash solution to the union-firm bargaining problem to show that wage-risk tradeoffs may be either higher or lower than market ones, so that the relative impact of unionization on these tradeoffs is an empirical question.

A fairly substantial empirical literature supports the predictions of the median voter/surplus maximization models. Among the more important studies that focus on wage-risk tradeoffs exclusively, Viscusi (1980), Thaler and Rosen (1976), and Olson (1981) all find statistically significant positive union effects on wage-risk premiums. More recently, however, Dickens (1984) and Dillingham and Smith (1984) fail to find evidence of a significant union effect on the compensating risk differential.

Evidence of union effects on wage-benefit tradeoffs is less extensive. Until recently, the sole empirical study of the effect of unionization on the wage-benefit tradeoff (Dorsey and Walzer 1983) indicated that union worker wages increase with expected workers' compensation benefits, while nonunion workers in the same sample substituted wages for benefits. Although this finding is consistent with the Nash model, it may also be the result of data limitations or the specification of the model. These possibilities are explored in Chapter 8.

Benefit-Risk Tradeoffs

The other workers' compensation effect analyzed extensively in the literature seeks to establish the effects of benefit increases on risk levels. Like any insurance program, workers' compensation does more than compensate insured workers for the pecuniary costs (lost earnings and medical expenses) of their injuries. In particular, economic models of rational firm and worker behavior predict that insurance benefits for on-the-job injuries alter risk-taking behavior in fundamentally opposed ways. The two primary forces are the safety incentive effects of workers' compensation premiums on firms and the moral hazard effects of benefits on workers.

To the extent that firms' safety records are reflected in their premiums, workers compensation insurance will act as an injury tax on firms, providing financial incentives to increase workplace safety. Employer contributions to state funds are determined by an experience-rating procedure, so that premium levels potentially reflect a firm's safety record and, in effect, act as a tax on injuries. The importance of the injury tax role of workers' compensation is conditioned by the degree of this experience rating. In practice, larger firms are rated most closely in accordance with their actual experience. Such firms can also self-insure, if they have an approved means of doing so. Smaller firms are typically rated as a group and therefore do not pay the full cost of an accident in terms of increased premiums.

Since the financial losses to workers that result from workplace injuries are reduced by workers' compensation, increased benefits will at the same time result in reduced care by workers, which could offset the safety incentive effect. Of course, given the large implicit valuations that workers place on their health and safety, which are fundamentally irreplaceable, this particular form of moral hazard is probably not too important. Rather, moral hazard in the workers' compensation system takes the form of increases in the frequency of claims filed and in their duration.

Table 2.4 summarizes a broad sample of research on the effects of workers' compensation on measured job risks. The majority of these studies indicate that the moral hazard effects dominate the safety incentive effects, as the risk-benefit tradeoffs are positive in virtually every study presented in Table 2.4. The lone exceptions to this result are Chelius (1974, 1982, 1983) and Chapter 9 of this book. Interestingly, these are the only analyses reported in Table 2.4 that use fatality rates or severity-weighted injury risks as the risk measure.[5] This suggests the possibility that much of the observed increase in risk levels associated with benefit increases is the result of spurious claims. As is well known, it is notoriously difficult to ascertain the severity of many nonfatal injuries, particularly muscular and skeletal injuries, such as sprains and strains. Indeed, using data on the nature and timing of injury claims, Smith (1989) documents a significantly higher rate of claims for injuries of this type on Monday mornings, indicating that workers may postpone reporting and receiving treatment for weekend injuries until arriving at work in order to qualify for workers' compensation benefits. Filing a spurious claim for a severe injury or for a fatality is much more difficult, and it is possible that the findings of Chelius and our results in Chapter 9 reflect this fact.

The injury tax effects of workers' compensation are countered by the moral hazard problems that plague any insurance program. If benefits increase, participation in the program by workers should increase independently of any changes in the underlying risk levels. This increased participation takes the form of increases in the frequency of claims filed and in their duration. These influences, which have been analyzed by Butler and Worrall (1983, 1985), Worrall and Butler (1985), Krueger (1988), and others are quite substantial, as these analyses of the effects of benefit increases on program participation indicate that

TABLE 2.4
The Risk Effects of Workers' Compensation

Author(s)	Sample	Risk Variable	Benefit Variable	Estimated Effect
Chelius (1976)	Time series; constructed by author from various sources, 1900–1940	Accidental death rate	Workers' compensation law (0–1)	Negative and significant in four different time frames
Chelius (1982)	Constructed by author from BLS: varies by state, industry, and year, 1972–1975	Lost workdays by state, industry, and year relative to national average by industry and year	Weekly benefits by state, industry, and year relative to wages by state, industry, and year	0.08
Chelius (1982)	Constructed by author from BLS: varies by state, industry, and year, 1972–1975	Lost workday cases by state, industry, and year relative to national average by industry and year	Weekly benefits by state, industry, and year relative to wages by state, industry, and year	0.14[a]
Chelius (1982)	Constructed by author from BLS: varies by state, industry, and year, 1972–1975	Lost workdays per case by state, industry and year relative to national average by industry and year	Weekly benefits by state, industry, and year relative to wages by state, industry, and year	−0.09[a]
Chelius (1983)	Pooled time series—cross-section; constructed by author from BLS; varies by state, industry and year, 1972–1978	Lost workdays relative to national average (see previous entry)	Weekly benefits by state, industry, and year relative to wages by state, industry, and year	0.16[a]
Chelius (1983)	Pooled time series—cross-section; constructed by author from BLS; varies by state, industry and year, 1972–1978	Lost workday cases relative to national average (see previous entry)	Weekly benefits by state, industry, and year relative to wages by state, industry, and year	0.22[a]
Chelius (1983)	Pooled time series—cross-section; constructed by author from BLS; varies by state, industry and year, 1972–1978	Lost workdays per case relative to national average (see previous entry)	Weekly benefits by state, industry, and year relative to wages by state, industry, and year	−0.05[a]

TABLE 2.4, *cont.*

Author(s)	Sample	Risk Variable	Benefit Variable	Estimated Effect
Butler (1983)	Time series; South Carolina industrial data	*ln*(Risk index)	*ln*(Benefit index)	0.29[b]
Butler (1983)	Time series; South Carolina industrial data	*ln*(Risk index)	*ln*(Expected benefits)	1.02[a]
Chelius and Smith (1983)	Constructed by authors from BLS data; varies by state, industry, and firm size group	Lost workday cases	Expected weekly benefits	Small majority negative, few significant
Butler and Worrall (1983)	Pooled time series—cross-section; constructed by authors from various sources	*ln*(Injury rate): number of claims filed per 1,000 employees	*ln*(Average weekly benefits) for temporary total disability, minor permanent partial disability, and major permanent partial disability	Largely positive and significant or insignificant
Butler and Worrall (1985)	Longitudinal; National Council on Compensation Insurance (NCCI)	Duration of workers' compensation claim for lower back injury	Replacement rate Replacement rate	0.187[b] 0.374[c]
Butler and Worrall (1985)	Longitudinal; National Council on Compensation Insurance (NCCI)	Duration of workers' compensation claim for lower back injury	Weekly benefits	0.463[b]
Ruser (1985a)	Cross-section; constructed by author from BLS industry data	Injury rate	Average weekly benefits	0.089
Ruser (1985a)	Cross-section; constructed by author from BLS industry data	Injury rate	Proportion of lost workdays per injury that is compensable	1.194[a]
Ruser (1985a)	Cross-section; constructed by author from BLS industry data	Lost workday cases	Average weekly benefits	0.449[a]
Ruser (1985a)	Cross-section; constructed by author from BLS industry data	Lost workday cases	Proportion of lost workdays per injury that is compensable	0.559[a]

32

TABLE 2.4, *cont.*

Author(s)	Sample	Risk Variable	Benefit Variable	Estimated Effect
Fishback (1987)	Pooled time series—cross-section; constructed by author from various sources	Fatal accident rate	Liability rule (1 if other than strict liability, 0 otherwise)	0.369[a]
Fishback (1987)	Pooled time series—cross-section; constructed by author from various sources	Fatal accident rate	Exclusive state workers' compensation fund (0–1)	0.489[a]
Fishback (1987)	Pooled time series—cross-section; constructed by author from various sources	Fatal accident rate	State or private workers' compensation fund (0–1)	0.431[a]
Fishback (1987)	Pooled time series—cross-section; constructed by author from various sources	Fatal accident rate	No state fund	0.333
Krueger (1988)	Longitudinal; current population surveys, 1983–1984 or 1984–1985	Participation in workers' compensation program (0–1)	Expected weekly benefits	0.478[b]
Krueger and Burton (1988)	Pooled time series—cross-section; 29 states for years 1972, 1975, 1978, and 1983; provided by NCCI	ln(Workers' compensation premiums	ln(Weekly benefits)	Range of estimates; no significant effect of benefits on injury rates implied by results
Moore and Viscusi (see Chapter 9)	PSID, 1982	NTOF death rate	Weekly benefits	−.013[a]

[a] Statistically significant at the 0.05 confidence level, one-tailed test.
[b] Significance level information unavailable.
[c] Estimates from hazard model allowing for duration depencence.

reported accident rates and the durations of claims rise with benefit levels. Thus, moral hazard effects dominate safety incentive effects for less severe injuries. Since moral hazard effects provide an alternative explanation for the benefit adequacy results in Chapter 3, their importance is critical.

Workers' Compensation and Tort Liability

The essential characteristic of all workers' compensation programs from a legal perspective is that employers, in effect, have absolute liability for workplace accidents. In return, employers gain a limitation on their firms' liability, as almost all states have adopted workers' compensation as the exclusive remedy against the employer and capped benefit amounts. However, particularly in recent years, injured workers have sought to circumvent the limits imposed upon their compensation by suing the manufacturers of products involved in their on-the-job accidents through the tort liability system. For example, a lumberjack who suffers a dismemberment while working may sue a chain saw manufacturer in a product liability action for a sum far in excess of the benefits guaranteed under workers' compensation. Furthermore, the workers' compensation carrier or the employer could initiate a subrogation action against the chain saw producer.

The nature of the relationship between the two systems is highly complex, given the intricate possible set of interactions. Many of the applicable legal provisions vary by state and with the particular nature of the industry. Despite the growing importance of common law remedies for job accidents, there has been no comprehensive empirical analysis of this class of injuries. Our discussion in Chapter 10 represents the first such attempt to grapple with the wide range of issues raised by conventional tort liability remedies for job accidents. In particular, we explore both the scope of such actions and the influence of various legal rules on a variety of aspects of the litigation process, such as the propensity to drop a claim, the likelihood of a settlement, and the amount of any award or settlement.

Three

The Performance of Workers' Compensation as a Social Insurance Program

THE STARTING POINT for our analysis is an exploration of how the wage and workers' compensation mechanisms interact. Although there has been a decade of literature on empirical estimates of compensating differentials for job hazards,[1] analysts have only recently begun to focus on the role of the workers' compensation system in affecting these differentials.[2] From a conceptual standpoint, one would expect workers' compensation to play a significant role, since the employer can compensate workers for job risks either through ex ante compensation (compensating wage differentials) or ex post compensation (such as workers' compensation benefits). The relative importance of the two forms of compensation depends on the degree to which workers wish to insure the income risks of job injury—a value that hinges on such factors as the degree of wage loss and the effect of the accident on the marginal utility of consumption.

One could omit workers' compensation from wage equations if there were uniformity in the benefit levels. From an econometric standpoint, one could not assess the wage effects of workers' compensation in this instance. There are, however, substantial variations both in benefits across states and according to the worker's wage level. For example, the usual formula for temporary and permanent total disabilities provides for two-thirds wage replacement with a benefit cap, so that the lower-paid workers effectively receive higher rates of income replacement. The principal differences among states are with respect to such features as benefit caps, benefit floors, dependency allowances, and time limits for benefit payment.

In view of this variation, one would expect the level of workers' compensation to play an important role in analyses of the compensation package. Benefits do not simply shift wages downward; rather, there is an important effect on the structure of wages for workers in jobs of differing riskiness. Unfortunately, the research results to date are somewhat mixed, in part because the influence of workers' compensation has often been modeled incorrectly.

Thus far there has been no link between empirical issues of this type and the more policy-oriented themes in the workers' compensation literature. A continuing open question, in the forefront of job safety policy since *The Report of the National Commission on State Workmen's Compensation Laws* (1972), is whether workers' compensation benefit levels are adequate.[3] Nominal workers' compensation earnings replacement rates have traditionally been below 1.0, except for very low income workers whose wages are exceeded by a benefits floor. Replacement rates taking into account the benefits' favorable tax status are higher. Whether partial compensation is optimal is, however, more difficult to ascertain. If a job injury lowers the worker's marginal utility of consumption for any given consumption level, as is often assumed in the health literature, then less than full compensation is desirable.[4] A worker would not choose to equalize income levels in the healthy and injured states if the injury impaired his or her ability to derive utility from the expenditures. How far below 1.0 the optimal replacement rate should be and whether current replacement rates are optimal remain open issues. Although it is plausible that less than full replacement is optimal, this theoretical proposition in no way implies that the current departure from full replacement is optimal.

Obtaining a general sense of whether workers' compensation benefits are adequate is particularly important since this wage-benefit component is not the result of a voluntary market transaction. Workers do not bargain with employers for these benefits. States set the benefit floors for different classes of injury; thus, it is not possible to infer that actual benefits are those that the workers would choose. Firms cannot reduce the benefit levels, and the transaction costs involved in setting up a separate program to augment existing benefit levels may discourage efforts to overcome the shortcomings that arise from inadequate benefits.

The purposes of this chapter are threefold. First, the theoretical framework we develop enables us to assess the economic implications of the tradeoff between wages and workers' compensation. We explore this tradeoff using data from the 1977 Quality of Employment Survey coupled with information on industry risk levels and state workers' compensation benefits. Second, we refine the empirical estimates of the effect of workers' compensation on wage levels and on compensating differentials for job risks. Our approach uses a theoretically based empirical framework that takes into account the role of differing levels of job risk in affecting workers' valuation of the benefits. Our analysis differs from previous studies in that the workers' compensation variable is worker specific, rather than a state benefit average, and it incorporates the favorable tax status afforded benefits. Furthermore, the diversity of the risk measures and the set of other nonpecuniary characteristics included is broader than in earlier studies. Most important, we include an individual-specific measure of job hazards in a number of our equations.

As a final product of this research, we generate the first reported implicit values of the nonpecuniary aspects of job injuries. Thus, we can break down workers' valuation of injuries into the valuation of monetary and nonmonetary losses. This general area of concern, often referred to as the cost of pain and suffering and nonwork disability, has been of great policy importance, but thus far has not been addressed empirically.

Conceptual Framework

The empirical analysis in this chapter focuses on the tradeoff between wages and workers' compensation in the total compensation package for hazardous jobs. For much the same reason that we observe positive compensating wage differentials for job risks and other unpleasant job attributes, we should observe negative wage differentials for desirable aspects of the overall compensation package, such as workers' compensation. The purpose of this section is not to reiterate this basic result, which follows directly from the work of Adam Smith, but rather to investigate the properties of the tradeoff between wages and workers' compensation. In particular, what is the efficient rate of substitution between these two compensation components? The expression we derive for this tradeoff provides the benchmark for the empirical work on ascertaining whether workers' compensation levels are appropriate, which we present in this and the following chapter.

The formulation of the model, which entails very few restrictive assumptions, parallels the health state utility function approach of Viscusi (1978). Suppose that there are two possible health states. In state 1 the worker is healthy and experiences utility $U^1(x)$ from any given consumption level x. In state 2 the worker experiences a job injury and has utility $U^2(x)$. For any given level of consumption, the worker would rather be healthy than not ($U^1(x) > U^2(x) > 0$), has a greater marginal utility of consumption when healthy than when injured ($U^1_x(x) > U^2_x(x) > 0$), and has a diminishing marginal utility of consumption ($U^1_{xx}, U^2_{xx} < 0$).

Let p denote the risk of an on-the-job injury, that is, the probability that state 2 prevails. Similarly, $1 - p$ is the probability that the worker will remain healthy. We assume that workers do not update their subjective probabilities over time. Worker learning can be introduced, and we do so in Chapter 7, but the basic elements of the model are not affected by it. Let w and b represent the wage the worker is paid when healthy and the level of workers' compensation when he or she is injured, respectively. For simplicity, all other income the worker receives when injured, such as social security benefits, is subsumed into the functional form of $U^2(x)$.

Supplementary benefits are a significant source of income support.[5] While the level of such benefits affects the welfare of workers, there is no loss in generality in excluding them from the analysis by incorporating them into $U^2(x)$, provided that the assumptions above are satisfied. Unlike workers' compensation, social security benefits are not merit rated to any degree, so there is no tradeoff between wages and benefits within the particular job contract. The benefit value does, however, have an indirect effect by raising the level of $U^2(x)$ and possibly altering its shape. The analysis below addresses the workers' welfare net of any such influences. Viewed somewhat differently, it addresses the adequacy of workers' compensation benefits, given the existence of these other social insurance programs.[6]

To facilitate the conceptual analysis, assume all disabilities are temporary and total. Unlike earlier analyses of workers' compensation, this model and the subsequent empirical analysis explicitly recognize the favorable tax status afforded benefits. There is a proportional tax rate t on wages. We assume that the role of assets in affecting consumption is subsumed in the functional form of the utility functions, so that consumption levels in states 1 and 2 are $(1 - t)w$ and b.

The focus here is on the rate of substitution between wages and workers' compensation for a worker at a job with risk p. For simplicity, we abstract from problems of moral hazard. Analytically, the initial part of the development follows Diamond (1977) and Viscusi (1980b). The worker's expected utility, G, is given by

(3.1) $(1 - p)U^1[(1 - t)w] + pU^2(b) = G.$

The rate of tradeoff between wages and workers' compensation that maintains the worker's level of welfare is

(3.2) $\dfrac{dw}{db} = \dfrac{-G_b}{G_w} = \dfrac{-pU^2_x}{(1 - p)(1 - t)U^1_x}.$

If the job risk p equals zero then dw/db also equals zero. The existence of a tradeoff between wages and workers' compensation consequently hinges on the existence of some risk that state 2 will prevail. For this reason any empirical specification of the wage–workers' compensation tradeoff must recognize the dependence of this relationship on the risk level.

In a situation in which the tax rate is zero and there is workers' compensation insurance available on an actuarially fair basis, from Viscusi

(1980b) we have the result that income will be allocated across the two states so that U_x^1 equals U_x^2. In this perfect markets case, equation 3.2 reduces to

$$\frac{dw}{db} = \frac{-p}{1-p}.$$

For the workers in the sample considered below, and using the lost workday case injury rate as the value of p, this condition implies a tradeoff of −.04. In effect, workers will sacrifice four cents of compensation (that is, wages, fringes, etc.) when they are healthy for an additional one dollar in compensation when they are injured (that is, workers' compensation) if there are no taxes and if insurance is available on an actuarially fair basis.

The manner in which these relationships are altered under the existing compensation system can be ascertained by comparing observed wage-benefits tradeoffs to the optimal tradeoff implied by the model. Observed deviations from the optimal tradeoff can then be used to determine whether compensation levels are appropriate and, if not, how they differ from the optimal amount.

In addition to the presence of tax rates, actual social insurance schemes incur associated administrative costs. These costs lead to a divergence of the insurance price from the expected cost to the insurer; this gap is known as insurance loading. Suppose that the degree of insurance loading is such that for each dollar of expected compensation in state 2 the insured worker must sacrifice $1 + a$ dollars of compensation in state 1. Furthermore, the worker must break even on an actuarial basis, given this degree of loading. The total limit on expected reimbursement, including the administrative costs of insurance, is the worker's marginal product, z. For a competitive firm, the worker's marginal product equals his or her expected wages and workers' compensation benefits plus an additional fee, apb, to cover the administrative costs of all benefits received. The actuarial constraint is consequently

(3.3) $(1 - p)w + (1 + a)pb - z = 0.$

The optimal insurance scheme is obtained by maximizing the worker's expected utility subject to equation 3.3, or

$$\text{Max } V = (1 - p)U^1[(1 - t)w] + pU^2(b) - \\ \text{w,b,}\lambda \quad \lambda [(1 - p)w + (1 + a)pb - z],$$

which yields

$$\lambda = (1 - t)U_x^1 = U_x^2/(1 + a),$$

or

(3.4) $U_x^2 = (1-t)(1+a)U_x^{1.7}$

The presence of taxes and deviations from actuarially fair rates lead to optimal levels of insurance that do not equate the marginal utility of income in the two health states unless $(1-t)(1+a)$ equals one. An appropriate combination of tax rates and insurance loading could produce this outcome. If $(1-t)(1+a)$ exceeds 1, as when tax rates are low and the degree of insurance loading is high, then the optimal marginal utility of consumption in state 2 will be greater than in state 1. To produce this higher marginal utility in state 2, one must decrease the level of consumption in state 2. This result is expected, since shifting resources to state 2 is more costly in the presence of taxes and actuarially unfair insurance rates, leading to a lower level of state 2 consumption and a higher associated marginal utility. Similarly, if $(1-t)(1+a)$ is below 1, U_x^1 will exceed U_x^2.

The principal issue considered here is how, given optimal workers' compensation benefit conditions as characterized by equation 3.4, the tradeoff between compensation in the two states is affected. Substituting the value of U_x^2 from equation 3.4 into equation 3.2, we have

(3.5) $$\frac{dw}{db} = \frac{-p(1-t)(1+a)U_x^1}{(1-p)(1-t)U_x^1} = \frac{-p(1+a)}{1-p}.$$

With current levels of insurance loading, beneficiaries receive approximately eighty cents of each dollar of insurance premiums, according to calculations based on the net earned premium valuation method in Burton and Krueger (1986).[8] The average value of dw/db for both the risk level in our sample and for the typical manufacturing worker will consequently be -0.05. Workers should be willing to trade off five cents of wages per additional dollar of workers' compensation benefits.

If the level of workers' compensation benefits is suboptimal, as a variety of observers have suggested, then the observed rate of tradeoff should exceed five cents per dollar. Similarly, if benefit levels are excessive, then the observed tradeoff of wages that workers are willing to sacrifice for more workers' compensation will be below this level. In the subsequent empirical analysis, we ascertain how estimated rates of compensation substitution compare with the reference point provided by equation 3.5.[9]

It should be noted, however, that these tests for optimality pertain only to the private valuation by the worker. The analysis does not address the role of workers' neglect of the external altruistic concern of society in their own welfare when making a job choice. If, however, benefits are found to be too low, consideration of these altruistic interests will simply reinforce the result.

A factor that works in the opposite direction is the adverse incentives or moral hazard problems associated with insurance. If workers' compensation leads workers to be less careful in avoiding accidents, as the majority of the studies in Table 2.4 indicate, then the efficient level of insurance will be lower. As a result, observing that insurance is inadequate from the standpoint of meeting workers' financial insurance needs might not necessarily imply that the outcome is inefficient. Other causes of an observed excess of the estimated rate over the optimal rate include the option value of risky jobs (Viscusi 1979b) in contexts in which there is worker learning and the value of leisure during injury-induced layoffs.

Empirical Formulation and Sample Characteristics

The data used to estimate the model are drawn from the 1977 Quality of Employment Survey (QES). The subsample that we examine contains 485 observations, consisting of nonfarm heads of households who were not self-employed and who worked at least twenty hours a week in the year of the survey.

The two central variables in this study are the job risk and workers' compensation variables. We capture the health and safety risks to which the worker is exposed in three different ways. First, the survey includes subjective, individual-specific responses to a series of questions concerning exposure to job hazards. If a worker cited any health and safety risks of his or her job, the binary hazard perception variable assumes a value of 1. The remaining two risk variables are based on the U.S. Bureau of Labor Statistics (1979) data on industrial injuries and illnesses, which are matched to workers by the three-digit industry code. These two variables represent the rates of lost workday cases and total recorded cases of injury and illness per one hundred workers.

The second variable of interest is the measure of workers' compensation benefits. The measure we constructed took into account not only the favorable tax status of workers' compensation benefits but also the manner in which the benefit formulas pertained to the particular individual rather than to the average worker. The worker-specific replacement rates including recognition of tax factors differ from those in the literature in varying degrees. Dorsey and Walzer (1983) use an industry- and state-specific rate based on insurance premiums that is then matched to workers by use of census industry codes. Butler (1983) uses two measures, each at the industry level. The first is actual benefits paid for death, temporary total disability, and other injury categories, which are included as regressors in a pooled time series/cross-section regression of industry average wages on human capital, injury and death rates, actual benefits, and other variables. His second measure is the industry average replacement rate for each year, which corresponds more closely to expected benefits and is consequently better suited to the theoretical model. Arnould and Nichols (1983) use state gross replacement rates from the *Compendium on Workmen's Compensation* (Rosenblum 1973) matched to workers in the 1970 census 1/10,000 sample. Finally, Ruser (1985b) uses an individual-specific measure similar to ours, but does not include the effect of tax status on the replacement rate.

Each of these measures yields mixed results. Compensating differentials are often insignificant, and sometimes do not have the theoretically predicted sign. Likewise, the workers' compensation effects are usually weak. Dorsey and Walzer (1983), in fact, find a positive relationship between wages and workers' compensation in the union portion of their sample. Note also that insurance premiums should be positively related to accident rates and are less likely to reflect the negative effect of ex ante insurance on wages.

Each of the previous studies attempts to identify an additive effect of workers' compensation on wages, and in some instances (Butler 1983) an interactive effect with job risks as well. In the purely additive models, workers' compensation variables usually have the expected negative signs, and are sometimes significant. The addition of higher-order terms consistently results in a dilution of this result. The interactive effects are usually negative, but are seldom significantly different from zero.

This previous research, although suggestive, appears to suffer from two principal shortcomings. First, as shown in equation 3.5, workers' compensation affects wages only at positive risk levels, thus making an interactive model theoretically appropriate in the absence of risk aversion. Second, most of the aforementioned studies measure individual insurance levels with substantial error.

The workers' compensation variable used in the analysis in this and other chapters is the weekly wage replacement rate. Unfortunately, no single benefits measure is ideal. States have often complex benefit formulas that provide for lump sum benefits and benefits depending on the duration of the disability. The waiting periods for these benefits may vary, and there are differences in the benefit structure according to family structure, the degree and type of disability, and whether a fatality was involved.

The approach we adopted was to base our benefits variable on the benefit formulas for temporary total disability by state.[10] This benefit category accounts for three-fourths of all claims and one-fifth of all cash benefits.[11] The formulas for permanent total disability are almost identical, except that the duration of these benefits is greater. Similarly, the category of permanent partial disability benefits, which plays a substantial role in terms of the total benefit distribution, is positively correlated with temporary total disability.[12] Ideally, one might wish to obtain actuarial valuation of expected benefit levels by state, but such calculations are a substantial research task for which we did not have access to the pertinent data. Because of the positive correlation among benefit categories, we will use the temporary total benefit formulas as a proxy for state differences in workers' compensation benefit levels.

Where it was appropriate to do so, we adjusted the benefit levels, using information on the survey respondents' marital status and number of dependents, and entered the resulting benefit figure as the numerator in the replacement ratio R_i:

$$R_i = \frac{b_i}{w_i(1 - t_i)}.$$

Since benefits are not taxed, the tax rate does not appear in the numerator of the expression for R_i. The denominator in R_i is the after-tax wage, $w_i(1 - t_i)$, where w_i is the weekly wage and t_i the marginal tax rate. We used the earnings, hours, and weeks worked information in the QES to calculate a wage variable. In computing the tax rate, we assumed that all workers took the standard deduction, with the number of exemptions based on the reported number of dependents.[13]

Unlike previous measures of workers' compensation replacement rates, the value of R_i is individual specific. As a result, it more closely measures the actual rate workers use in making their decisions. Observable determinants of w_i and t_i render R_i endogenous. To correct for this endogeneity, we regress R_i on a vector of characteristics (Z_i) and state dummy variables.[14] The predicted value of R_i serves as the exogenous measure of the replacement ratio.[15]

A detailed list of variable definitions appears in Table 3.1, and Table 3.2 summarizes the means and standard deviations. The dependent variable in the subsequent analysis is the worker's hourly wage or its natural logarithm. Each equation also includes a set of variables pertaining to the worker's personal characteristics, such as the worker's sex, race, presence of health impairments, years of work experience since the age of sixteen, and whether the worker has less than twelve years of schooling, exactly twelve years, some college, or has completed at least a college degree.

TABLE 3.1
QES Variable Definitions

Variable	Definition
Wage	Computed hourly after-tax wage measure
Sex	Sex dummy variable (d.v.): 1 if worker is female, 0 otherwise
Race	Race d.v.: 1 if worker is black, 0 otherwise
Poor health status	Severity of health limitation d.v.: 1 if limiting physical or nervous condition has created either sizable or great problems in working on or in getting jobs, 0 otherwise
Experience	Experience variable: Years worked for pay since age 16
Less than high school education	Education d.v.: 1 if worker did not finish high school, 0 otherwise
High school education	Education d.v.: 1 if worker finished high school, 0 otherwise
Some college education	Education d.v.: 1 if worker has some college education, 0 otherwise.
College degree	Education d.v.: 1 if worker has at least a college degree, 0 otherwise.
Marginal tax rate	Marginal tax rate
Hazard perceptions	Hazardous working conditions d.v.: 1 if worker answered "yes" to "does your job at any time expose you to what you feel are physical dangers or unhealthy conditions," 0 otherwise
Lost workday cases	BLS industry hazard variable: annual rate of injuries and illnesses involving lost workdays
Total cases	BLS industry hazard variable: annual rate of total injuries and illnesses
Replacement rate	Workers' compensation replacement rate: benefit level/(Wage [1 − marginal tax rate])
Fast work pace	Work pace d.v.: 1 if job requires worker to work very fast a lot, 0 otherwise
No decisionmaking	Absence of worker decisions on job d.v.: 1 if it is not at all true that the worker makes a lot of decisions on the job, 0 otherwise
Overtime work requirements	Overtime work d.v.: 1 if worker works overtime often, 0 otherwise
Weighted replacement rate	Interaction of replacement rate and one of the three risk measures
Job security	Job security d.v.: 1 if it is "very true" that the worker's job security is good, 0 otherwise
Firm size	Firm size: midpoints assigned to intervals for number of workers at the firm (hundreds of workers)

TABLE 3.1, *cont.*

Variable	Definition
Supervisory status	Supervisor d.v.: 1 if worker supervises anyone as part of his or her job, 0 otherwise
Availability of training	Training program d.v.: 1 if employer makes available a training program to improve worker skills, 0 otherwise
Union status	Union status d.v.: 1 if worker belongs to a union or employee's association, 0 otherwise.
Residence in the Northeast region	Northeast region d.v.: 1 if worker lives in northeastern United States, 0 otherwise
Residence in the South region	Southern region d.v.: 1 if worker lives in southeastern United States, 0 otherwise
Residence in the North Central region	North Central region d.v.: 1 if worker lives in north central United States, 0 otherwise
Residence in the Western region	Western region d.v.: 1 if worker lives in western United States, 0 otherwise
City size	Urban area d.v.: 1 if worker lives in a major SMSA, 0 otherwise
Occupation categories	Occupation d.v.s: for worker's reported single-digit occupation (professional, managerial, sales, clerical, craftsperson, non-transport operative, transport operative, unskilled, or service)

Pertinent job characteristics include the worker's marginal tax rate, which was used in constructing the replacement rate variable, the subjective risk assessment variable, the lost workday accident rate, the total recorded injury and illness rate, the predicted value of the workers' compensation replacement rate, whether the job requires the worker to work fast, whether the job permits the worker to make decisions, whether the worker works overtime often, whether the worker has good job security, the number of employees at the workplace, whether the worker is a supervisor, whether the employer offers a training program, and whether the worker is a union member. Occupation dummy variables were entered to control for unobservable occupation-specific characteristics. The particular set of nonpecuniary rewards variables that was selected closely followed the group utilized in the earnings equations for the earlier Survey of Working Conditions esults reported in Viscusi (1978).

Finally, we included a set of regional dummy variables for whether the respondent lived in the Northeast, in the South, in the North Cen-

TABLE 3.2
Descriptive Statistics, 1977 QES Sample (N = 485)

Variable	Mean	SD
Wage	7.676	3.779
Sex	0.162	0.369
Race	0.068	0.252
Poor health status	0.029	0.167
Experience	20.901	12.078
Less than high school education	0.191	0.393
High school education	0.351	0.477
Some college education	0.226	0.419
College degree	0.232	0.423
Marginal tax rate	0.264	0.095
Hazard perceptions	0.798	0.402
Lost workday cases	3.810	2.418
Total cases	9.738	5.627
Replacement rate	0.835	0.315
Fast work pace	0.162	0.369
No decisionmaking	0.016	0.127
Overtime work requirements	0.347	0.477
Job security	0.427	0.495
Firm size	6.698	10.265
Supervisory status	0.351	0.478
Availability of training	0.511	0.500
Union status	0.341	0.474

tral states, in the West, and in an urban area. Detailed industry and occupation responses for each worker also made it possible to create pertinent job-related dummy variables and to merge the BLS risk data with the sample information at the three-digit industry level.[16] Overall, the sample was broadly representative of the working population.

The wage equations differ in three ways. First, the functional form of the dependent variable, which is theoretically arbitrary, is either the wage or its natural logarithm. The second distinction among the regressions is in the nature of the three job hazard measures. The third difference is that the manner in which the replacement rate variable is entered varies, partly for purposes of comparison with previous research.[17] We first omit the replacement rate from the regressions, and then enter it separately to provide a comparison with earlier research. Finally, the theoretically preferable interactions of the replacement rate with the risk variables, which capture the weighted replacement rates, are included. Not reported below are results from regressions in which the replacement rate variable is entered both interactively and additively. The additive term was never significant in any of these, while the interactive term performed well.

For example, the three equations for person i, using lost workday cases as the hazard measure, are[18]

(3.6) $\ln \text{Wage}_i = X_i\beta + \gamma_w\text{Lost workday cases}_i + \varepsilon_i$,

(3.7) $\ln \text{Wage}_i = X_i\beta + \gamma_w\text{Lost workday cases}_i + \mu\text{Replacement rate}_i + \varepsilon_i$,

and

(3.8) $\ln \text{Wage}_i = X_i\beta + \gamma_w\text{Lost workday cases}_i + \delta_w\text{Lost workday cases}_i \times \text{Replacement rate}_i + \varepsilon_i$.

Equation 3.6 corresponds to the usual hedonic wage regression that fails to account for insurance. Equation 3.7 is similar to those estimated by several other investigators.[19] In Arnould and Nichols (1983), inclusion of the workers' compensation variable boosted the value of the risk coefficient by 12 percent and was associated with a statistically significant wage reduction, as expected. These modest effects may stem in part from their use of the death risk as a proxy for compensable job-related injuries. It is worth noting that all previous research has omitted other workplace characteristics, which is a potential source of bias. Moreover, the individual-specific hazard perception variable has heretofore not been used in any study of workers' compensation.

Compensating Differential Estimates

The focus of our empirical analysis is on a series of equations including different combinations of risk and workers' compensation variables. The basic structure of the wage equation is, however, unchanged. In Table 3.3 we report detailed estimates for a representative $\ln$ wage equation with the lost workday cases variable and the weighted replacement rate. This specification is the most important, since it is the lost workday accident rate and the weighted replacement rate that best reflect the impact of the workers' compensation system.

Overall, the $\ln$ wage equation performs in the expected manner. There is a positive but diminishing effect of work experience on earnings. Workers in the college-educated group tend to earn more income, as do union members. Moreover, the performance of the explanatory variables, such as union status, is quite robust with respect to specification of the risk variables.

TABLE 3.3
Wage Equation Estimates

Independent Variable	Coefficient	SD
Sex	−0.230[a]	0.051
Race	−0.124[a]	0.068
Poor health status	−0.210[a]	0.097
Experience	0.031[a]	0.006
Experience^2	$-1.0E-3$[a]	$0.2E-3$
Less than high school education	−0.098[a]	0.048
High school education	−0.018	0.046
College degree	0.185[a]	0.056
Lost workday cases	0.041[a]	0.014
Weighted replacement rate	−0.031[a]	0.015
Fast work pace	−0.068	0.044
No decisionmaking	0.140	0.128
Overtime work requirements	−0.042	0.035
Job security	0.085[a]	0.033
Firm size	0.007	0.018
Adjusted R-squared	0.477	—

[a] Statistically significant at the 0.05 confidence level, one-tailed test.

The focus of the analysis is on the various risk and workers' compensation measures. Results for the different combinations of risk and compensation variables utilized appear in Table 3.4. In each case, we first included a risk variable by itself, then with the weighted replacement rate variable, and finally with the replacement rate variable not interacted with the risk. Although we estimated eighteen equations in all, the principal patterns of influence were common across all of these variants. In ten of twelve cases, inclusion of the workers' compensation variables boosted the statistical significance of the risk variable alone. Inclusion of the replacement rate variable had little effect on the risk variable coefficient. This was not the case for the interactive regressions 2, 5, and 8. Finally, the weighted replacement rate variable was consistently negative and statistically significant.

The Implicit Value of Job Injuries

Although addition of the weighted replacement rate variable greatly boosts the coefficient on the job risk variable, after taking into account the role of both the risk and the interaction term, there is not a large

TABLE 3.4
Summary of Risk and Workers' Compensation Effects

Independent Variable	Coefficients and Standard Deviations for Equation:								
	(1)	(2)	(3)	(4)	(5)	(6)	(7)	(8)	(9)
Wage equations									
Lost workday cases	0.099 (0.065)	0.282[a] (0.122)	0.101 (0.065)	—	—	—	—	—	—
Total cases	—	—	—	0.037 (0.028)	0.113[a] (0.050)	0.038 (0.028)	—	—	—
Hazard assessment	—	—	—	—	—	—	0.270 (0.378)	1.057[a] (0.637)	0.2? (0.3?
Lost workday cases × replacement rate	—	−0.230[a] (0.129)	—	—	—	—	—	—	—
Total cases × replacement rate	—	—	—	—	−0.096[a] (0.053)	—	—	—	—
Hazard assessment × replacement rate	—	—	—	—	—	—	—	−0.999 (0.651)	—
Replacement rate	—	—	−0.606 (0.564)	—	—	−0.610 (0.563)	—	—	−0.5? (0.5?
Adjusted R-squared	0.374	0.374	0.372	0.373	0.411	0.371	0.372	0.371	0.3?
ln **Wage equations**									
Lost workday cases	0.017[a] (0.008)	0.041 (0.014)	0.017[a] (0.065)	—	—	—	—	—	—
Total cases	—	—	—	0.007[a] (0.003)	0.018[a] (0.006)	0.007[a] (0.003)	—	—	—
Hazard assessment	—	—	—	—	—	—	0.029 (0.045)	0.148[a] (0.074)	0.0? (0.0?
Lost workday cases × replacement rate	—	−0.031[a] (0.015)	—	—	—	—	—	—	—
Total cases × replacement rate	—	—	—	—	−0.012[a] (0.005)	—	—	—	—
Hazard assessment × replacement rate	—	—	—	—	—	—	—	−0.153[a] (0.076)	—
Replacement rate	—	—	−0.080 (0.065)	—	—	−0.081 (0.065)	—	—	−0.0? (0.0?
Adjusted R-squared	0.479	0.477	0.474	0.478	0.477	0.473	0.474	0.472	0.4?

[a] Statistically significant at the 0.05 confidence level, one-tailed test.

difference in the implicit value of job injuries when they are evaluated at current workers' compensation levels. The implicit value of a lost workday accident remains at $47,000 for the *ln* wage equation and rises from $35,000 to $39,000 for the wage equation upon inclusion of the interaction term.[20] To put these values in perspective, the average injury severity led to a loss of thirteen days of work on average. Each of these estimates is consistent with past estimates of the implicit value of injuries, as found in Viscusi (1978, 1983). Furthermore, the implicit injury values are somewhat greater than in studies of all job injuries, which represent a less severe injury mix than the lost workday injuries considered here.

These estimates, however, do not take into account the depressing influence that workers' compensation has on the level of risk premiums. If workers' compensation benefits dropped to zero, the required wage premium would rise substantially because of the income risks workers would face. One measure of this increase is the increased implicit value of a job injury, which would rise to $105,000 for the wage equation and to $122,000 for its *ln* wage counterpart. Similarly, full earnings replacement would lead to implicit values of injuries of $18,500 for the wage equation and $28,000 for the semilogarithmic form.

Although extrapolations of this nature are not as reliable as estimates pertaining to current levels of compensation, the overall suggestion of the results is clear. If there were no program providing earnings replacement to injured workers, the level of risk premiums would increase greatly. The reduction in risk premiums from additional increases in workers' compensation is much more modest.

The results for the full compensation case are of interest in their own right, since they isolate the earnings risk from the health status risk associated with job injuries. The findings here imply that at least half of current implicit valuations of injuries represent implicit values of the nonmonetary aspects of injuries. In effect, the $18,500 and $28,000 estimates above represent the value of the nonmonetary health losses associated with accidents.

These results are the first estimates of nonpecuniary health impacts that have ever been obtained. The valuations pertain to both the value of pain and suffering and the more general welfare losses from what Burton (1983) has termed "nonwork disability." To the extent that analysts wish to place a value on these nonmonetary considerations for policy evaluation or in a judicial proceeding, these empirical estimates provide a beginning for the process of trying to assess these amounts, which in the past have been based entirely on speculation. At current compensation levels, about half of the compensation for injuries is for nonpecuniary consequences. If there were no income replacement program, the relative importance of the health aspects would be far less.

Are Benefits Levels Optimal?

The fundamental and more immediate policy concern that this chapter addresses is whether the workers' compensation system provides an adequate level of earnings replacement. The results most pertinent to an assessment of the rate of substitution between wages and workers' compensation are in column 2 of Table 3.4, which includes both lost workday cases and the weighted replacement rate variable. The lost workday accident rate is the risk variable that most closely corresponds to the probability of receiving workers' compensation benefits for temporary total disability or permanent total disability. Similarly, the expected replacement rate is the appropriate measure of insurance.

The interaction term approach to assessing the role of workers' compensation is preferable because the value of workers' compensation coverage hinges on the risk level. Workers in completely safe jobs receive no benefits from the existence of such a compensation scheme. The weighted benefits are the product of the risk level and benefits level; in this case, we use the replacement rate as the benefit variable. The interaction variable appears in columns 2, 5, and 8 of Table 3.4.

The rate of substitution between wages and workers' compensation implied by these equations is quite substantial. On the basis of the empirical results, one can calculate how changes in the benefit formula affect the wage level.

Calculation of the rate of tradeoff is straightforward. Equation 3.8 can be rewritten, dropping the i subscript for convenience, as

$$ln \text{ Wage} = X\beta + \gamma_w \text{Lost workday cases} +$$

$$\delta_w \frac{\text{Lost workday cases} \times \text{benefits}}{40 \times \text{Wage}}$$

plus a random error term. The last term is the risk level multiplied by the weekly wage replacement rate. The weekly replacement rate equals the value of the weekly insurance payments divided by 40 times the wage, where the wage is the after-tax hourly wage and forty hours is the average full-time work week.

Multiplying both sides of the equation by $40 \times$ Wage,

$$40 \times \text{Wage} \times ln \text{ Wage} = (X\beta + \gamma_w \text{Lost workday cases}) \times$$
$$40 \times \text{Wage} +$$
$$\delta_w \text{Lost workday cases} \times \text{Benefits}.$$

Totally differentiating the above expression and collecting terms, we get the expression for the rate of tradeoff between the weekly wage and weekly benefits,

$$40 \times \frac{\partial \text{Wage}}{\partial \text{Benefits}} = \left(\frac{\delta_w \text{Lost workday cases}}{1 + ln \text{ Wage} - X\beta - \gamma_w \text{Lost workday cases}} \right).$$

For both the wage and ln wage equations, an additional one dollar in workers' compensation benefits leads to a twelve-cent reduction in wages. In each case, the rate of substitution is more than twice the five cents per dollar tradeoff one would expect given current rates of insurance loading and injury rates.

Not only is there substitution between wages and workers' compensation, but workers are willing to sacrifice more wages when they are healthy than would be dictated by the added insurance costs. Taken at face value, these results imply that existing levels of workers' compensation benefits are suboptimal from the standpoint of insuring income levels. Such underprovision of benefits may nevertheless be efficient if moral hazard is an important concern. As shown in Table 2.4, most research indicates that the elasticity of injuries with respect to the level of benefits is positive.

Several other implications of the results are also noteworthy. First, we have calculated the benefit levels necessary to provide full insurance to equate the marginal utility for the healthy and injured states and found that an increase of $111 from the weekly average of $266 would achieve this result. Second, and finally, it is not possible to calculate the benefit level necessary to reach the desired wage tradeoff of five cents per dollar of benefits. This requires information on preferences, which is not available from hedonic wage equations, such as we have estimated here.

Conclusion

The workers' compensation variables proved to be of fundamental importance in analyzing the structure of job risk compensation for workers in the Quality of Employment Survey. Higher levels of workers' compensation lead to a reduction in the base wage level that workers are paid. In addition, the size of the estimated wage-risk tradeoff is enhanced by inclusion of the replacement rate variables, thus strengthening findings in the compensating differential literature. Overall, the strongest results were those associated with the interactive variable, as would be expected on theoretical grounds.

Two of the implications of the results in this chapter extend to concerns of a much broader nature. First, the observed rate at which workers are willing to substitute base wage rates for higher levels of workers' compensation greatly exceeds the actuarial rate of tradeoff, even taking into account administrative costs. These results suggest that benefit levels in 1976 were suboptimal, provided that one abstracts from moral hazard considerations.

Finally, the results suggest that a large portion of compensating differentials for job hazards is for the nonmonetary aspects of the potential loss. However, if there were no workers' compensation system the role of income losses would predominate. The estimate that job hazards have an associated health impact of $18,500 to $28,000 is the first estimate of the role of the nonmonetary costs of job risks. In this case it is clear that the welfare implications of job risks extend well beyond their financial implications.

Four _____

Net Workers' Compensation Costs: Implications of the Wage Offset

SINCE THE EARLY 1970s, there has been a dramatic change in the market for hazardous jobs. The government began direct control of workplace technology through occupational safety and health regulations, while the judicial system became an active player in the area of ex post compensation of job risks.[1] This compensation for long-term health risks, particularly for asbestos workers, may run in the tens of billions of dollars.[2]

Much of the reason for the focus of public attention on these developments is that they represented a change in the role that these institutions played. Although the federal government has long had specific interests in particular areas of safety, such as the working conditions of longshoremen and maritime workers, the advent of the Occupational Safety and Health Administration marked a sweeping expansion of these responsibilities. Similarly, the emergence of an important role for judicial compensation of job accidents in product liability suits did not represent an entirely new area of the law, but the advent of mass tort cases at the very least did represent a quantum leap in the degree of activity.

Perhaps because of these developments, there has not been sufficient attention devoted to the equally important shift in the role of workers' compensation.[3] The state workers' compensation system has long been one of the principal sources of nonwage costs borne by employers. Although by no means as large a component of compensation as social security taxes, workers' compensation premiums have traditionally been of comparable importance to other nonwage costs.[4]

The Rising Costs of Workers' Compensation

In the early 1970s, the National Commission on State Workmen's Compensation Laws sought a somewhat more ambitious role for workers' compensation. In a series of recommendations, the Commission urged that benefits be raised in order to reduce the extent of wage loss (Report of the National Commission on State Workmen's Compensation Laws

1972). In response, there has been a major shift in the level of workers' compensation premiums, which have risen from $6.8 billion in 1973 to $22.9 billion in 1983. As a percentage of total compensation, workers' compensation also increased its importance in that decade, constituting about 1 percent of compensation in 1973 and 1.67 percent in 1983.

This dramatic increase in costs has not gone unnoticed by employers, who nominally bear the costs through payment of premiums. The rapid increase in the compensation burden in the late 1970s was a particular cause for alarm. Taking these cost increases at face value as a measure of the total cost of the system is not, however, appropriate from an economic standpoint.

A $16.1 billion increase in annual workers' compensation premiums is not tantamount to a general tax levy of $16.1 billion used to provide for contributions to the overall federal budget. The benefits to injured workers have also risen, and as a result, workers will view compensation for hazardous jobs as greater than before. From a conceptual standpoint, workers should willingly accept some reduction in wages for the added benefits, and if the level of benefits provided is not as high as they would like, the results in Chapter 3 imply that the workers will accept a wage reduction that exceeds the actuarial cost of the awards.[5]

There may be additional ramifications as well. More generous benefit levels may boost the number of injuries for which claims are filed and may lead workers to prolong the period of recovery. Although the magnitude of such influences remains controversial, the existence of some moral hazard problems of this type is suggested by the research cited in Chapter 2. These effects and existing evidence on their magnitudes are discussed below.

In this chapter we explore the extent to which the effect of higher workers' compensation costs is offset by these economic effects. The principal building block for our analysis is an estimate of the wage reductions induced by higher benefit levels. To estimate this relationship, we employ three different sets of survey data for the years 1977 and 1982, which enable us to estimate not only the rate of tradeoff but also changes in the rate of tradeoff over time. These results consequently serve both to track the change in the wage–workers' compensation tradeoff over time and to provide a robustness test for the results in Chapter 3.

The regression results in Chapter 3 indicate a substantial tradeoff between the base wage rate and workers' compensation benefits, which exceeds the actuarial cost of the benefits. These findings are used in this chapter to calculate the cost of the increase in workers' compensation premiums net of the wage reductions. In all of the cases considered, benefit increases have more than paid for themselves through wage reductions.

The magnitude of this economic "free lunch" is reduced, however, if higher benefit levels induce workers to collect benefits for a longer duration and for more injuries. The role of these factors is discussed in an exploratory analysis. Recognition of the offsets resulting from higher benefits greatly reduces the net benefit impact of higher premium levels, and helps reconcile the "free lunch" finding with the observed opposition of many firms to the workers' compensation system.

The Samples and the Variables

The general approach we take is to estimate a wage equation in which we isolate the effects of worker characteristics, job characteristics (including job risks), and workers' compensation on wages. The estimated relationship then provides the basis for assessing the wage–workers' compensation tradeoff.

This estimation relies on two large data sets pertaining to the labor market situation of individual workers. More specifically, the data used to estimate the parameters of interest are drawn from the University of Michigan Panel Study of Income Dynamics (PSID) and the 1977 Quality of Employment Survey (QES). Two years of the PSID are considered: 1977 and 1982. We use the 1977 data to allow comparison of the results reported below with those in Chapter 3 and the 1982 data to capture the relationship between wages and workers' compensation of a more recent vintage.

Although it is possible to exploit the panel nature of the PSID, we do not do so here, choosing instead to treat each year as a distinct cross-section. After exclusion of the nonrandom poverty subsample of the PSID, self-employed individuals, farmers, and individuals who are not heads of households and who experienced long-term unemployment in each year, 1329 and 1106 observations, respectively, remain in the 1977 and 1982 waves. The QES sample used in Chapter 3 contained 485 observations.

As in Chapter 3, the variables of primary interest in this study are the lost workday case rate and replacement rate variables. Since the PSID does not ascertain injury risks for individual workers, it is necessary to match injury rate data to each worker by industry. Unfortunately, the detail afforded by three-digit industry data is not available in the PSID until 1981. Thus, the 1977 risk data in the PSID are more highly aggregated than the 1982 data, which causes more error to be introduced into the earlier measure.

The theoretical model developed in Chapter 3 defines risk as the probability of an injury. This suggests the use of the lost workday case rate as the empirical measure of risk, since the number of accidents is a better measure of frequency than the alternative—total lost workdays. Thus, the risk measure is the lost workday case rate reported by the Bureau of Labor Statistics and matched to individual workers by two-digit industry in the 1977 PSID and three-digit industry in the 1977 QES and 1982 PSID. As noted in Chapter 3, use of the injury rate ignores such issues as the duration and severity of wage loss. Injury frequency data capture sufficiently the effects we wish to analyze here, however, and are more directly comparable to earlier results, so we abstract from duration issues. We capture the ex post component of job risk compensation by the workers' compensation wage replacement rate described in Chapter 3.

A detailed list of the variables used in the empirical analysis has already been presented in Chapter 3. Worker characteristics include years of schooling, years worked since completion of schooling, years worked on the current job, race, sex, and health status. Job characteristics include whether or not the worker's job is covered by a union contract, the BLS lost workday case rate, the expected replacement rate, and a blue-collar occupation dummy variable. The basic measure of pecuniary compensation is the after-tax hourly wage. The wage variable is computed from information on annual labor earnings and hours and the marginal tax rate, which is reported directly in the PSID, and computed as described earlier in the QES.

Table 4.1 presents descriptive statistics for the PSID samples. Each sample appears representative of the U.S. working population. In addition, time-dependent measures, such as experience and education, are consistently larger in 1982. Wages increase substantially, primarily because of inflation: The average nominal wage for 1981, the year covered by the 1982 PSID, is approximately $7.29, compared with the 1976 average of $4.88; however, the 1981 wage in 1976 dollars is only $4.85. Finally, there is a substantial increase in the average risk level in the later sample.

The risk and workers' compensation variables reflect the experiences of a typical U.S. worker. The mean risk levels suggest that for these samples the average risk of a lost workday injury ranged from 4–5 per 100 workers annually. These levels are comparable to figures for the average U.S. worker. The injury rate of 3.56 for the 1977 PSID subsample, which reflects working conditions in 1976, is very close to the 1976 private sector average lost workday rate of 3.5 per 100 workers. The 1982 PSID sample rate of 4.56 for employment experiences in 1981 is somewhat greater than the 1981 national average of 3.8 injuries per 100

TABLE 4.1
Descriptive Statistics, 1977 and 1982 PSID Samples: Means and
Standard Deviations

Variable	1977	1982
Wage	4.88	7.29
	(1.99)	(2.42)
Sex	0.17	0.12
	(0.37)	(0.32)
Race	0.07	0.07
	(0.26)	(0.26)
Poor health status	0.06	0.08
	(0.24)	(0.28)
Experience	19.71	21.68
	(13.27)	(11.84)
Job tenure	5.64	6.01
	(6.24)	(6.05)
Education	12.23	12.75
	(3.03)	(2.82)
Lost workday cases	3.56	4.56
	(1.72)	(2.93)
Replacement rate	0.94	0.92
	(0.54)	(0.50)
City size	0.53	0.53
	(0.50)	(0.50)
Weighted replacement rate	3.26	4.28
	(2.47)	(3.98)
Union status	0.30	0.31
	(0.46)	(0.46)
Blue collar	0.50	0.49
	(0.50)	(0.50)
Residence in the Northeast region	0.21	0.20
	(0.41)	(0.40)
Residence in the North Central region	0.32	0.32
	(0.47)	(0.47)
Residence in the South region	0.29	0.28
	(0.45)	(0.45)
Residence in the West region	0.18	0.19
	(0.45)	(0.46)

[a] Variable was coded differently in the QES sample.

workers, but it is less than the manufacturing average lost workday
case rate of 5.1 per 100 workers.

The magnitudes of the workers' compensation variables suggest that
the degree of coverage is quite extensive. Taking into account the fa-

vorable tax status of the benefits, workers' compensation replaces over 90 percent of the worker's wage in each of the sample years. The duration of these benefits is not, however, unlimited, so the effective replacement rate for injuries of long duration may be less. The weighted replacement rate, which is the probability of suffering an injury times the replacement rate of wages, equals 3.26 for 1977 and 4.28 for 1982.

The blue-collar dummy variable is intended to capture important differences in job attributes other than risk that might influence the wage premium that a job commands. Thus, this variable is intended to act as a proxy for other job attributes, such as whether the job involves unpleasant working conditions. Inclusion of such nonpecuniary attributes has been the exception in the literature, as only a minority of compensating differential studies (for example, Viscusi 1979a) include such measures. Since the PSID does not include such job attribute measures, we rely on the blue-collar dummy variable as a proxy for these conditions.

Estimates of the Wage Equations

We estimated two equations for each PSID cross-section, using post-tax wages and their natural logarithms as the dependent variables. The principal variables of interest are lost workday cases and the weighted replacement rate. Higher risk levels should boost worker wages, since workers will demand a compensating differential for hazardous jobs. Similarly, higher weighted replacement rates for injuries will lower the level of compensation; thus, the benefit variable, which reflects the interactive influence of the risk level and the replacement rate, should have a negative sign.

Table 4.2 summarizes estimates of a wage equation identical to equation 3.8 in the previous chapter.

(4.1) $ln \text{ Wage}_i = X_i\beta + \gamma_w\text{Lost workday cases}_i +$
$\delta_w\text{Lost workday cases}_i \times \text{Replacement rate}_i + \varepsilon_i$

for each sample. Since the results using the wage variable were quite similar to those using ln wage as the dependent variable, only the semilogarithmic results are reported in detail.

In both the 1977 and 1982 samples, the equations perform as expected in terms of the usual components of an earnings equation. An additional year of education results in a 3–4 percent increase in wages. Experience and job tenure both increase wages at a decreasing rate. Black and female workers earn substantially lower wages, as do workers with health limitations. Finally, the estimated wage premium for

TABLE 4.2
Wage Equation Estimates: Coefficients and Standard Deviations

Variable	1977	1982
Sex	−0.305	−0.284
	(0.028)	(0.028)
Race	−0.130	−0.135
	(0.040)	(0.036)
Poor health status	−0.098	−0.094
	(0.042)	(0.032)
Experience	0.023	0.016
	(0.003)	(0.004)
Experience^2	$-3.7E-4$	$-2.5E-4$
	$(0.7E-4)$	$(0.7E-4)$
Job tenure	0.017	0.011
	(0.005)	(0.003)
Job tenure^2	$-4.5E-4$	$-1.9E-4$
	$(1.8E-4)$	$(1.2E-4)$
Education	0.045	0.032
	(0.004)	(0.004)
Lost workday cases	0.034	0.023
	(0.008)	(0.005)
Weighted replacement rate	−0.010	−0.015
	(0.006)	(0.004)
City size	0.116	0.063
	(0.021)	(0.019)
Union status	0.169	0.153
	(0.024)	(0.021)
Blue collar	−0.131	−0.075
	(0.024)	(0.023)
Residence in the Northeast region	$-0.4E-2$	−0.054
	$(3.1E-2)$	(0.028)
Residence in the North Central region	$1.6E-2$	−0.042
	$(2.9E-2)$	(0.025)
Residence in the Southern region	$-6.7E-2$	−0.089
	$(3.0E-2)$	(0.027)
Constant	0.589	1.319
	(0.080)	(0.079)
Adjusted R-squared	0.38	0.31

workers covered by a collective bargaining agreement is about 16 percent.

The variables of particular interest in Table 4.2 are lost workday cases and the weighted replacement rate. In both samples, higher non-

TABLE 4.3
Wage-Benefit Elasticities: Coefficients and Standard Deviations

Wage Equations	After-Tax Wage		After-Tax ln Wage	
	1977[a]	1982	1977[a]	1982
Lost workday cases	0.158	0.107	0.036	0.015
	(0.035)	(0.037)	(0.008)	(0.005)
Weighted replacement rate	−0.140	−0.185	−0.031	−0.031
	(0.072)	(0.129)	(0.016)	(0.018)
Rates of tradeoff	−0.10	−0.06	−0.12	−0.08

[a] The 1977 results are taken from Chapter 3.

fatal injury risks increase wages significantly. Likewise, ex post compensation for injuries reduces wages, affecting the ex ante compensation for risk provided through the injury risk compensating differential. In both years the replacement rate effect is statistically significant at the 0.05 confidence level.

Table 4.3 summarizes the estimated risk and insurance elasticities. The results include the equations reported in Table 4.2, estimates for equations using the wage as the dependent variable, and results that we obtained with the 1977 University of Michigan Quality of Employment data (described in Chapter 3). The evidence is consistent across the three sets of data and two dependent variables in terms of the nature of the influences. There is strong support for the prediction that risks increase wages and that workers' compensation insurance reduces wages, conditional on the risk level. In each of the two models estimated with the 1982 data, the risk and insurance effects have the predicted signs and are significant at the 0.01 confidence level. The same is true of the lost workday case coefficient in both 1977 samples. Likewise, the workers' compensation variable has the predicted sign and performs quite well in both the before- and after-tax log wage equations, and is negative and significant in three of the four equations we estimated using the 1977 samples. Furthermore, in every equation estimated, the risk and insurance variables have the correct signs and are jointly significant.

Wage-Benefit Tradeoffs

The parameter of primary importance that can be calculated from these estimates is the implied rate of tradeoff between wages and workers' compensation. This estimate has interesting policy implications. Our focus in this chapter is the extent to which benefit increases are financed by workers through wage reductions. In addition, as shown in Chapter 3, estimation of this rate of tradeoff enables us to determine whether or not benefit levels are optimal by comparing the observed rate with that which would occur in an idealized world, recognizing the existence of administrative costs of the insurance program.

The bottom row in Table 4.3 summarizes the estimated rates of tradeoff derived by use of this formula in conjunction with the estimated regression coefficients. The most striking result apparent in Table 4.3 is the size of the estimated rate of tradeoff in the 1977 QES and the 1982 PSID. These results are estimated with a less aggregative risk variable than are the 1977 PSID estimates and are consequently less subject to measurement error bias.

The results indicate that benefit levels are too low relative to the rate of tradeoff that would be observed if the level of insurance were optimal. Assuming $a = 0.25$, which is a reasonable approximation of the national average (see Chapter 3), and given the accident probabilities of 0.035 (1977 QES), 0.047 (1977 PSID), and 0.046 (1982 PSID) in our samples, the optimal tradeoffs are −0.05 (1977 QES), −0.06 (1977 PSID), and −0.06 (1982 PSID). The actual tradeoffs calculated from the data are always much larger (in absolute value) than those for the 1977 QES. The 1977 PSID results are smallest in absolute magnitude, perhaps in part because of the greater measurement error in the risk variable, which is based on two-digit industry matchups of injuries to workers, whereas the 1977 QES and the 1982 PSID results are based on more refined three-digit matchups. The 1982 results indicate benefit levels fairly close to the optimal insurance amount excluding the role of moral hazard, which may imply that benefit levels are too high.

If we focus on the PSID data, it appears that there has been an increase in benefit inadequacy over the five-year period, since workers are increasingly willing to trade off wages for workers' compensation benefits. Some rough calculations could be made to explain this finding. First, although the average weekly benefit level in our sample rose from $148 to $235, the average after-tax weekly wage based on a forty-hour week rose from $195 to $292. Thus, in our sample, the average weekly earnings replacement rate fell over time by 9 percentage points. A further calculation shows that when weekly benefits in 1981 are translated into 1976 dollars by using the appropriate price deflator for the period, real benefits are largely unchanged. Since these real benefits are the worker's concern, and since we would expect the demand for real benefits to rise with the observed increase in the injury level, the observed trends in the rates of tradeoff are plausible. Nevertheless, in all likelihood, the difference reflects primarily the higher quality of the risk data in the 1982 PSID; thus, one should be cautious in taking the 1977 PSID results at face value.

For purposes of the subsequent calculations, the general implications of the results are the following. Consider a situation in which the actuarial cost of benefits (plus administrative costs) leads to a five- to six-cent expected additional cost to employers for each additional dollar in benefit levels. Since administrative costs are not high, workers receive an expected benefit of four to five cents. In return for these higher expected benefits, they are willing to take a considerably higher wage cut, on the order of twelve cents for the 1977 QES. For this sample, higher workers' compensation benefits produce wage reductions several times greater than their dollar cost.

In the case of the 1977 PSID results, the higher benefits do not pay their own way. These estimates, which counter the others, are subject to much more substantial measurement error than are the 1977 QES estimates because of the more aggregative industry risk-worker matchups. They do not appear to be a reliable reflection of worker preferences, particularly given the much different and more precise results derived from three-digit matchups.

Finally, for the 1982 PSID, higher workers' compensation benefits lead to wage reductions comparable to the levels that one would expect if insurance for injuries were set at an optimal level. If one uses the 1977 QES results as the reference point for the tradeoff four years earlier, then there appears to have been a substantial drop in the rate at which workers will sacrifice wages for higher workers' compensation benefits. Thus, the level of workers' compensation benefits that would be observed with fully efficient insurance markets is similar to that provided in 1981 and above the amount provided in 1976.

Estimates of the Total Wage Offset

Table 4.4 explores the net cost of workers' compensation after taking into account the wage offset effects. Column 2 in each panel of the table is identical, summarizing the before-tax levels of total workers' compensation payments.[6] Before-tax premium levels rose from $10.9 billion in 1976 to $22.9 billion in 1983. Assuming that the marginal tax rate faced by firms is 0.30,[7] the after-tax payments for workers' compensation reported in column 3 of each panel rose from $7.6 billion to $16.0 billion over the same period. Most of this increase occurred during 1976–1979, as after-tax payments almost doubled in this period, rising from $7.6 billion to $14.1 billion.

Panels A to F in Table 4.4 present calculations of the wage reduction and the net cost of workers' compensation benefits, based on the data in columns 2 and 3. The key assumptions made, which are summarized in the panel headings, pertain to the rate of tradeoff between wages and workers' compensation and the manner in which benefits relate to workers' compensation payments.

In addition, since the 1977 QES results had a tradeoff of greater absolute magnitude than the 1982 PSID tradeoff, we explored the possible influence of a diminishing magnitude of the rate of tradeoff over time. In Panel C and Panel F the −0.12 tradeoff is assumed to decrease linearly by 0.008 annually. As a result, the assumed rate of tradeoff in 1983 is −0.064, and the rate of tradeoff in 1981 is −0.08, the result obtained with use of the 1982 PSID sample A diminishing of the rate of tradeoff is expected on theoretical grounds as benefit levels increase, since the marginal value of insurance declines. This result abstracts from possible moral hazard problems.

Calculation of the wage reductions requires assumptions concerning the relationship between payments, which are made ex post, and benefits, which generate ex ante wage changes. The basic relationship utilized is that total premiums (*TP*) will equal benefits (*b*) times the probability of an accident (*p*), plus the associated administrative costs:

Total Premiums = Benefits × Probability of an
Accident + Administrative Costs.

If administrative costs equal *a* cents per dollar of expected benefits, then

$$TP = pb(1 + a).$$

Thus, using information on total premiums and accident probabilities and the loading factor $a = 0.25$, we can compute the benefit level as

(4.2) $b = TP/(1.25)p.$

Once we know *b*, we can determine the wage reduction due to *b* by multiplying *b* by the estimated wage reduction rate. Panels A–F are based on this formula. In Panels A, B, and C, the 1976 risk level of 0.035 is taken as the measure of *p*, while in Panels D, E, and F the 1981 risk level of 0.045 is used. The results in columns 2–4 are all reported in after-tax dollars, assuming a corporate tax rate of 0.30.

Based on these assumptions, column 4 in each panel presents the wage reduction effects. For simplicity, let us focus on Panels A–C. With the −0.12 wage reduction rate in Panel A, the wage savings values range from $20.3 billion to $42.7 billion, each of which is far in excess of the level of insurance payments. With a tradeoff of −0.08 in Panel B, the wage effects are one-third lower than in Panel A, as they reach a peak of $28.5 billion in 1983. Finally, in Panel C, in which the rate goes linearly from −0.12 in 1976 to −0.08 in 1981 and −0.064 in 1983, the wage

TABLE 4.4
Wage Effects and the Net Cost of Workers' Compensation
(in billions of dollars)

Panel A: Wage reduction rate = 0.12; Risk level = 0.035;
$p(1 + a) = 0.045$

Year	Total Premiums[a]	Total Payments[b]	Wage Reduction[c]	Net Cost[d]
1976	10.9	7.6	20.3	−12.7
1977	14.0	9.8	26.1	−16.3
1978	16.6	11.6	30.9	−19.3
1979	20.2	14.1	37.6	−23.5
1980	22.0	15.4	41.1	−25.7
1981	22.9	16.0	42.7	−26.7
1982	22.5	15.8	42.1	−26.3
1983	22.9	16.0	42.7	−26.7

Panel B: Wage reduction rate = 0.08; Risk level = 0.035;
$p(1 + a) = 0.045$

Year	Total Premiums[a]	Total Payments[b]	Wage Reduction[c]	Net Cost[d]
1976	10.9	7.6	13.5	−5.9
1977	14.0	9.8	17.4	−7.6
1978	16.6	11.6	20.6	−9.0
1979	20.2	14.1	25.1	−11.0
1980	22.0	15.4	27.4	−12.0
1981	22.9	16.0	28.5	−12.5
1982	22.5	15.8	28.0	−12.2
1983	22.9	16.0	28.5	−12.5

Panel C: Wage reduction rate = 0.12 in 1976, decreases linearly
by 0.008/year; Risk level = 0.035; $p(1 + a) = 0.045$

Year	Total Premiums[a]	Total Payments[b]	Wage Reduction[c]	Net Cost[d]
1976	10.9	7.6	20.3	−12.7
1977	14.0	9.8	24.4	−14.6
1978	16.6	11.6	26.8	−15.2
1979	20.2	14.1	30.1	−16.0
1980	22.0	15.4	30.1	−14.7
1981	22.9	16.0	28.4	−12.4
1982	22.5	15.8	25.3	−9.5
1983	22.9	16.0	22.8	−6.8

[a] Data are taken from "Workers' Compensation: Coverage, Benefits, and
Costs," *Social Security Bulletin*, for each year in the table.

TABLE 4.4, *cont.*

Panel D: Wage reduction rate = 0.12; Risk level = 0.045; $p(1 + a) = 0.056$

Year	Total Premiums[a]	Total Payments[b]	Wage Reduction[c]	Net Cost[d]
1976	10.9	7.6	16.3	−8.7
1977	14.0	9.8	21.0	−11.2
1978	16.6	11.6	24.9	−13.3
1979	20.2	14.1	30.2	−16.1
1980	22.0	15.4	33.0	−17.6
1981	22.9	16.0	34.3	−18.3
1982	22.5	15.8	33.9	−18.1
1983	22.9	16.0	34.3	−18.3

Panel E: Wage reduction rate = 0.08; Risk level = 0.045; $p(1 + a) = 0.056$

Year	Total Premiums[a]	Total Payments[b]	Wage Reduction[c]	Net Cost[d]
1976	10.9	7.6	10.9	−3.3
1977	14.0	9.8	14.0	−4.2
1978	16.6	11.6	16.6	−5.0
1979	20.2	14.1	20.1	−6.0
1980	22.0	15.4	22.0	−6.6
1981	22.9	16.0	22.9	−6.9
1982	22.5	15.8	22.6	−6.8
1983	22.9	16.0	22.9	−6.9

Panel F: Wage reduction rate = 0.12 in 1976, decreases linearly by 0.008/year; Risk level = 0.045; $p(1 + a) = 0.056$

Year	Total Premiums[a]	Total Payments[b]	Wage Reduction[c]	Net Cost[d]
1976	10.9	7.6	16.3	−8.7
1977	14.0	9.8	19.6	−9.8
1978	16.6	11.6	21.5	−9.9
1979	20.2	14.1	24.2	−10.1
1980	22.0	15.4	24.2	−8.8
1981	22.9	16.0	22.9	−6.9
1982	22.5	15.8	20.3	−4.5
1983	22.9	16.0	18.3	−2.3

[b] Total payments = premium costs net of taxes. Assume tax rate = 0.30.
[c] Wage reduction = [total payments/$p(1 + a)$] × wage reduction rate.
[d] Net cost = total payments − wage reduction.

reduction goes from $20.3 billion in 1976 (as in Panel A) to $22.8 billion in 1983.

The final column of each panel is the net cost of workers' compensation, which is simply the difference between total after-tax premiums paid (column 3) and the wage reduction (column 4). In every case considered, workers' compensation benefits have more than paid for themselves in all years through the wage offset.

The most favorable evidence of the desirability of workers' compensation is in Panel A. Increasing workers' compensation premiums from $10.9 billion in 1976 to $22.9 billion in 1983 did not cost firms an extra $12 billion before taxes. Rather, it saved them an extra $14.0 billion through the influence of the wage offsets. For the results in Panel B, the additional net cost went from −$5.9 billion in 1976 to −$12.5 billion in 1983, and in Panel C it went from −$12.7 billion in 1976 to −$6.8 billion in 1983. More modest savings result if we use the injury rate of 0.045, as shown in Panels D-F.

The results in Panel C are a bit deceptive since they seem to suggest that workers' compensation increases reduce costs. Overall, the net cost is negative, as is true in every other case considered. However, if it is the higher level of workers' compensation benefits that has led to the dampening of the rate of tradeoff between wages and workers' compensation, as one would expect theoretically, then the higher level of benefits is not cost reducing. In particular, the net cost went from −$12.7 billion in 1976 to −$6.8 billion in 1983, which represents a cost increase of $5.9 billion. Overall costs remain negative, but the costs of benefit increases are positive.

This pattern is not unique to Panel C. Panel F also has a larger cost reduction in 1976 than in 1983. These are both cases in which the rate of tradeoff declines over time, and the dampening of the tradeoff is attributed to the more generous levels of workers' compensation benefits. In these cases, benefit increases do not pay for themselves through wage reductions, since the net cost of the benefit increases is positive.

The results in Table 4.4 are strengthened when the net cost of benefits is computed in real terms. In particular, in Panels C and F, where nominal net costs are falling over time, real net costs are falling at an even faster rate, because of the effects of the chronic inflation experienced during the period. In Panel C, for instance, the net cost of workers' compensation decreased by 46 percent in nominal terms during 1976–1983. Given the increase in the price level during that period, real benefits fell by $8.6 billion, or over 67 percent.

Three general sets of conclusions emerge from Table 4.4. First, recognition of the wage reductions generated by workers' compensation leads to a lower net cost than the total premiums suggest. The highest annual real net cost estimated was –$2.3 billion (Panel E, 1983), and the lowest was –$26.7 billion (Panel A, 1981). Second, in every instance the annual net cost of workers' compensation is negative. Finally, even though the annual net costs may be negative, the incremental real costs of higher benefits are typically positive if one assumes that the observed changes in the wage–workers' compensation tradeoff from 1976 to 1983 are due to the higher benefit levels.

Moral Hazard and Related Factors

One potential drawback of the higher workers' compensation benefits from the standpoint of the firm is that they may increase the number of injuries, or at least claims of injuries, and their duration. As the degree of coverage of the income loss from job injuries is increased, workers have less of a financial incentive to avoid the injury since the size of the loss has been reduced. Similarly, the duration of injuries may increase since workers have less of an incentive to return to work if they receive close to full earnings replacement without working.

Each of these effects follows directly from standard economic models, but the magnitude of these effects has long been controversial. Recent research by Butler (1983) and Butler and Worrall (1983, 1985) indicates that these influences can be substantial—with an elasticity of injury claims with respect to benefits of 0.4 and a duration elasticity of 0.23.[8] The calculations in Table 4.4 take into account the effects of moral hazard on benefits, since total net costs, including the costs due to more frequent or prolonged injuries, are reflected in the total premiums.

Two additional classes of costs have not been considered. First, if there are more frequent injuries, costs to the firm in terms of interruptions of production and the replacement of injured workers will rise. Empirical evidence on the effect of benefit levels on injury rates is not conclusive. Of the studies summarized in Table 2.4, most indicate a substantial moral hazard effect. However, evidence in Chelius (1976, 1982, 1983) and the results reported in Chapter 9 indicate that this may not be true for more severe injuries, where productivity losses are the largest.

Second, higher injury rates may boost the level of wages workers require to work on the job. In general, there are substantial compensating differentials for job risks that increase as the injury level rises, as reflected in the positive risk coefficients in Table 4.3. If, however, the underlying level of workplace safety has not changed but workers, in effect, choose to have a higher accident rate because more generous benefit levels diminish their optimal level of safety precautions, the standard relationship between wages and injury rates will not hold. At the very minimum, there will be some offset of the compensating differential effect because of the diminished safety precautions that are taken. These indirect effects are analyzed in Chapter 9.

The only plausible case for a substantial wage increase for greater job risks stemming from diminished precautions must be based on either the ability of unions to use a bad safety record for negotiating purposes or a failure of other workers to perceive the true source of the greater apparent riskiness. Because of the speculative nature of such adjustments, we did not modify the results in Table 4.4 to take such factors into account.

Conclusion

The most fundamental purpose of this chapter has been to show that one cannot take workers' compensation premium levels at face value as an estimate of the costs to firms of the system. Under a wide range of assumptions a substantial wage offset is generated by the provision of benefits. This offset is expected on economic grounds since boosting one attractive feature of the compensation mix (workers' compensation) will reduce the wages needed to make a hazardous job acceptable to the worker.

One can take two perspectives on the wage offsets. In terms of the level of net costs (that is, premiums less wage reductions), workers' compensation more than pays for itself. When viewed incrementally, however, the change in net cost is positive because of a substantial diminishing of the rate of tradeoff between wages and workers' compensation as the benefit levels increase. The incremental benefit increases do impose net costs on firms, so the complaints that have been voiced regarding benefit hikes are not irrational. Real cost increases to the firm are involved. Although workers' compensation increases do not provide an economic "free lunch" to firms, they are cheaper fare on average than is generally believed.

Five

Workers' Implicit Value of Life

ONE VERY PROMINENT and controversial application of benefit assessment is the valuation of policies that reduce the risks to human life.[1] From a conceptual standpoint, the task of valuing life is no different from that of any other public policy. The appropriate benefit measure for a safety-enhancing policy is society's willingness to pay for the expected number of lives extended as a result of the policy.[2]

Policy analysts typically estimate the value of life from labor markets because the availability of information on risks in labor markets and the associated wage rates that workers receive enable estimation of the market-generated wage-risk tradeoff. Analysts interpret the observed market tradeoff between dollars and mortality risk as an indication of the compensation a worker would forgo for a reduction in risk. They then statistically extrapolate to generate the dollar value of life. Almost without exception, labor market studies of the value of life utilize risk measures based on U.S. Bureau of Labor Statistics (BLS) death risk data.[3]

The release of a new and more refined data series on occupational death risks calls into question the accuracy of the estimates obtained using this approach. In order to provide a more reliable statistical basis for assessing job-related deaths, the National Institute of Occupational Safety and Health (NIOSH) initiated its own occupational death statistics system. The first set of death statistics, released in 1987, implied that the overall number of deaths experienced by workers was 84 percent greater than indicated by the BLS data. More important, as the comparisons presented in this chapter indicate, the bias in reported deaths is not uniform—most industry risks exceed the BLS levels, but by differing amounts, while two major industry groups have a risk level in the NIOSH data below that in the BLS data. Such an extensive revamping of the death rate statistics potentially undermines the validity of the value of life estimates based on BLS risk data. At the very least, there is a need for a fundamental reexamination of the value of life results.

This chapter explores the implications of this new risk data series for labor market estimates of the value of life. Will statistically significant wage-risk tradeoffs still be observed, and how will they differ from estimates derived from BLS data? In the next section, we discuss the data base used to explore these issues and provide a detailed comparison of the NIOSH and BLS risk data that represent the pivotal components of the analysis. We then report wage equation estimates using the new occupational death risk data, as well as comparable equations using BLS risk data. The reassuring aspect of the results is that there is a powerful and statistically significant positive relationship between job risks and worker wages. The magnitude of this tradeoff is, however, substantially underestimated by use of the BLS data. Our estimates indicate that use of the more accurate risk measure approximately doubles the estimated value of life.

The Sample and the Variables

The building block for the empirical analysis is a large set of data on worker wages and characteristics of individual workers, which provides the basis for relating wages to NIOSH data for workers in different states and industries. Several employment data sets, such as those used in the previous chapter, could serve this function adequately. To analyze this particular issue we selected the 1982 wave of the University of Michigan Panel Study of Income Dynamics (PSID). The PSID is a widely used national survey of employment patterns for which we can select a survey year that is appropriate for both the NIOSH and the BLS risk data, because the PSID survey is repeated annually. The 1982 wave of the PSID summarizes the work experiences of workers in 1981. This wave of the PSID covers the only year that is included in both of the fatality risk measures used below and is consequently most appropriate for estimation purposes.

The PSID includes a random sample of families and a nonrandom group of families who were selected because their incomes fell below a prespecified poverty line. To maintain the representativeness of our sample, this latter group is excluded from the sample we use in our estimation. Also excluded are workers for whom no NIOSH death risk data are available—principally farmers, farm managers, and government employees. We also excluded non–household heads and blacks because intermittent labor supply and the influence of racial discrimination may distort estimates of the wage equations for these groups. The remaining sample contains 1,349 complete observations.

The general approach in this chapter, as in the literature, is to regress the worker's wage or its natural logarithm on a series of explanatory variables, including the worker's personal characteristics, job characteristics, and risk level. An accurate assessment of the wage-risk tradeoff must hold these nonrisk characteristics constant in measuring the effect of changes in death risk on the wage. The coefficient of the death

TABLE 5.1
PSID Variable Definitions

Variable	Definition
NTOF death risk	NTOF death rate variable: number of fatal accidents per 100,000 workers
BLS death risk	BLS death rate variable: number of fatal accidents per 100,000 workers
Weighted replacement rate	Workers' compensation fatality benefits replacement rate, weighted by death risk

risk variable then yields the risk-dollar tradeoff that is used to calculate the implied value of life. This value represents the value of a statistical life based on the rate of tradeoff implied by the amount workers require as compensation for exposure to small risks of death.

One can view such estimates in either of two ways. First, the estimated value of life represents the total amount of compensation that a group of workers requires to face a job risk that is expected to kill one additional worker. Second, it represents the compensation required per unit of risk that is faced, with the rate of tradeoff estimated for small risks used to provide an index of the tradeoff society should have in dealing with larger-scale risk reduction policies.

Table 5.1 summarizes the definitions of new variables used in the empirical analysis in this chapter. The dependent variable once again is the worker's after-tax hourly wage or its natural logarithm. Since the PSID included either an hourly wage variable or information that could be used to construct an hourly wage, it was not necessary to use annual earnings as a proxy for wages, as was necessary in some of the earlier studies in this area. A more novel aspect of our formulation is the tax adjustment of wages, which is the procedure we used in Chapters 3 and 4 as well. This adjustment is not common in the compensating differential literature, despite the fact that it is the theoretically appropriate measure, because it is the after-tax wage that drives worker behavior. In those studies that have adjusted for taxes, such as our two earlier analyses in Chapters 3 and 4, use of the after-tax wage led to significant changes in the results. The explanatory variables that we included as regressors to control for the wage variation that is not attributable to variation in risk mirror those in the previous chapters.

The impact of the workers' compensation system is again captured by including the weighted replacement rate variable; the annuity to survivors is used as the benefit measure. This variable also serves as a proxy for other forms of workers' compensation benefits, including

TABLE 5.2
Selected PSID Sample Characteristics (N = 1,349)

Variable	Mean	SD
Wage	7.010	2.416
Age	37.142	11.605
Experience	11.906	10.565
Sex	0.154	0.361
Education	12.984	2.504
Poor health status	0.072	0.258
Blue collar occupation	0.518	0.500
Union status	0.285	0.451
NTOF death risk (fatalities/100,000 workers)	7.918	9.737
BLS death risk (fatalities/100,000 workers)	5.209	10.178
Weighted replacement rate	0.544	0.190

medical coverage and earnings replacement for nonfatal injuries. The weighted replacement rate variable is similar to those included in the previous chapters, which analyzed the role of insurance for nonfatal injuries. The replacement rate measure used here is the predicted value of the annual replacement rate of after-tax wages by fatality insurance benefits.[4]

Table 5.2 summarizes the descriptive statistics for key variables in our sample, which is broadly representative of the working population. The average worker has a high school degree, has twelve years of experience, and is thirty-seven years old. Approximately 50 percent of the sample members hold blue-collar jobs, and 30 percent are covered by union contracts. The relatively small proportion of women is common in studies of this kind, and is attributable primarily to the restriction of the sample to household heads. The difference in sample size between the PSID subsample used in this chapter and those used previously primarily reflects different coverage of the risk variables.

The Death Risk Variables

To establish the worker's death risk, one must link workers to death risk measures based on reported industry. The death risk data most often used for this task, the BLS occupational fatality data, are measured only at highly aggregative levels and do not allow a precise matching of risk exposure on the job to individual workers. Furthermore, the BLS data are estimated on the basis of a survey of industries, so some sampling error is present in the data. The BLS data used in this chapter were obtained from unpublished statistics available at the U.S. Bureau of

Labor Statistics office. Industry death rates were available at the two-digit Standard Industrial Classification (SIC) code level, and we averaged these death statistics over the 1972–1982 period to remove the distortions that arise because of the effects of catastrophic accidents in any particular year.

To provide a sounder statistical basis for assessing death risks, NIOSH has collected data on occupational fatalities as part of its National Traumatic Occupational Fatality (NTOF) project. The NTOF data differ from the BLS data in several important ways. Most important, a partial sample is not used to project national death risks. Rather, the NTOF data are based on a census of all occupational fatalities recorded on death certificates during the years 1980–1984; thus, no sampling error is present in the data. The mix of injuries covered is also more extensive, as the NTOF data include all work-related traumatic fatalities. The types of fatal injuries covered include industrial accidents (for example, slips and falls), fire-related deaths, homicides, and suicides. Of the recorded deaths, 84 percent were due to unintentional injuries, 13 percent resulted from homicides, and 3 percent were suicides. Although it is unlikely that suicides are a component of job risks for which workers will receive compensation, they constitute a very small portion of the sample and should not affect the results significantly. The NTOF data are classified by state and by one-digit SIC industry code, yielding 450 distinct observations of the death risk faced by workers. This state-specific aspect of the data, in particular, makes possible a more precise match of the death risk with the measure of death insurance benefit than is possible with available BLS data.

A comparison of the BLS data and the NTOF data provides two striking empirical differences in the perspectives on job risks. The first is in the overall riskiness of the job. The BLS reports 3,750 occupational fatalities in 1984, with similar magnitudes reported for adjacent years. The NTOF system, on the other hand, recorded average annual deaths of 6,901 for the period 1980–1984, which is 84 percent larger than the BLS total, or almost double the risk measured by the BLS. On the other hand, the NTOF average is slightly greater than one-half the average for the same period reported by the National Safety Council in *Accident Facts, 1988*.

In constructing our measures of the death risk, we assign the NTOF data to workers by reported state of residence and industry, and assign the BLS data only by industry. The mean NTOF death risk in our sample is 7.9 deaths per 100,000 workers, while the average fatality rate reported in the BLS data is 5.2 deaths per 100,000 workers; for the particular mix of workers in our sample the NTOF risk levels exceed the BLS risk by over 50 percent. There is also substantial variation in the risk, as the standard deviation of each risk variable is at least 1.5 times greater than its mean.

The understatement of death risks in the BLS measure has a direct impact on the value of life calculations. Systematic understatement of death risks by a factor of about two will cause regression-based value of life estimates to roughly double in magnitude. This is due to the nature of value of life calculations based on regression estimates. If the death risk measure is cut in half, its associated regression coefficient, which provides the basis of the calculation, is doubled.

This bias assumes, of course, that worker behavior is governed by the true death risks rather than the death statistics published by BLS. In particular, suppose that the true risk level is equal to the NTOF measure, so that the average of the true death risk is 7.9 deaths per 100,000 workers Using the wage-risk tradeoff that we estimate below (that is, an 0.4 percent increase in wages per unit increase in risk), a doubling of the true risk to 15.8 deaths per 100,000 workers would yield an increase in the hourly wage of twenty-two cents, evaluated at the sample mean wage of seven dollars per hour. If the risk level observed by the researcher is given by the BLS measure, however, it will appear that the twenty-two cent increase was generated by a risk increase of only 5.2 deaths, or double the mean BLS risk. This observed tradeoff would then imply an estimated wage-risk tradeoff of 0.6 percent, which is roughly 1.5 times as large as the true tradeoff, and value of life estimates based on the observed tradeoff would be overstated by 50 percent.

This result derives from the fact that by introducing the smaller observed risk with no change in the true underlying risk, the estimated wage-risk tradeoffs must rise. If, on the other hand, worker perceptions of risks are equal to the published statistics, introduction of the new risk information will increase wages also, and there will be no change in the observed wage-risk tradeoff. This latter case does not appear likely. The BLS publishes death rates only at the one-digit level and does not publicize these figures. It is highly unlikely that worker perceptions have been distorted by the available BLS statistics.

Nevertheless, the relationship of workers' risk perceptions to the two death risk measures is a central issue for interpreting the empirical results linking the objective risk measures and workers' wages. The available evidence suggests that workers utilize diverse forms of information in a reasonable fashion to form their risk judgments.[5] Although there are no available data on workers' perceptions of fatality risks, overall assessments of nonfatal risk levels follow expected patterns. In particular, workers' risk perceptions are strongly correlated with BLS nonfatal injury risk measures and are influenced in the expected manner by opportunities for learning on the job. These influences include experiencing an injury oneself, hearing of injuries to other workers, seeing hazard warning signs, and observing whether the physical conditions at the workplace are pleasant.

TABLE 5.3
Industry Risk Comparison: Means and Standard Deviations

Industry	Number of Observations	Mean and SD	
		NTOF	BLS
Mining	(25)	40.010	18.736
		(19.977)	(4.932)
Construction	(108)	32.738	28.698
		(6.253)	(16.450)
Manufacturing	(503)	4.369	1.503
		(2.852)	(1.391)
Transportation, communications, and			
public utilities	(164)	20.244	10.702
		(9.806)	(12.442)
Wholesale trade	(59)	2.233	2.658
		(0.120)	(0.584)
Retail trade	(149)	3.176	2.020
		(0.905)	(1.122)
Finance, insurance, and real estate	(62)	2.348	4.030
		(0.184)	(2.283)
Services	(279)	3.428	0.866
		(1.498)	(0.679)
Total	(1349)	7.918	5.209
		(9.737)	(10.178)

Comparable data are not available to assess the extent of the correspondence between subjective risk perceptions and actual fatality risk levels. It is, however, noteworthy that fatality risks are several orders of magnitude smaller than nonfatal risks. To the extent that any systematic bias arises in risk perceptions, it is that individuals generally display a tendency to overestimate small probabilities and underestimate large probabilities. Any perceptual bias is likely to increase the validity of the NTOF risk measure as a reflection of workers' risk perceptions, since these risk levels are larger than those reflected in the BLS measure. To the extent that workers have sound assessments of the risk level, a basic underlying assumption in the compensating differential literature, use of the more accurate NTOF risk variable should enhance the reliability of the empirical estimates.

Table 5.3 presents an industry-specific comparison of the two risk measures. As anticipated, the NTOF data usually yield a higher average risk level within industries. The most extreme relative difference in the risk levels is for services, where the NTOF risk level is almost four times as great as the BLS risk level. In the most representative industry—man-

FIGURE 5.1

BLS vs. NTOF death risk by major industry category (1 = Manufacturing; 2 = Wholesale Trade; 3 = Retail Trade; 4 = Finance, Insurance, and Real Estate; 5 = Services)

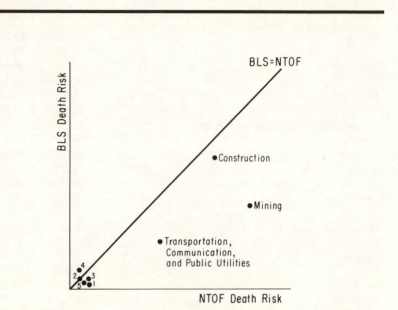

ufacturing—the NTOF-based fatality risk measure is almost three times as large as its BLS counterpart. The differences are narrower in the case of the construction industry, for which there is only a 14 percent discrepancy. A somewhat different pattern is in evidence in two of the white-collar industries, the wholesale trade industry and the finance, insurance, and real estate industry. In those instances, the BLS risk level is somewhat greater.

The statistics in Table 5.3 illustrate the second key difference between the two data sources. The BLS statistics do not differ from the NTOF data by a simple scale factor. Rather, the extent of the bias varies substantially across industries. Thus, in addition to the scale factor bias documented above, there consequently is a substantial random measurement error in the BLS death risk variable, which will bias past estimates of the value of life downward and also render the estimates less precise.

Figure 5.1 depicts the within-industry risk differences graphically. If the two risk measures are identical, the BLS/NTOF industry risk pairs pictured in Figure 5.1 will lie on the 45° line BLS = NTOF. Likewise, if the

NTOF risk is larger by a simple scale factor, the risk pairs will lie approximately on a straight line below BLS = NTOF. Because neither of these conditions hold, the presence of random measurement error in the BLS data is indicated.

One potential cause of the error portrayed in Figure 5.1 is the difference in the data collection methodologies. The NTOF data are based on a census of occupational fatalities, while the BLS conducts a survey and uses the results to predict fatalities in industries. Whether the impact of the reduced measurement error on the estimated value of life offsets the scale factor bias, which operates in the opposite direction, is an empirical question that we answer below.

Wage Equations and the Value of Life

Table 5.4 reports selected regression results using the natural logarithm of the wage rate as the dependent variable, and Table 5.5 summarizes the key estimated risk coefficients for a variety of specifications. Although most wage equation studies in labor economics utilize the natural logarithm of the wage as the dependent variable because of the nature of the theoretical relationship between wages and human capital variables, there is no comparable theory specifying the functional form linking wages and death risks. Consequently, we report both wage and *ln* wage regression results in Table 5.5. We also report estimates using the flexible functional form estimator known as the Box-Cox transformation in Appendix A. These results indicate that the appropriate form of the dependent variable is closer to the semilogarithmic than to the linear one; thus, our discussion will focus primarily on the *ln* wage equation results.

The overall performance of the equations reported in Table 5.4 accords with the wage equations in the literature, in terms of both the magnitudes and the directions of the coefficients.[6] Worker wages rise at a declining rate with experience, increase with education and union status, and are lower if the worker has a health impairment, is a blue-collar worker, or is a woman.

The main variables of interest are the fatality risk variables, for which the regression results are summarized across a variety of specifications in Table 5.5. The results for the *ln* wage equations appear in the first two rows of Table 5.5, and those for the wage equations appear in the bottom two rows. Equations (1) and (2) employ the NTOF risk measure, while equations (3) and (4) utilize the BLS risk measure. In each case, results are first reported excluding the workers' compensation variable, because most studies in the literature have not controlled for this

TABLE 5.4
Wage Equation Estimates: Coefficients and Standard Deviations

Variable[a]	Estimates Using NTOF Risk Measure	Estimates Using BLS Risk Measures
Experience	0.028[b]	0.028[b]
	(0.003)	(0.003)
Experience^2	$-6.0E-4$[b]	$-5.9E-4$[b]
	$(0.8E-4)$	$(0.8E-4)$
Sex	-0.288[b]	-0.293[b]
	(0.024)	(0.024)
Education	0.044[b]	0.044[b]
	(0.004)	(0.004)
Poor health status	-0.079[b]	-0.082[b]
	(0.032)	(0.032)
Blue collar	-0.064[b]	-0.061[b]
	(0.021)	(0.021)
Union status	0.182[b]	0.191[b]
	(0.020)	(0.020)
Death risk	$7.5E-3$[b]	$2.7E-3$
	$(2.2E-3)$	$(2.0E-3)$
Weighted replacement rate	$-8.1E-3$[b]	$-2.8E-3$
	$(4.2E-3)$	$(3.4E-3)$
Adjusted R-squared	0.335	0.327

[a] Other variables included in the wage equations are the region dummy variables.

[b] Significant at the 0.05 confidence level.

aspect of compensation. Equations 5.2 and 5.4 include the workers' compensation variable, which is clearly preferable from a conceptual standpoint and has been included in more recent work.[7]

The NTOF death risk variable consistently outperforms the BLS risk measure. Although the BLS fatality variable coefficient is always positive, the largest t-ratio observed is 1.625, so that this measure at best has coefficients just shy of the level needed (1.645) to achieve statistical significance. In contrast, the coefficients based on the NTOF variable are always positive, are several times larger than the comparable BLS coefficients, and never have t-ratios smaller than 3.35, thus passing even the most demanding tests for statistical significance. These results provide strong evidence of an errors in variables problem in the BLS data.

Table 5.5 also reports the associated value of life estimates, using the price level from 1988. These estimates range from \$2 million for the BLS risk measure to \$5–\$7 million for the NTOF measure. The means by which these values are calculated is straightforward. The coefficient on

TABLE 5.5
Summary of Death Risk and Replacement Rate Effects:
Coefficients and Standard Deviations

Variable	NTOF Risk Measure for Equation:		BLS Risk Measure for Equation:	
	(1)	*(2)*	*(3)*	*(4)*
ln Wage equations				
Death risk	0.00354[a]	0.00747[a]	0.00126	0.00272
	(0.00090)	(0.00223)	(0.00083)	(0.00196)
Weighted replacement rate	—	−0.00805[a]	—	−0.00276
	(0.00419)		(0.00336)	
Adjusted *R*-squared	0.334	0.335	0.327	0.327
Value of life	$6,193,000	$5,407,750	$2,200,000	$2,132,112
Wage equations				
Death risk	0.027[a]	0.052[a]	0.008	0.017
	(0.006)	(0.015)	(0.006)	(0.013)
Weighted replacement rate	—	−0.050[a]	—	−0.016
	(0.028)		(0.023)	
Adjusted *R*-squared	0.315	0.316	0.306	0.306
Value of life	$6,810,500	$6,111,000	$1,997,000	$2,070,000

[a] Statistically significant at the 0.05 confidence level.

the death risk variable in the wage regression equation measures the amount by which a worker's wage will increase or decrease for corresponding increases or decreases in the risk that he or she faces on the job. Conceptually, the wage-risk tradeoff is interpreted as the dollar amount of wages that a worker requires to face a small additional amount of risk. The risk coefficient measures the required compensation for a risk increase; thus, it is a "willingness to accept" measure. For small changes in risk, this willingness to accept risk increases equals the willingness to pay for risk reductions. We extrapolate the individual worker's willingness to pay for a small risk reduction linearly to calculate the collective willingness to pay for a statistical life.

As an example, consider a worker who works for an hourly after-tax wage that is 2.5 cents higher for every increase in the annual probability of a fatal accident of 1/100,000. On an annual basis, this worker will require $50 for a risk reduction of 1/100,000. Furthermore, 100,000 similar workers will collectively accept this increase in risk in return for $5 million in wage compensation. On average, one life will be saved among this group. Hence, the workers place a collective value of $5 million on the one statistical life saved.

Let us analyze the implications of the estimates of the *ln* wage equation reported in column 2 of Table 5.5. Consider the effect of a unit increase in the NTOF death risk, so that the annual death risk has risen by 1/100,000. The effect on the value of the log of workers' wages equals 0.00747 − 0.00805 × Weighted replacement rate. Evaluated at the mean levels of the wage and weighted replacement rate of 7.01 and 0.544, this calculation yields an estimated tradeoff of 0.021667 between the hourly wage and the risk. Multiplying this number by 2,000 hours to annualize the figure and by 100,000 to reflect the scale of the risk variable yields a tradeoff in 1981 dollars of $4.34 million per statistical life. Using the GNP deflator to express this nominal value in 1988 dollars transforms the result into the current estimated value of life of $5.408 million.

In the case of the *ln* wage equations, the BLS estimates imply a value of life in the $2 million range, whereas use of NIOSH's NTOF measure yields a value of life in the $5 million to $6 million range. Switching from the BLS to the NTOF measure more than doubles the estimated value of life.

A similar pattern occurs for the wage equation, except that the extent of the increase is even greater. The BLS measure yields value of life figures in the $2 million range, whereas the NTOF data imply a value of life on the order of $6 million to $6.5 million. Although the upper end of the range is relatively large, it is not implausibly large, as evidenced by the estimates reported in Chapter 2.[8]

Overall, the NTOF results suggest a value of life in the $5.4 million to $6.8 million range and, on average, the value of life is over double that obtained by use of the BLS risk estimates. If one is willing to select a particular functional form for the wage equation, then the variation in the value of life across different specifications is much less. Exploration of the optimal wage transformations for use as the dependent variable (see Appendix A) indicates that the value of life estimates from the equation specifications that are most consistent with the data range between $5.56 million and $5.70 million.

Because of the precision in the estimates made possible by the NTOF data, we can pinpoint the value of life much more accurately than did previous studies. To provide a range that can be used as a frame of reference for risk control policies, we can construct confidence intervals for the value of life, using the coefficient estimates and their standard errors. Consider the *ln* wage results, which are more consistent with the functional form exploration provided in Appendix A. The coefficients on the NTOF risk variables in Table 5.5, column 2, indicate that the value of life will fall between $5.34 million and $5.70 million 95 percent of the time. The BLS-based estimates, on the other hand, yield much less precise estimates, as the asymptotic 95 percent confidence interval for the value of life includes all values between $1.68 million and $2.58 million. Thus, the upper end of the NTOF confidence interval is less than 10 percent higher than the bottom end, whereas for the BLS data the variation is just over 50 percent.

Conclusion

The development of a new and more comprehensive occupational death risk series by NIOSH provides a new reference point for assessing the wage-risk tradeoff that governs estimates of the value of life. Overall death risks are roughly double the rate estimated by BLS. Based solely on the average scales of the overall risk levels, the value of life estimates in the PSID sample were expected to fall by about 50 percent through use of this new variable. The additional influence of random measurement error in the BLS death risk measures, however, apparently exerted a substantial depressing effect on previous value of life estimates, so that replacing the BLS measure with NIOSH's NTOF risk variable boosts the risk coefficient by a factor of more than two. Overall, the new estimates of the value of life are at least double the levels obtained using BLS risk data. It is also noteworthy that the death risk coefficients are dramatically stronger in terms of statistical significance, so that the statistical confidence one can place in the value of life estimates is greatly enhanced by the use of the new occupational risk data. The sensitivity of the results to the risk measure used indicates a need to reestimate the value of life with other employment data sets to provide a broader empirical basis for selecting a consensus value of life estimate to use in policy contexts.

Six _____

The Value of Life:
Quantity Adjustments and
Implicit Rates of Time Preference

THE FOCUS of the preceding chapter was on the value of the statistical life of the average worker. This emphasis is in keeping with the literature on this topic, but it does not fully reflect all of the dimensions of exposures to risk of death. Two simplifying assumptions are made in Chapter 5 and elsewhere. First, the measure of risk used—the probability of a fatal or nonfatal accident—abstracts altogether from life cycle issues, such as variation across individuals in the potential losses resulting from death or injury.[1]

Second, upon incorporating life cycle effects, the choice of an appropriate discount rate becomes an issue. Some losses, such as immediate pain and suffering and medical expenses, are likely to be similar across individuals for similar accidents. In the case of nonfatal accidents, it is probably not too great a simplification to assume that these losses are similar for different persons, since the duration of a given injury type is not highly variable. There may be greater differences, however, in the financial losses and the associated reduction in utility that result from a permanent change in health status, particularly with respect to the extreme loss of welfare that results from death.

In the case of fatalities, a young person loses a much greater amount of lifetime utility than does an older person, a source of variation in risk that has not been reflected in past empirical studies of the value of life. In this chapter, we incorporate this variation by weighting the standard death risk measure by the remaining life of each sample member. More specifically, we use information on expected lifetimes, the worker's current age, a discount rate that is computed as part of the estimation process, and measures of death risk. This information enables us to calculate the worker's expected remaining life at risk, reflecting the fact that the worker's principal concern is not simply the probability of a fatal accident, but the discounted duration of life and the associated lifetime utility at risk on the job. We will refer to this discounted duration of life at risk as the quantity-adjusted death risk and utilize it in calculating the quantity-adjusted value of life. The quantity-adjusted value of life differs from conventional estimates of the value of life in that the tradeoff is not between wages and death risk probabilities but between wages and death risks that have been weighted by the discounted number of potential years of life lost.

Obtaining a quantity-adjusted measure of the value of life also has potentially important policy implications. Analysts have long noted that the appropriate value of life for policy analysis cannot be divorced from the duration of life involved, since lives can only be extended, not permanently saved.[2] The task of actually developing a measure of the value of life that incorporates changes in expected lifetime utility has never been undertaken, however, in large part because there was no sound empirical basis for doing so. The results reported here will take into account quite explicitly the influence of the duration of life.

A related issue arises in obtaining these quantity-adjusted measures: What discount rate do people use in valuing their future utilities? Estimates of discount rates have appeared elsewhere in the literature, as in the studies by Fuchs (1982), Hausman (1979), Lang and Ruud (1986), and Weiss (1972), but none of these studies addressed the job risk problem. The closest of these studies to the health risk issues considered here is that of Fuchs. His analysis obtained rates of time preference from survey questions relating to financial opportunities at different dates, which he then related to health concerns, such as cigarette smoking.

Estimated discount rates that diverge substantially from the financial market rates faced by workers are of interest in their own right to the extent that these diversions provide evidence pertaining to irrationality in the valuation of future health losses. It has long been suggested that people are myopic in their risk-taking decisions. We address this issue quite explicitly by comparing our estimated discount rates to financial market interest rates for the period. These estimated rates are also of interest in that they suggest the appropriate rate of time preference to use in discounting future effects of health and safety policy.

A second simplification that, until recently, has been applied universally in wage-risk studies is the omission of expected ex post compensation for accidents in the form of accident insurance benefits available to workers.[3] Practically every state now provides workers' compensation insurance, with approximately 90 percent of the work force now covered by some form of accident insurance. From a conceptual standpoint, increases in ex post compensation for accidents should reduce ex ante compensation and should, if possible, be incorporated explicitly in any analysis of the relationship between wages and job risks. We take ex post compensation into account by including in our estimating equation a death benefit variable that reflects the worker's marital status, spouse's remaining life, number of dependents, and characteristics of the state workers' compensation system covering each worker. These benefits are also discounted at a rate that is calculated in the process of estimation.

In this chapter we couple the data used on our analysis in Chapter 3, the 1977 University of Michigan Quality of Employment Survey (QES), with risk and insurance variables that are collected from external sources and matched to workers in the sample.[4] We then present estimates of compensating differential equations that include both the quantity-adjusted risks to life and the present value of death benefits to the surviving spouse as regressors. We also report estimates that condition the industry risk measures on individual assessments of working conditions, thus controlling partially for the measurement error that has impeded many previous attempts to match industry data to workers in micro data sets.

In all of the cases considered, we obtain strong support of the hypothesized rationality of employment decisions. Workers receive wage premiums for exposure to risk that reflect the remaining lifetime at risk. They trade ex post for ex ante compensation for exposure to risks, and they discount future utilities and the utilities of their heirs at rates consistent with observed explicit interest rates.

The Sample and the Variables

The empirical analysis utilizes the 1977 QES, which was discussed in detail in Chapter 3. Table 6.1 summarizes many of the principal characteristics of the QES subsample of 317 workers, which is smaller than the earlier sample because of the death risk data used in this chapter. The sample has an average age of thirty-eight, 6 percent black workers, and 8 percent female workers. About one-fifth of the workers have not completed high school, one-fourth have some college education, less than one-fifth have a college degree plus additional training, and the remaining two-fifths have a high school diploma. The average firm size for the workers is 783 employees. Almost two-thirds of the workers hold blue-collar jobs, and 39 percent are union members.

The dependent variable in the analysis is the worker's after-tax hourly wage rate. Since workers' compensation benefits are included in the equation in their after-tax form (benefits are tax exempt), for comparability the wage variable is the worker's after-tax hourly wage in 1976 dollars. These taxes include both state and federal income taxes and are calculated using information on the worker's wage rate and family structure.[5] We assume that each worker took the standard deduction.

TABLE 6.1
Selected QES Sample Characteristics

Variable	Mean	SD
Age	38.09	12.22
Race	0.06	0.24
Sex	0.08	0.27
Less than high school education	0.22	0.41
Some college education	0.25	0.44
College degree	0.13	0.33
Experience	21.30	12.49
Firm size	783.82	1,110.54
Blue-collar occupation	0.63	0.48
Union status	0.39	0.49
Wage (after taxes)	5.49	1.88
Fatal accident rate (per 100,000 workers)	5.89	8.98
Lost workday accident rate (per 100 workers)	4.68	2.38
Hazard perceptions	0.85	0.36
Replacement rate	0.79	0.35

Three job risk variables are used in the analysis. The first and most important is the worker's death risk. The approach used matches the workers in the sample to a death risk variable based on death risk statistics for the worker's two-digit industry.[6] Since death risks involve a low probability of death (on the order of 5/100,000 per worker in this sample), even at this level of aggregation death risks may vary substantially across years, particularly if there is a major catastrophe that results in multiple deaths. To eliminate the distorting influence of such random fluctuations, we use as our death risk measure the average probability of death over the 1973–1976 period. Unlike the nonfatal accident statistics, death rate data were not subject to the classification problems that were present in the early 1970s under the new reporting requirements. Use of shorter-term average measures yielded little change in our results.

The main focus of this chapter is on the quantity of life adjustment of the standard death risk measure. To accomplish this, we use information on the worker's age, race, sex, and remaining life data from life expectancy tables to calculate the remaining life of worker i, RL_i.[7] Discounted remaining life years are then

$$RL_i = \int_0^{RL_i} e^{-rt}dt,$$

and

Discounted remaining life$_i$ = $(1/r)[1 - \exp(-rRL_i)]$,

where r is the worker's rate of time preference. Weighting the discounted remaining life by the probability of a fatality yields the weighted discounted life years lost variable,

$$\text{Weighted life years lost}_i = \text{Death risk}_i \times \text{Discounted remaining life}_i.$$

The variable representing life years lost is inserted as a regressor in a compensating differential equation to estimate the effect of changes in remaining lifetime on wages. Since this particular risk variable is a nonlinear function of the discount rate parameter, it is necessary to estimate the model using nonlinear regression techniques.

It is useful to interpret the effect of life years lost on wages in the context of Arthur's (1981) theoretical paper on the value of extensions to life. In a general equilibrium intertemporal consumption-loans model, Arthur shows that the welfare gains associated with a reduction in age-specific risks consist of three forces affecting consumption—the increase due to lengthened life and the increased work years and increased births over the extended life span that result in increased productivity. These gains are offset to an unknown degree by the fact that the increased consumption during later years must be financed by someone's decreased consumption. This last term is shown by Arthur to depend upon the consumption elasticity of utility, a parameter that has been estimated elsewhere by Rosen (1988). If this elasticity has a value close to zero, financing considerations can effectively be ignored, since extended life affects utility independently of the changes in consumption that it entails. In Rosen (1988) this parameter estimate equals about 0.25, suggesting that the financing considerations associated with life extension are not of major consequence.

The remaining influences will be reflected in our wage equation if decreasing death risks increases productivity as well as utility. Otherwise, firms will not compensate workers for placing their life years, productivity, and fertility at risk, and workers who care little about risks will sort themselves into more risky jobs. In principle, empirical separation of these influences is possible. In addition to the information on life years at risk, estimation of these effects would require data on both fertility and labor force participation over the life cycle. These factors could then be incorporated into the model to hold constant the fertility and productivity effects, allowing estimation of the "pure" value of extended life. Since we do not incorporate these effects in our analyses, our gross estimates of the quantity-adjusted value of life are overstated if expected life years lost are correlated with expected labor force participation and fertility gains effects and if these factors increase wages.[8]

The second job risk measure included is the nonfatal lost workday accident rate for the worker's three-digit industry. This measure pertains to the incidence of nonfatal accidents that entail at least one lost day of work. Workers in the sample have an average annual probability of a lost workday injury of 1/20. This accident measure is a more reliable index of injuries than the total injury and illness rate, since the definition of what constitutes an accident is clear-cut. Inclusion of this measure prevents the fatality risk variable from capturing the omitted influence of nonfatal risks.

The final accident measure is the worker's subjective assessment of whether the job exposes him or her to dangerous or unhealthy conditions. This binary (0,1) variable assumes a value of 1 if the worker cites one or more hazards of his or her job. Unlike the danger perception question in the Survey of Working Conditions data analyzed in Viscusi (1979a), the 1977 Quality of Employment Survey does not ascertain explicitly whether a job poses any hazards but instead inquires whether the worker can cite specific risks. This change in wording contributed to a higher rate of danger perception than in previous surveys, with 85 percent of the sample viewing their jobs as exposing them to some health or safety risk.

A well-known problem with the use of industry data to measure individual-level risks is that workers in the same industry face different risks in different occupations. Some of these job-specific variations can be taken into account by utilizing the question in the Quality of Employment Survey asking for the worker's own perception of the presence or absence of hazards. In other words we can condition the industry-level risk data by the presence of a perceived hazard, as in Viscusi (1979a). Multiplication of the binary hazard perception variable by the fatal and nonfatal industry injury rates yields a risk measure that equals zero if a worker perceives no risk on the job and equals the industry risk level if the worker reports the job as hazardous.

Our interpretation of weighted life years lost is as a measure of lifetime exposure to job risk. The implication of our use of this measure is that, for given characteristics of the job and the worker, the lifetime utility at risk is greater for a younger person than for an older one. An alternative interpretation is that the quantity adjustment serves as a proxy for "tastes for risks," that is, that younger workers have a lower aversion to risk and therefore choose a higher value of expected life years lost. If this were so, weighted life years lost would not be a valid measure of risk, since it would be subject to the sorting problems inherent in the compensating differential model. In the case of pure taste sorting, there would be no evidence of a risk premium for any given point on firms' offer curves. It is more likely, however, that younger workers (who typically work on more dangerous jobs) do so because they are more productive in those jobs than older workers, and that firms are willing to compensate workers with greater exposure for their greater productivity.

Besides ex ante wage compensation for risk, workers also receive ex post compensation through the state workers' compensation programs. Higher workers' compensation levels should reduce the wage rates for workers in hazardous jobs. As shown in Chapter 3, the theoretically appropriate measure of compensation for nonfatal injuries is the weighted benefit amount, which equals the probability of an injury multiplied by the benefit level. As a measure of insurance for nonfatal injuries, we use the predicted value of the expected earnings replacement rate, following the procedure discussed in Chapter 3.

The final benefit measure is the discounted expected annuity for survivors. Estimation of the wage equation using a wage replacement rate for death insurance produced results consistent with those reported below. However, since death benefits are a measure of lifetime compensation, the discounted lifetime annuity captures the nature of the benefit better than does a current period replacement rate, and we therefore report its effects below.

On the basis of the state death benefit formulas and the worker's wage rate, family structure, and state of residence, one can calculate the annual annuity amount, $A(b_i)$.[9] The value of these benefits to the family of the deceased worker also depends on their duration. Using information on the spouse's age, race, and sex and life expectancy tables, one can calculate the spouse's expected remaining lifetime SL_i. The discounted value of the annuity is consequently

$$\text{Discounted Annuity}_i = (1/r)A(b_i)[1 - \exp(-rSL_i)].$$

When there are no heirs, the annuity is assigned a value of zero.

For the purpose of the empirical analysis, the appropriate benefit variable conditions the worker's annuity by the risk level:

$$\text{Weighted Annuity}_i = \text{Death Risk}_i \times \text{Discounted Annuity}_i.$$

Estimates of the parameter r in the regressions using nonlinear techniques are reported below.

In principle, the discount rates applied to a worker's future utility and to the utilities of his or her heirs need not be equal. As a preliminary step in the analysis, we tested this restriction, and could not reject the hypothesis that workers weight the utilities of other family members equally. It should be noted, however, that estimation of two separate discount rates substantially increases the demands placed upon our data. The unconstrained estimates were therefore less precise than the single estimate reported below, and this imprecision is partially responsible for the failure to reject the restriction. In the unrestricted estimation, the worker's own discount rate has a statistically significant effect, as in the restricted estimates reported below.

Finally, each equation includes a detailed set of other variables pertaining to the worker and his or her job. These variables include work experience (years worked since age sixteen) and dummy variables indicating health status, speed of work, job security, whether the worker is a supervisor, overtime work requirements, training program availability, and residence in an urban area, the South, the West, or the North Central states. Of particular importance in the estimation are the job characteristic variables. These detailed job variables are not available in the larger data sets often used to estimate compensating differentials for working conditions, and in their absence, industry dummy variables are necessary as a proxy for capturing differences in jobs correlated with the worker's industry. Inclusion of such industry dummy variables makes it difficult to estimate the effects of an industry-based job risk measure that is constructed from the industry information. Since our equations include several job-specific measures of job attributes, industry dummy variables are not necessary to control for industry differences in job characteristics.

Empirical Results

The empirical analysis focuses on a series of wage equations. Both the after-tax wage and its natural logarithm are used as dependent variables to control for sensitivity of the results to this aspect of model specification. For each equation, we estimate both a version that conditions the death risk variables by the dummy hazard perception variable and an unconditional estimate.

The basic form of the model is given by the equation

(6.1) $\text{Wage}_i = X_i\beta + \lambda_1\text{Weighted Life Years Lost}_i +$
$\delta_1\text{Weighted Annuity}_i + \lambda_2\text{Lost workday cases}_i +$
$\delta_2\text{Weighted Replacement Rate}_i + \varepsilon_i,$

and its semilogarithmic counterpart, where the X_i are the aforementioned variables pertaining to the worker and job.

This equation is in the same general spirit as the conventional compensating differential equation, with four important differences. First, the dependent variable is the after-tax hourly wage rate. An after-tax measure is especially appropriate to put wages and workers' compensation benefits on a comparable basis. Further, since it is the after-tax wage that is relevant to worker decisions, use of the before-tax wages will introduce error into the dependent measure. Second, this is the first such equation to include the discounted value of the annuity in the estimating equation. Third, whereas some studies have included a workers' compensation variable analogous to the weighted replacement rate, no such analyses using micro data have also included a fatality risk measure in the wage equation.[10] Finally, and most important, the death risk measure (weighted life years lost) takes into consideration the discounted duration of remaining life that is at risk on the job. Weighted life years lost is the worker's discounted remaining life multiplied by the death risk, or discounted weighted life years lost. This adjustment of the standard death risk variable reflects the fact that what is at stake is not death per se, but loss of years of life, that the amount of life lost is of consequence, and that individuals discount the utility attached to future years of life. The discount rate used in adjusting remaining life is computed in the estimation process. The procedure does not constrain the discount rate to be nonzero, so the possibility that workers do not discount is not ruled out a priori.

Finally, we report both weighted and unweighted estimates. Heteroskedasticity, which is common in cross-section data, is usually ignored in compensating differential studies. However, given the nonlinear nature of our model, controlling for heteroskedasticity is crucial, since bias in estimates of standard errors carries over to estimates of the coefficients in this case. As shown below, weighting produced important changes in some significance levels.

In constructing the weights, it was assumed that the variances of the individual error terms, ε_i, were approximately a linear function of the vector Z. This vector Z included worker experience in both linear and squared forms, nonfatal and fatal risks, and annuity terms. These variables were chosen on the basis of residual plots from unweighted estimates and entered as regressors in an equation with e_i^2 as the dependent variable, where e_i is the nonlinear least squares residual. This procedure was iterated twice, yielding estimates of weights that are asymptotically normal and consistent.

Table 6.2 reports weighted and unweighted nonlinear least squares estimates of equation 6.1. A nonlinear least squares technique was required to estimate the worker's implicit discount rate. The control variables (X_i) generally perform as expected.[11] Education increases wages, as does residence in an urban area; and black and female workers earn significantly lower wages. The race variable is not statistically significant, no doubt because there were only nineteen black workers in the sample. In the unweighted results, a year of experience increases

TABLE 6.2
Wage Equation Estimates of Unconditional Risk Model: Coefficients
and Standard Deviations

Variable[a]	Unweighted	Weighted
Race	−0.028	−0.085
	(0.071)	(0.073)
Sex	−0.255[b]	−0.273[b]
	(0.066)	(0.068)
Poor health status	−0.139	−0.124
	(0.096)	(0.100)
Less than high school education	−0.095[b]	−0.071
	(0.046)	(0.047)
Some college education	−0.034	−0.023
	(0.043)	(0.045)
College degree	0.096[b]	0.123[b]
	(0.046)	(0.062)
Experience	0.003[b]	0.002
	(0.001)	(0.002)
Firm size	$5.2E-5$[b]	$4.9E-5$[b]
	$(1.7E-5)$	$(1.9E-5)$
Blue-collar occupation	−0.128[b]	−0.148[b]
	(0.042)	(0.043)
Union status	0.141[b]	0.145[b]
	(0.041)	(0.042)
Fast work pace	−0.069	−0.072
	(0.045)	(0.048)
Job security	0.051	0.060[b]
	(0.034)	(0.035)
Supervisory status	0.065[b]	0.043
	(0.038)	(0.039)
Overtime work requirements	−0.043	−0.041
	(0.036)	(0.038)
Availability of training	0.044	0.035
	(0.037)	(0.039)
Lost workday accident rate	0.049[b]	0.058[b]
	(0.013)	(0.014)
Weighted replacement rate	−0.048[b]	−0.055[b]
	(0.013)	(0.013)
Weighted life years lost	11.945[b]	17.732[b]
	(6.861)	(5.880)

[a] Each equation also included dummy variables pertaining to the worker's residence in an urban area, and the South, the West, or the North Central United States.
[b] Statistically significant at the 0.05 confidence level, one-tailed test.

TABLE 6.2, *cont.*

Variable[a]	Unweighted	Weighted
Weighted annuity	$-1.4E - 3$[b]	$-2.4E - 3$[b]
	$(0.7E - 3)$	$(0.8E - 3)$
Discount rate	0.096	0.122[b]
	(0.063)	(0.043)
Adjusted *R*-squared	0.387	0.390

wages by 0.3 percent. Poor health causes a reduction in wages of 14 percent that is in the expected direction but is not significantly different from zero.

The effects of the job-related variables are similar to those found in studies that used the earlier surveys—the 1970 Survey of Working Conditions (SWC) and the 1973 QES.[12] Union members receive a wage premium of 14 percent, and workers in large firms have higher wages, consistent with previous research. Workers in blue-collar occupations earn, on average, 13 percent less than do those in white-collar jobs. Of those job characteristic variables measuring nonpecuniary attributes, only the supervisory status dummy variable has a statistically significant effect among the subsidiary working condition variables, and its sign is in the expected direction. In most other cases, the coefficients approach significance at the 0.05 level, so the variables are included to separate their effects from those of the risk variables.

The results of primary interest are the estimated effects of the injury rate variables, the insurance variables, and the estimate of r—the worker's implicit discount rate. In the unweighted estimates, each effect has the expected sign. Furthermore, all of the injury and insurance variables are statistically significant at the 0.05 confidence level (one-tailed test).

The importance of weighting is seen by comparing estimates of the discount rate. In the unweighted regressions, the estimated real discount rate of 9.6 percent is not statistically significant at the 0.05 level, with a *t*-ratio of 1.52. The two-stage weighting, however, causes an increase in significance for many variables, including the accident and insurance variables. Most pertinent to our interests here is that it also causes an increase in the estimated discount rate to 12.2 percent and a decrease in the standard error to 0.043, rendering the estimate significant at the 0.01 level. Based on this estimate, one can reject both extreme alternative hypotheses that workers exhibit a zero discount rate or an infinite discount rate when making their job choices.

To compare our estimate of the discount rate to observed explicit rates for the year 1976, it is necessary to convert it to a nominal rate. Using the increase in the GNP deflator of 6 percent in 1976 as a measure of the expected rate of inflation yields a nominal discount rate of 18 percent for the weighted regressions. This discount rate is above the 9 percent nominal rate for new home mortgages in 1976 but equal to the 18 percent rate of interest charged in most states by credit card companies.[13] Our estimated rate of time preference is thus consistent with a hypothesis of rationality of workers' intertemporal tradeoffs.

This estimate is also among the most reasonable estimates of implicit discount rates in the literature. The estimated rate of time preference for life years is in a more plausible range than that for consumers' implicit rates of discount for appliance energy efficiency, which Hausman (1979) found to be around 20 percent or more and Gately (1980) found to be between 45 and 300 percent. Similarly, Fuchs (1982) generated survey data on consumers' rates of time preference that implied a mean implicit rate of time preference of 30 percent. During the recent low inflation period, corporate executives have also been found to use nominal rates of discount on the order of 15 percent or more, so our estimated nominal rates of 18 percent for this equation should not be viewed as unreasonably large.[14]

Similar estimates are obtained with other specifications as well. Table 6.3 summarizes the key parameters in a weighted estimation of the unconditional equations in which the job risk variables appear in their conventional form. In addition, Table 6.3 includes conditional equations in which the risk variable represents the interaction of the objective risk measure and the subjective hazard perception dummy variable. Workers will not demand wage premiums for jobs that they do not perceive as dangerous, and the subjective risk perception variable is incorporated in the risk measure to capture this effect. It is important to note that the conditional estimates eliminate some of the measurement error involved in the matching of average industry risks to workers. As expected, coefficients on the conditional estimates are uniformly larger than their unconditional counterparts for the death risk variables. However, the opposite holds for the injury risk coefficients.

Although the worker's subjective risk perception is the theoretically appropriate variable, the hazard perception variable may not represent the ideal adjustment for these subjective factors. The wording of the hazard perception question, which requires that the worker cite specific hazards, may not elicit perceptions of very small risks. In particular, how large must the risk be before it passes the worker's threshold

TABLE 6.3

Summary of Selected Estimates for Wage Equations with Discounted Expected Life Years Lost: Coefficients and Standard Errors

Independent Variable[a]	Unconditional Risk Measure		Conditional Risk Measure	
	Wage	ln Wage	Wage	ln Wage
Weighted life years lost	7.8E + 1	1.8E + 1	1.0E + 2	1.9E + 1
	(3.7E + 1)	(0.6E + 1)	(0.5E + 2)	(0.5E + 1)
Weighted annuity	−8.6E − 3	−2.4E − 3	−1.3E − 2	−2.5E − 3
	(4.2E − 3)	(0.8E − 3)	(0.7E − 2)	(0.8E − 4)
Lost workday accident rate	0.235	0.058	0.184	0.047
	(0.071)	(0.014)	(0.071)	(0.014)
Weighted replacement rate	−0.255	−0.055	−0.247	−0.053
	(0.075)	(0.013)	(0.080)	(0.014)
Discount rate	0.096	0.122	0.122	0.122
	(0.052)	(0.043)	(0.056)	(0.034)
Implicit value of life (1986 dollars)[b]	$1.5E + 6	$1.2E + 6	$1.2E + 6	$1.2E + 6
Implicit value per life year[c]	$194,285	$177,143	$171,429	$177,143
Implicit value of remaining life[d]	$6.8E + 6	$6.2E + 6	$6.0E + 6	$6.2E + 6

[a] Each equation also included the variables pertaining to the worker's race, sex, experience, union status, blue-collar occupation, firm size, health status, education, speed of work, job security, supervisory status, overtime work, training, and residence in an urban area, the South, the West, or the North Central United States.

[b] Calculated as the product $\partial w / \partial p \times 2000$ hours $\times 1.891$, where 1.891 is the price inflator and p is the probability of a fatal accident.

[c] Calculated as the Implicit Value of Life/Discounted Remaining Life.

[d] Calculated as the Implicit Value per Life Year $\times$ Undiscounted Remaining Life.

for categorization as dangerous or unhealthy? Since the conditional risk measure is not necessarily more meaningful than the unconditional, we present both sets of findings to explore the robustness of the results. The estimates reported in Table 6.4 for the conditional and unconditional measures are very similar.

The rates of discount individuals use to discount years of life are significantly different from zero at the 0.05 level of confidence in all cases and range in magnitude from 10 to 12 percent. One can thus reject the hypothesis that workers have a zero rate of time preference. Similarly, one can reject the other extreme hypothesis that workers are myopic and, in effect, have infinite rates of discount. The 95 percent confidence interval for rates of discount is restricted to generally plausible values.

The findings in Table 6.3 also offer striking support for the theoretical predictions regarding risks and the compensation mix. Both risk measures are consistently positive and statistically significant at the 0.05 level of confidence. The implicit values per additional expected year of life are in the $175,000–$206,000 range, which is remarkably consistent across the four equations, given the wide range of life values reported previously in the literature. If we use the discounted number of life years as the denominator in this calculation the average value of a year of life rises to almost $750,000.

These values represent the average willingness to pay for an additional year of life in present value terms. More important for policy purposes is the marginal value of a life year. If a worker expects to live thirty-five more years, then a one-year life extension is worth only $11,000 now. An older worker, however, who expects to live only five more years will value an additional year of life at approximately $410,000.

The value of life extension also depends on the discount rate. If the real rate of time preference is lower, additional life years increase in value. The worker described above with thirty-five years of life remaining who values an extra year at $11,000 when the discount rate is 12 percent will value the marginal year of life at over $129,000 if the discount rate is 5 percent. Likewise, the older worker with five years of life remaining will pay $590,000 for an additional year when the discount rate is 5 percent.

As the figures at the bottom of Table 6.3 indicate, the value of life estimates on the order of $6.2 million (1988 prices) are similar to those obtained in many traditional estimates, but larger in magnitude than estimates for high-risk samples, such as those of Thaler and Rosen (1976). Thaler and Rosen calculate the implicit value of life at about $620,000 in 1988 prices, using occupational risk data. Viscusi (1981), on the other hand, generates value of life estimates of $5.5 million, again in 1988 prices, using industry risk data. It should be noted also that the annual death risk level for our sample of 5/100,000 is below the 1/1000 value in Thaler and Rosen (1976) and the 1/10,000 value in Viscusi (1979a). Our discounted value of life estimates are larger than the average value of life for these two studies. Given the self-selection of workers with lower values of life into higher-risk jobs, our results are quite consistent with the literature.

Similar calculations of the willingness to pay to avoid a nonfatal injury indicate that individuals value this element of job safety at between $15,500 and $31,000 per accident. Although not as stable as the value of life estimates, these values are also consistent with those found elsewhere in the literature that have controlled for the role of accident insurance and with those of Viscusi (1979a), whose estimated values in current dollars range from $15,000 to $26,000. Since the value of the nonfatal accident wage replacement rate is 0.80, these values represent the implicit costs of pain and suffering and the uninsured wage losses.

The annuity and workers' compensation variables have the expected sign and in every instance they are statistically significant at the 0.05 level (one-tailed). An additional dollar of weekly workers' compensation benefits for disabilities leads to a weekly wage reduction of eighteen cents. As in the Chapter 3 analysis, this is higher than the optimal rate of tradeoff between wages and benefits (–6 cents) that would exist if there were perfect insurance markets. Likewise, the rate of tradeoff between wages and the discounted annuity, which equals –0.8 cents in our estimates, is much larger than the ideal rate of –0.06 cents. If we abstract from the problems of moral hazard, which may be considerable, these estimated rates of tradeoff imply that benefit levels were too low in 1976. Estimates from a more recent data set, reported in Chapter 4, however, indicate that the dramatic increase in benefit levels since 1976 has lowered the rate of tradeoff so that benefit levels are no longer suboptimal. The principal implication of these results is that there is an important tradeoff between ex ante wage compensation and ex post insurance compensation for job risks.

Conclusion

Consideration of the implications of fatality risks for workers' future lifetimes enables assessment of the roles of the duration of life lost and workers' implicit rates of time preference with respect to future life years. The most notable result is that workers discount future life years at real rates of 9.6 to 12 percent. Since these values converted to nominal rates are bounded from below by the prevailing home mortgage interest rate and bounded from above by credit card interest rates, there is no evidence of substantial intertemporal irrationality.

Consideration of the duration of life lost also makes it possible to consider the value of each year of life lost. This value, which averaged more than $176,000 in 1988 prices, was associated with an implicit value of one's future life of about $6.2 million. The valuation level greatly exceeds workers' annual earnings, which is not necessarily inconsistent, since it represents the rate of risk-dollar tradeoff for very small risks, not the amount that workers would pay for certain life extension. Compared with the estimates of other studies, this estimated value of life is toward the higher end of the spectrum, but it is generally consistent with past estimates for workers with jobs of similar riskiness.

The ex post compensation for fatalities and nonfatal injuries played a more prominent role in this chapter than in previous analyses in the literature. Both forms of ex post compensation led to a reduction in ex ante compensation through wage reductions. Rewards for exposure to job risk thus involve two components of compensation: ex ante wage compensation and ex post insurance compensation.

In all of the aspects of our analysis, recognition of the role of the temporal dimension of job risks bolsters the support for an economic model of rational job choice. Although temporal misallocations may exist, the magnitude of any departure from rationality appears small.

Seven

Worker Learning and the Valuation of the Compensation Package

THE COMPENSATING wage differential model underlying the analysis in the preceding chapters assumed that workers value their wage and workers' compensation components on the basis of full job risk information. In this situation, market forces generate positive wage differentials for ex ante compensation for exposure to this risk. Similarly, there are wage offsets for the increases in ex post compensation for risk embodied in workers' compensation benefits.

The general character of this result remains unaffected even if one takes into account potential imperfections in worker information, as in Viscusi (1979a, 1979b, 1980a, 1980b, 1980c). However, the potential for learning about the risk introduces a new market response through worker quitting after the acquisition of adverse risk information. In a full information world, no job risk–quit relationship will be observed unless risks are changing over time, a factor from which we choose to abstract because of data limitations. In the more realistic imperfect information model, sufficiently adverse new information acquired by the worker on the job may lead the worker to quit. Moreover, this evolution in workers' risk perceptions will create changes in the valuation of workers' compensation.

With the exception of the experimental results reported in Viscusi and O'Connor (1984), in which worker responses to alternative chemical labels were monitored, tests of the standard compensating differential model and of the learning models have been distinct, as each focuses on a different aspect of labor market behavior. The literature in support of compensating risk differentials is similar in spirit to the discussion in Chapters 3–6. Higher levels of job risks boost worker wages, and workers are willing to accept a wage cut in return for higher workers' compensation benefits.[1] These results are the main predictions of the standard compensating differential theory, and they continue to hold if learning is introduced. Market tests of the role of worker learning have focused on two empirical issues—the effect of injury experiences on workers' risk perceptions and the positive effect of job risks on worker quitting.[2]

The focus of this chapter is broader than the separate analyses of the wage and quit effects of job risks in that we use the main relationships that are estimated and tested in the standard compensating differential theory to test the job risk learning model as well. In particular, we examine the tradeoff between wages and workers' compensation benefits and differences in the tradeoff across worker groups. Wage equation estimates generate these tradeoff levels for the new hires, who are likely to be the least well informed with respect to job risks. If, however, we focus on the quit–no quit margin, we ascertain information on the wage–workers' compensation tradeoff of many individuals who have acquired adverse information about job risks. If the adaptive model of job choice is correct, then these workers should place a higher value on workers' compensation relative to wages, since their subjective probability of an accident is greater.

In the next section of this chapter, we develop these theoretical underpinnings formally. A discussion of the data set as well as the wage and quit equation estimates then follows. The implied tradeoff levels that are calculated support the predictions regarding the structure of compensating differentials for wages and workers' compensation, The higher tradeoff between wages and workers' compensation on the quit margin suggests that worker learning is important in determining workers' valuations of the compensation package.

Conceptual Framework

Our overall objective is to develop a relationship between the wage–workers' compensation tradeoff for workers overall and for workers on the quit–no quit margin. The theoretical basis for the wage–workers' compensation tradeoff analysis is an extension of the model in Chapter 3 and in Viscusi (1980a, 1980b, 1980c).[3]

The essential ideas can be captured in a two-period model. As in the Chapter 3 analysis, there are two states: healthy and injured. In the good health state, the worker receives a wage rate w, from which he or she derives utility $U^1(w)$. In the injured state, the worker receives workers' compensation benefits b, where $w \geq b$. We continue to assume that the worker would rather be healthy than not (that is, $U^1(x) > U^2(x)$; that he or she has a higher marginal utility of income when healthy, that is, $U^1_x > U^2_x(x)$; and that he or she is either risk averse or risk neutral, that is, $U^1_{xx}, U^2_{xx} \leq 0$. The worker values these payoffs over time using a discount factor Ψ, which equals the reciprocal of 1 plus the discount rate.

Suppose that there are two possible jobs, a risky job and a certain job. We can assume with no loss of generality that the certain job poses no risk of injury.[4] The certain job offers a payoff w_0 forever. The risky job offers the worker an initial perceived probability of not being injured equal to $1 - p$ and a p chance of suffering an injury that lasts a single period. If the worker is injured in period 1, he or she revises the assessed probability of being injured downward to $p(\text{bad})$. If the worker is not injured, the assessed injury probability is $p(\text{good})$. This revision follows a standard Bayesian learning process, where

(7.1) $p(\text{good}) > p > p(\text{bad}).$

The initial job choice of the worker involves a choice between two periods of work on the certain job or initial work on the uncertain job, after which the worker can quit if he or she is injured in period 1. Problems of this type fall into the class of two-armed bandit models of sequential decisionmaking (DeGroot, 1970). For this class of problems, it is shown in Viscusi (1979a, 1979b, 1980a, 1980b, 1980c) that the stay-on-a-winner rule is always optimal.[5] The worker will not leave the certain job once he or she starts on it and will not leave the uncertain job after a favorable experience in period 1.

The wage package for the marginal worker attracted to the firm must satisfy the condition that expected lifetime utility, V, is equal between the two jobs, given the opportunity the worker has to switch from the risky job following an unfavorable period 1 outcome:

$$V = U^1(w_0)(1 + \Psi) = (1 - p)U^1(w) + pU^2(b) +$$
$$\Psi(1 - p)[(1 - p(\text{good}))U^1(w) + p(\text{good})U^2(b)] +$$
$$\Psi p \text{Max}[U^1(w_0),(1 - p(\text{bad}))U^1(w) + p(\text{bad})U^2(b)].$$

If we set $U^1(w_0) = 0$, with no loss of generality we have

$$V = 0 = (1 - p)U^1(w) + pU^2(b) + \Psi(1 - p)[(1 - p(\text{good}))U^1(w) +$$
$$p(\text{good})U^2(b)] + \Psi p \text{Max}[0,(1 - p(\text{bad}))U^1(w) +$$
$$p(\text{bad})U^2(b)].$$

Not all workers will quit their jobs in period 2 after an unfavorable job experience. However, the focus here is on the marginal worker and on the pay package that will attract the worker to the job initially. The marginal worker will quit after an adverse experience in period 1; thus, the wage-benefit package (w,b) sufficient to attract the worker initially will satisfy

(7.2) $V = 0 = (1 - p)U^1(w) + pU^2(b) + \Psi(1 - p)[(1 - p(\text{good}))U^1(w) +$
$p(\text{good})U^2(b)],$

since $\Psi U^1(w_0)$ equals zero after an unfavorable period 1 experience.

The first issue is the wage–workers' compensation tradeoff that will be reflected in the (w,b) package for new hires. Upon implicit differentiation of equation 7.2, we have

(7.3) $\quad \dfrac{\partial w}{\partial b} = \dfrac{-V_b}{V_w} = \dfrac{-U_x^2[p+\Psi(1-p)p(\text{good})]}{U_x^1[(1-p)+\Psi(1-p(\text{good}))]}$.

This equals the wage offset in response to b for the new hire in a two-period job choice problem. The initial wage package (w,b) will be adequate to retain the worker if his or her on the job experiences are favorable.

The worker on the quit–no quit margin at the start of period 2 has an expected utility Z equal to

(7.4) $\quad Z = 0 = (1 - p(\text{bad}))U^1(w) + p(\text{bad})U^2(b)$,

since he or she is indifferent between leaving—where $U^1(w_0) = 0$—and staying on the risky job. The wage–workers' compensation tradeoff for a worker on the quit–no quit margin is given by

(7.5) $\quad \dfrac{\partial w}{\partial b} = \dfrac{-Z_b}{Z_w} = \dfrac{-p(\text{bad})U_x^2}{(1-p(\text{bad}))U_x^1}$.

The principal issue is the relative magnitude of the wage–workers' compensation tradeoffs in equations 7.3 and 7.5. Workers who have experienced an on-the-job injury should value workers' compensation more highly since their assessed probability of receiving such benefits will be greater. In particular, one would expect

		Quit Margin Tradeoff	New Hire Tradeoff
(7.6)	$\dfrac{\partial w}{\partial b} \quad =$	$\dfrac{-Z_b}{Z_w} \quad <$	$\dfrac{-V_b}{V_w}$,

or

(7.7) $\quad \dfrac{p(\text{bad})U_x^2}{1-p(\text{bad})U_x^1} < \dfrac{-U_x^2[p + \Psi(1-p)p(\text{good})]}{U_x^1[(1-p) + \Psi(1-p)(1-p(\text{good}))]}$.

After some algebraic manipulation, equation 7.7 reduces to

(7.8) $\quad p(\text{bad}) < p(\text{good})$.

Given the restrictions on probabilities outlined in equation 7.1 above, equation 7.8 always holds.

The overall wage structure of the firm will, of course, include returns to worker experience and performance. This wage structure can be viewed as defining the pecuniary returns to the worker over time. As is standard in agency theory models of wages, it is the new hires and workers on the margin of leaving the firm that are of greatest concern. Inframarginal workers are not of consequence for the firm's wage structure since they are already earning an economic rent. By altering the entering wage level, the firm ensures a flow of new workers to the firm. Higher wages also diminish the tendency to quit, but since quitters tend to be workers with particularly adverse job experiences, learning-induced quits will continue to occur. Because of the difference in risk perceptions of the potential quitters, the second compensation component—workers' compensation—should be more highly valued by this group than by the worker group that has a lower assessment of the job risk.

The principal prediction that we will explore below is that for workers on the quit margin, the wage–workers' compensation tradeoff should have a higher absolute magnitude, as indicated by equation 7.6. This relationship arises because of the higher value these workers attach to receiving benefits as a result of their on-the-job learning about the risks.

The Sample and the Variables

The main requirement with respect to the survey data for the study is that it include information on wage rates, quit behavior, the worker's state of residence (to establish matchups to workers' compensation benefit formulas) and the worker's industry (to establish matchups with industry risk data). The principal data source that we will use is the 1982 wave of the University of Michigan Panel Study of Income Dynamics (PSID), which has been used earlier in Chapters 4 and 5. These data are matched to information on the risk of an on-the-job fatality by use of the NTOF data introduced in Chapter 5.

The workers' compensation data, which are described in detail in Chapter 3, are based upon benefits for temporary total disabilities. In recent years benefit maximums for temporary disabilities and for permanent partial disabilities, which represent the largest dollar component of total claims, have become equal in practically all states.[6] Likewise, fatality benefit ceilings are now roughly equal to those for the above two categories, although there are some exceptions. This standardization of the benefit structure allows a more representative measure of ex post accident compensation than was available in most earlier studies. The state benefit levels are matched to workers in the PSID sample by state. They are then used in conjunction with information on the worker's wage and family size to determine the weekly benefit for which the worker qualifies. This benefit is then divided by the worker's after-tax weekly wage to construct the wage replacement rate measure that is used in the empirical analysis.

For purposes of estimation, workers who report their occupation as professional, managerial, or farming are excluded from the sample. The remaining exclusions consist of workers whose reported hourly wage is below the statutory minimum of approximately three dollars an hour, non–heads of households, and workers who are over sixty-five years old or are not in the labor force. Cases with missing data are also excluded. The remaining sample consists of 709 workers. The mix of the workers in the sample follows the expected patterns, given the occupational mix, which is predominately blue-collar. The sample consists primarily of workers in industrial contexts, for whom job hazards are likely to be of consequence. In particular, the sample restrictions we have imposed yield a sample that is over four fifths blue-collar and is 40 percent unionized.

The average after-tax weekly wage is $254. We calculated the tax component of wages using information on marginal tax rates provided by the PSID. As in the previous chapters, we make this adjustment to put wages and workers' compensation in comparable after-tax terms.

The death risk measure, which was described earlier, implies an average death risk of 8/100,000 for members of the sample. This risk level is only slightly different from the national average NTOF risk measure of 9/100,000; thus, the sample is representative of the industry mix captured in the NTOF data set. The roughly 1/10,000 death risk level should be viewed as a typical risk sample rather than a high-risk sample. We will use the death risk variable as a proxy for the overall job risk, since this measure is available on a state-specific basis, whereas nonfatal injury data are not.

The basic workers' compensation variable is the dollar value of the state weekly workers' compensation benefit (weekly benefits), which averages $220. Benefits are computed by using information on the worker's state of residence, marital status, and number of dependents. Insurance benefits are once again captured by the weighted replacement rate.

Empirical Results

The empirical tests of the worker learning hypothesis compare the wage-benefit tradeoffs estimated in two basic equations. Estimates of the parameters of the quit equation provide information on the behavior of workers on the quit–no quit margin, while estimates of the parameters of the wage equation provide information on the preferences of

TABLE 7.1
Descriptive Statistics and Definitions of New Variables

Variable	Mean and SD	Definition
Actual quits	0.05 (0.22)	Quit behavior dummy variable (d.v.): 1 if worker quit his job during the year, 0 otherwise
Quit intentions	0.20 (0.40)	Quit intention d.v.: 1 if worker is thinking of finding a new job, 0 otherwise
	(N = 709)	

the newly hired worker. Our principal hypothesis is that the wage–benefit tradeoff for the newly hired worker group will be lower in absolute value than that of the worker group on the quit–no quit margin, which will tend to include many workers who have acquired adverse information about risks on the job.

The quit equation is estimated with two different measures of quit behavior. Table 7.1 defines these two variables. The first is a dummy variable that equals one if the worker actually quit his or her job in the year following the survey. The second is a dummy variable measuring the worker's quit intentions. If a worker answers "yes" to a question asking whether he or she is considering looking for a new job, this quit intention variable is assigned a value of one.

The quit equation to be estimated is

(7.9) $\text{Actual Quit}_i = [1 + \exp(Z_i \beta_q + \phi_q \text{Wage}_i + \gamma_q \text{Risk}_i + \delta_q \text{Weighted Replacement Rate}_i)]^{-1} + \varepsilon_{qi}.$

In addition to equation 7.9, an equation is estimated with the quit intention dummy variable as the dependent variable. Because of the binary nature of the dependent variable in each of these equations and the presence of the endogenous wage variable on the right-hand side of equation 7.9, nonlinear two-stage least squares is used to estimate the parameters of the model. Instrumental variables include all of the explanatory variables in the quit and wage equations and state and industry dummy variables.

Higher worker wages should reduce quitting by increasing the attractiveness of the worker's current job. Quit rates should increase with risk levels if there are learning induced quits, and higher workers' compensation rates should diminish quitting. The key coefficients of interest are ϕ_q and δ_q, which we will use to calculate the wage–workers' compensation tradeoff for workers on the quit–no quit margin.

The other variables included in equation 7.9 include a fairly standard set of demographic and job characteristic variables. Perhaps the most influential is tenure of less than one year, which is an indicator of workers with very little job experience. The results in Viscusi (1980a, 1980b, 1980d) indicate that this variable has a strong positive effect on quitting, as it captures the quit behavior of workers who have a very weak job attachment or who are at an early stage of the process of learning about the main uncertainties posed by the job. Union members should be less likely to quit because of the union "voice" function discussed by Freeman (1976, 1980).

The wage equation is a standard compensating differential equation, similar to the equation found in Chapter 3. The form of the wage equation is

(7.10) $\ln \text{Wage}_i = X_i\beta_w + \gamma_w\text{Risk}_i +$
$\delta_w\text{Weighted Replacement Rate}_i + \varepsilon_{wi}.$

The key variables in the wage equation are the risk and weighted replacement rate measures. Job risks should increase wages based on the standard compensating differential arguments. The expected negative coefficient on the replacement rate variable, δ_w, is used to compute the wage-benefit tradeoff for the new hire.

Table 7.2 presents estimates of equation 7.9 using each quit variable. Actual quit behavior is more relevant than quit intentions, which may measure quit behavior with substantial error, so we focus on the actual quit equation results. Nevertheless, the quit intention variable may provide a useful measure of the job satisfaction of workers once on the job, with the role of worker learning in affecting the wage–workers' compensation tradeoff for the quit intentions equation similar to that for actual quitting.

The Table 7.2 results are broadly consistent with a priori expectations. The coefficients of the actual quit equation indicate that workers with more education are less likely to actually quit their jobs, suggesting that the specific human capital effect may be dominant. There are no significant differences in the quit behaviors of women, blacks, or workers with children. Workers with a health limitation are more likely to quit their jobs, suggesting that it is difficult for an impaired worker to find a good job match. Single workers are less likely to quit, possibly because they do not have another potential source of support while searching for a new job.

The effects of job tenure do not appear substantial for workers with more than one year of tenure.[7] Workers who have been at a firm for less than a year show a significantly higher quit propensity, however, reflecting the larger amount of job experimentation that is conducted in

TABLE 7.2
Quit Equation Estimates: Coefficients and Standard Deviations

Independent Variables[a]	Actual Quits	Quit Intentions
Education	−0.104[b]	0.125[b]
	(0.025)	(0.065)
Sex	−0.050	0.052
	(0.351)	(0.286)
Race	−0.012	−1.224[b]
	(0.231)	(0.512)
Poor health status	0.449[b]	0.717[b]
	(0.224)	(0.346)
Number of dependents	0.013	0.062
	(0.029)	(0.093)
Marital status	−0.484[b]	0.118
	(0.261)	(0.232)
Job tenure	−0.012	0.003
	(0.037)	(0.026)
Tenure of less than one year	1.274[b]	0.348
	(0.390)	(0.166)
Blue collar	−0.822[b]	−0.315
	(0.332)	(0.240)
Union status	−0.206	−0.450
	(0.200)	(0.275)
Wage	$-7.8E-3$[b]	$-3.7E-3$
	$(3.7E-3)$	$(-2.3E-3)$
Death risk	0.034	0.052[b]
	(0.044)	(0.027)
Weighted replacement rate	−0.100[b]	−0.084[b]
	(0.054)	(0.045)
Total effects[c]		
Wage	$2.35E-4$[b]	$2.09E-4$
	$(1.41E-4)$	$(3.58E-4)$
Weekly benefits	$-1.57E-4$[b]	$-4.48E-4$[b]
	$(0.85E-4)$	$(2.38E-4)$

[a] Also included as explanatory variables are three regional dummy variables and a city size variable.

[b] Statistically significant at the 0.05 confidence level.

[c] Total effects equal partial derivatives of equation 7.9 with respect to the appropriate explanatory variable. For example, if $R(q)$ equals the right-hand side of equation 6.9, then the total workers' compensation benefit (b) effect is $\partial R(q)/\partial b = (\delta_q \times \text{Risk}/\text{Wage} \times R(q) \times [1 - R(q)]$. The mean value of $R(q) = 0.05$ is used for these calculations.

early stages of the job. Finally, there appears to be less quitting among blue-collar workers.

As expected, increases in a worker's wage exert a strong downward influence on quitting. Likewise, nonpecuniary compensation in the form of expected workers' compensation insurance benefits leads to lower quit probabilities. This is true for both the replacement rate variable and the dollar benefit level. The latter effect, which is calculated using the regression estimates, is reported at the bottom of Table 7.2, along with the total effects of the wage variable.

For the actual quit equation, and to a lesser extent for the quit intention equation, we have reasonably precise estimates of the parameters used to calculate the wage–workers' compensation tradeoff value. In terms of the total effects, both the wage and workers' compensation variables are significant at the 0.05 level or lower for actual quits. In the case of quit intentions, the workers' compensation variable is also significant at the 0.05 level, while the wage variable is insignificant.

Unlike the earlier quit studies of Viscusi (1979a, 1979b, 1980d) the risk variable does not have a significant effect on actual job quits in this sample. This result appears to be primarily attributable to collinearity with the weighted workers' compensation variable, which also varies by state and interacts with the risk variable. In the quit intentions equation, however, the risk variable is positive and statistically significant, as expected, so that even with the inclusion of the workers' compensation variable, an effect of risk on quit intentions is evident.

Table 7.3 presents estimates of the *ln* wage equation given in equation 7.10 above. The estimates of this equation are consistent with our expectations of the effects of the explanatory variables. The risk and insurance coefficients that are our primary focus have strong effects that are in the expected direction. Consistent with the results discussed in previous chapters, the ex post compensation variable has a significant downward effect on wages, indicating that workers are willing to sacrifice current earnings for insurance payments that are contingent upon an injury. Moreover, even if there were full earnings replacement, the results in Table 7.3 imply that there would still be some ex ante compensation for risk. This compensation provides further evidence of the nontrivial welfare losses associated with the health and disability components of accidents that go beyond the financial loss alone.[8]

Since the weighted replacement rate includes both risk and workers' compensation components, the total effects of the two variables of interest are calculated and summarized at the bottom of Table 7.3. Job risks have a positive effect on wages, and workers' compensation reduces wages. Each of these effects is significant at the 0.01 level.

TABLE 7.3
Wage Equation Estimates

Independent Variable[a]	Coefficient	SD
Sex	-0.345[b]	0.007
Race	-0.142[b]	0.041
Marital status	-0.070[b]	0.039
Number of dependents	0.020[b]	0.012
Education	0.042[b]	0.007
Job tenure	$9.85E-3$[b]	$4.96E-3$
Job tenure^2	$-2.13E-4$	$1.80E-4$
Experience	0.023[b]	0.004
Experience^2	$-3.8E-4$[b]	$0.9E-4$
Union status	0.219[b]	0.026
Blue collar	-0.021	0.034
Death risk	0.013[b]	0.003
Weighted replacement rate	$-7.9E-3$[b]	$2.6E-3$
Adjusted R-squared	0.493	
Total effects		
Death risk	$5.89E-3$[b]	$1.22E-3$
Weekly benefits	-0.071[b]	0.024

[a] Also included as explanatory variables are three regional dummy variables and a city size variable.
[b] Statistically significant at the 0.01 confidence level.

Tests of Worker Learning

The conceptual model predicts that the wage-benefit tradeoff should be greater in absolute value for workers on the quit–no quit margin than for the new hires, whose preferences are reflected in the wage equation coefficients. By using the results at the bottom of Tables 7.2 and 7.3, these tradeoffs can be calculated directly.

In the quit and quit intention equations, the wage-benefit tradeoff is computed as the negative of the ratio of the partial effect of a dollar increase in wages on quits or quit intentions, $(\partial q/\partial w)$, to the effect of a dollar increase in workers' compensation benefits on the same dependent variables, $(\partial q/\partial b)$, where b and w denote the weekly benefit and the weekly wage. Thus, we have the equation

$$(7.11) \quad \frac{\partial w}{\partial b} = \frac{-\partial q/\partial b}{\partial q/\partial w}.$$

Given the definitions of the variables used in equation 7.9, and letting p equal the death risk and $R(q)$ the right-hand side of equation 7.9, the partial effects of wages and benefits on quits and quit intentions are

$$\frac{\partial q}{\partial w} = (\phi_q - \delta_q pb/w^2) \times R(q) \times (1 \ R(q)),$$

and

$$\frac{\partial q}{\partial b} = (\delta_q p/w) \times R(q) \times (1 - R(q)).$$

Substituting into equation 7.11 yields

$$\frac{\partial q}{\partial w} = \frac{\delta_q p/w}{(\phi_q - \delta_q pb/w^2)}.$$

Evaluated at the mean values of risk, weekly benefits, and weekly wages of 8.42 injuries per 100 employees, $220, and $255, the wage-benefit tradeoffs from the quit and quit intention equations equal −0.667 and −2.122.

Similarly, one can use the wage equation estimates in Table 7.3 to assess the wage-benefit tradeoff of new hires. The total effect of a one-dollar increase in benefits on the wage is

$$\frac{\partial w}{\partial b} = \frac{\delta_w p}{[1 + \delta_w pb/w]}.$$

As indicated at the bottom of Table 7.3, this effect equals −0.071.

The evidence provided by these results thus supports the hypothesis that workers who have experimented with a job to discover its risk characteristics, found the job unsatisfactory, and decided to move on to a new job value workers' compensation benefits more highly than do marginal hires. In the quit equation the wage-benefit tradeoff is over nine times larger than in the wage equation, and many times larger in the quit intention equation.

Conclusion

The results reported in this chapter and elsewhere in this book suggest that the discussion of compensating differentials for risk should be viewed as a broader issue than is implied by the standard wage-risk tradeoff literature. Wages and workers' compensation serve as complementary compensation mechanisms, with wages providing ex ante risk compensation and workers' compensation providing ex post earnings replacement. Each of these wage components reduces worker quitting, and workers accept a lower wage in response to higher workers' compensation benefits. This result reflects the tradeoff workers are willing to make between different forms of risk compensation.

The more interesting aspect of the results arises when we use the wage and quit relationships to explore the differences in the wage–workers' compensation tradeoff for new hires and workers on the quit–no quit margin. Estimated tradeoffs indicate that workers on the quit–no quit margin place a much higher relative value on workers' compensation than do new hires. These findings are consistent with a model in which worker quits are induced in part by learning about risks on the job. There is heterogeneity in the valuation of different forms of risk compensation since workers at different stages of their employment history have different assessments of the risk. The wage–workers' compensation results provide a fairly refined test of the learning model.

The more general implication of these results is that further examination of workers' compensation not only illuminates the role of that institution but also enriches our understanding of overall labor market performance.

Eight

The Role of Unions
in Altering the Structure of
Risk Compensation

THE DISCUSSION thus far has addressed wages and workers' compensation in isolation from the labor market context of these compensation mechanisms. Perhaps the most salient omission is that unions have not entered the analysis. It has been well established that unions alter both the wage level and the nature of the compensation package, so it would be surprising if unions had no influence whatsoever on the wage–workers' compensation tradeoff as well.[1]

The union role is unclear, however, since benefit levels are set exogenously by state workers' compensation boards. Trade unions probably have little effect on actual benefit levels at a particular firm, although they may affect differences across states in the benefit structure. Unions can, however, alter the impact of insurance benefits on those aspects of compensation over which they have some control. Under median voter and maximum worker surplus models, average rather than marginal preferences determine the size of wage-risk and wage-benefit tradeoffs, so that we would expect a larger wage-risk tradeoff and a smaller wage-benefit tradeoff for union workers.[2]

The role of unions in altering the wage-risk-benefit relationship remains a largely unexplored issue. In the sole analysis of this topic, Dorsey and Walzer (1983) found, somewhat counterintuitively, that wages and benefits are positively related for union members.[3]

In this chapter, the role of unions in determining the composition of the total wage-risk-benefit package is assessed empirically. In the course of doing so, the counterintuitive finding of Dorsey and Walzer is first replicated, and then found to be attributable to problems associated with the risk variable. Estimated wage-risk and wage-benefit tradeoffs are compared for union and nonunion workers as a test of economic models of union influence. The estimated wage-benefit tradeoffs are also compared to the efficient tradeoff in the manner described in Chapter 3 to determine whether unions enhance the overall efficiency of workers' compensation programs.

Empirical Framework

The building block for the empirical analysis is a standard compensating differential wage equation of the form

(8.1)   Wage = $X\beta + \beta_u$Union status + γ_wDeath risk +
          δ_wWeighted weekly benefits + ε,

where the coefficient β_u measures the union wage effect, the coefficient γ_w measures the compensating differential for job risks, and the coefficient δ_w measures the effect of workers' compensation insurance benefits on wages.

The differential impacts of union membership on ex ante and ex post compensation for job risks are captured by adding interaction terms for union status and job risks and for union status and weighted workers' compensation benefits. The resulting equation is

(8.2)   Wage = $X\beta + \beta_u$Union status + γ_wDeath risk +
          δ_wWeighted weekly benefits + γ_uUnion status $\times$
          Death risk + δ_uUnion status $\times$
          Weighted weekly benefits + ε,

where γ_u and δ_u measure the union effects on the compensating differentials.

The principal hypotheses tested below are that union members receive larger wage increases for exposure to a given level of risk and less of a wage cut for increases in workers' compensation benefits. Implicit in these tests is the test of whether workers' compensation lowers the wages of nonunion workers, which is contrary to the sole finding reported in the literature. In terms of the coefficients of equation 8.2, the hypotheses tested below are

$$\frac{\partial \text{Wage}^U}{\partial \text{Risk}} > \frac{\partial \text{Wage}^N}{\partial \text{Risk}} > 0 \text{ and } \frac{\partial \text{Wage}^N}{\partial \text{Benefits}} < \frac{\partial \text{Wage}^U}{\partial \text{Benefits}} < 0,$$

where the U and N superscripts denote the union and the nonunion wage, and where, for example,

$$(\partial \text{Wage}^U/\partial \text{Risk}) = (\gamma_w + \gamma_u) + (\delta_w + \delta_u) \times \text{Weekly benefits}.$$

The workers' compensation variable used below is an individual-specific measure that is based on the state-mandated benefit levels and on the worker's own wage. The basic formula for a worker's weekly benefit specifies that benefits will equal two-thirds of the worker's pretax wage, within minimum and maximum benefit levels set independently by state workers' compensation boards. If two-thirds of the worker's wage exceeds the maximum, he or she qualifies for the maximum. Similarly, if two-thirds of the worker's wage falls below the minimum, he or she receives the minimum in the event of a qualifying injury. Very few workers' wages are so low that they qualify for the minimum, however, so the development and estimation of the model will ignore this aspect of the benefit structure.

To construct the benefit variable used in this chapter, first define the dummy variable, d, to equal one if the worker qualifies for the benefit maximum, and zero otherwise.[4] The weekly benefits that will accrue to a worker in the event of an injury are then expressed as the equation

(8.3)   Weekly benefits = d × Benefit Maximum + $(1 - d)$ ×
          (2/3) × Wage.

Substitution of this expression for the weekly benefit into equation 8.2 yields, after solving for the weekly wage, the estimating equation

(8.4)   Wage = $D^{-1}(X\beta + \beta_u$Union status + γ_wDeath Risk +
          δ_wDeath Risk × Benefit Maximum × d +
          γ_uUnion status × Death risk + δ_uUnion status ×
          Death risk × Benefit maximum × $d + \varepsilon)$,

where

$$D = 1 - \text{Death risk} \times (1 - d) \times (2/3) \times (\delta_w + \delta_u \text{Union status}).$$

Several features of equation 8.4 are worth noting. First, since the variable d is a function of the worker's wage, it must be treated as an endogenous variable for purposes of estimation. Second, the presence of the coefficients δ_w and δ_u in the denominator of equation 8.4 requires estimation by nonlinear methods. Third, and finally, the error term in equation 8.4 is heteroskedastic, since

$$D^{-1}\varepsilon = \varepsilon / (1 - \text{Death risk} \times (1 - d) \times (2/3) \times (\delta_w + \delta_u \text{Union status}),$$

and

$$\text{Var}(D^{-1}\varepsilon) = D^{-2}\sigma^2.$$

To circumvent these problems, equation 8.4 is estimated by using nonlinear two-stage least squares.[5] The coefficients are estimated in three identical equations using three separate years of data taken from the PSID, with the coefficients on the explanatory variables restricted to be equal across the equations.[6] To identify the model, the square of the benefit maximum variable and its interaction with a firm size variable are used as excluded instrumental variables. Since these particular measures vary only by state and industry, it is unlikely that they will be correlated with unexplained variation in wages at the individual level, which justifies their use as excluded instruments.[7]

The primary focus of the empirical analysis is on the treatment of the union status and the risk variables. An extensive literature on the econometric modeling of union effects in wage equations suggests that union status should be treated as an endogenous variable, since unobservable determinants of the worker's wage help determine the worker's choice of union status.[8] A less extensive but nonetheless sizable body of literature argues similarly that the risk variable in the wage equation must be treated as an endogenous variable, since in the compensating differential model wages and risk are jointly chosen.[9] A second argument for treating risk as an endogenous variable arises when industry-level risk data are matched to individual-level worker data, as is the case here, since this matching procedure introduces measurement error into the risk variable. In the results reported below, the sensitivity of the estimates of the wage-risk and wage-benefit tradeoffs for union and nonunion workers to these aspects of the specification of the model is evaluated by comparing estimates of the wage-risk and wage-benefit tradeoffs that treat union status and risk as endogenous to those treating each as exogenous.

The Sample and the Variables

Table 8.1 defines the key new variables used in the analysis, and Table 8.2 presents their means and standard deviations. Data for this study are taken from the PSID for the years 1981–1983. Nonfarm household heads who did not suffer any long-term unemployment during the sample period are included in the sample. Cases with missing data are excluded.

The dependent variable used in the analysis is the worker's after-tax hourly wage. The actual wage is used, rather than the more common logarithmic transformation, in order to implement the empirical model developed above. Wages for all three years are converted to 1983 dollars by use of the GNP deflator.

The auxiliary control variables include the standard wage equation variables representing human capital effects attributable to years of schooling, experience, and job tenure; personal characteristic dummy variables indicating the worker's race, sex, health status, and marital status; geographic indicators of city size and state of residence (state dummy variables); and an occupation dummy variable indicating whether the worker works in a blue-collar occupation. In addition to these variables, which are available in the PSID, a measure of average firm size taken from the *State and Metropolitan Area Data Book* is matched to workers by state of residence and one-digit industry.

TABLE 8.1
Key Variable Definitions

Variable	Definition
Union status	Union status dummy variable (d.v.): 1 if worker's job is covered by a collective bargaining agreement, 0 otherwise
Death risk	NTOF risk variable: number of fatal accidents per 100,000 workers in the worker's industry, on a state-specific basis
Benefit maximum	Maximum benefit level for temporary total disability under state workers' compensation program
Weekly benefits	Weekly benefits for temporary total disability under state workers' compensation program

TABLE 8.2
Selected Sample Characteristics, 1983 Variables: Means and Standard Deviations

Variable	Union Status = 0	Union Status = 1
Death risk	6.63	6.73
	(7.92)	(9.92)
Benefit maximum	243.85	251.03
	(85.84)	(91.23)
	(N = 490)	(N = 217)

The variables that are the primary focus of this study are those related to union status, job riskiness, and expected weekly workers' compensation benefits. Union status is measured by a dummy variable, which is assigned a value of 1 if the worker's job is covered by a collective bargaining agreement. Data on job risks are taken from the National Traumatic Occupational Fatality survey. These data have been described in detail in Chapter 5.

One limitation of the risk data used by Dorsey and Walzer (1983), which they note, is that their injury rate data varied only by industry, and not by state. The use of national-level risk data introduces error into the risk measure, since interstate variation in risk is ignored. To control for the bias that would be introduced into the estimates of the risk differential, Dorsey and Walzer include state dummies in the wage equations. Doing so produces no meaningful changes in the results reported for the nonunion portion of the sample, so the measurement error bias does not appear to be a problem in this case, as long as the heterogeneity is restricted to shifts of the regression intercept. Despite this apparent lack of bias, the risk data used below represent an improvement over the national aggregate risk data, in that they vary by both state and industry. Thus, bias due to omitted interstate differences in risk levels is not a problem that must be empirically assessed in the particular sample used here.[10]

The final compensation component used is the measure of weighted workers' compensation benefits. This variable, which is defined above in equation 8.3, is a function of the worker's wage and the maximum benefit level in his or her state. The benefit maximum variable is taken from the annual analyses of workers' compensation laws published by the U.S. Department of Commerce and matched to workers by their state of residence. The weighted benefit variable is then constructed by interacting the weekly benefits with the death risk variable.

Empirical Results

Table 8.3 presents four sets of estimates of the union-risk-benefit effects.[11] The results in column 1 treat both union status and job risks as exogenous, while the column 2 estimates treat union status as endogenous and the 3 estimates treat job risks as endogenous. The column 4 results describe estimates of a model that treats both union status and job risk as endogenous variables.

The individual coefficient estimates at the top of Table 8.3 reflect patterns of influence that are consistent across all four models. The union status and death risk differentials are both positive and statistically significant in all four equations, with the exception of the union effect in columns 1 and 3. The effects of measurement error bias are evidenced by comparing the risk coefficients in columns 1 and 2 to those in columns 3 and 4, which are about three times larger. The direct union status effects likewise increase by a factor of about two when union status is treated as endogenous. This could reflect reporting error in the union variable, which would cause downward bias in its estimated coefficient if left uncorrected.[12] Alternatively, the increase in the union effect observed in moving to the instrumental variable estimates could reflect negative selectivity in the union sector, which, although difficult to explain, has been documented empirically by Duncan and Leigh (1985), Cain, et al. (1981), and Adamache and Sloan (1982).

The two workers' compensation effects reported in Table 8.3 are consistently in the predicted direction and statistically significant. Expected ex post compensation for accidents replaces wages, as evi-

TABLE 8.3

Union Status, Death Risk, and Workers' Compensation Effects:
Coefficients and Standard Deviations

Variable	Exogenous Union Status/ Exogenous Death Risk	Endogenous Union Status/ Exogenous Death Risk	Exogenous Union Status/ Endogenous Death Risk	Endogenous Union Status/ Endogenous Death Risk
Union status (β_u)	0.341	0.685[a]	0.291	0.731[a]
	(0.240)	(0.372)	(0.258)	(0.391)
Death risk (γ_w)	0.078[a]	0.094[a]	0.238[a]	0.278[a]
	(0.025)	(0.027)	(0.057)	(0.065)
Weighted weekly benefits (δ_w)	$-2.58E - 4$[a]	$-3.09E - 4$[a]	$-8.91E - 4$[a]	$-1.04E - 3$[a]
	$(1.07E - 4)$	$(1.24E - 4)$	$(2.29E - 4)$	$(0.26E - 3)$
Union status × Death risk (γ_u)	-0.032	-0.044	-0.013	-0.110
	(0.037)	(0.051)	(0.078)	(0.103)
Union status × Weighted weekly benefits (δ_u)	$5.04E - 4$[a]	$5.51E - 4$[a]	$4.86E - 4$[a]	$8.71E - 4$[a]
	$(1.67E - 4)$	$(2.44E - 4)$	$(3.14E - 4)$	$(4.42E - 4)$
Total effects at sample means				
Union status (equation 8.5)	0.811	1.134	0.820	0.138
Union member				
Death risk (equation 8.6)	0.083	0.086	0.162	0.142
Benefit maximum				
(equation 8.7)	$1.36E - 3$	$1.33E - 3$	$-2.23E - 3$	$-0.931E - 4$
Nonunion member				
Death risk (equation 8.6)	0.043	0.052	0.111	0.128
Benefit maximum				
(equation 8.7)	$-9.60E - 4$	$-1.15E - 3$	$-3.32E - 3$	$-3.87E - 3$

[a] Statistically significant at the 0.05 confidence level, one-tailed test.

denced by the negative and statistically significant expected benefit effects. The extent of this wage replacement is decreased significantly for union members in all four cases.

The total effects of the union, risk, and benefit variables are reported at the bottom of Table 8.3. These total effects are computed by use of equation 8.4 above. Let w, p, U, and c denote the wage, death risk, union status, and benefit ceiling variables. Rearranging terms by multiplying through the denominator on the right-hand side of equation 8.4, and dropping the auxiliary control variables for convenience, we get the expression

$$w[1 - p(1 - d) \times (2/3)(\delta_w + \delta_u U)] = \beta_u U + \gamma_w p + \delta_w pcd + \gamma_u Up + \delta_u Upcd.$$

Totally differentiating this expression with respect to w, p, U, and c yields the expressions for the total effects

(8.5) $\dfrac{\partial w}{\partial U} = D^{-1}[\beta_u + \gamma_u p + \delta_u pcd + \delta_u wp(1-d)(2/3)],$

(8.6) $\dfrac{\partial w}{\partial p} = D^{-1}[\gamma_w + \delta_w cd + \gamma_u U + \delta_u Ucd + (1-d)(2/3)(\delta_w + \delta_u U)],$

and

(8.7) $\dfrac{\partial w}{\partial c} = D^{-1}(\delta_w pd + \delta_u Upd).$

These effects, which are the most informative, given the use of interaction terms in the wage equation, provide clear evidence on the source of observed positive wage-benefit tradeoffs for union members. The estimates in column 1 replicate Dorsey and Walzer's finding that wage-benefit tradeoffs are negative for nonunion workers and positive for union workers. This result persists when union status is treated as an endogenous variable and risk as exogenous, with little change in the magnitude of the wage-benefit tradeoff for either type of worker. However, when job risks are treated as endogenous, as in columns 3 and 4, the sign of the workers' compensation effect is reversed for union workers, regardless of the treatment of union status. Thus, the somewhat counterintuitive finding that union members receive wage increases for increases in workers' compensation benefits appears to be attributable to problems associated with the risk variables commonly used in wage equations. Once the problems of measurement error and endogeneity of job risks are controlled for, the counterintuitive result disappears, and the union wage-fringe tradeoff becomes consistent with a priori expectations.

The results in Table 8.3 are broadly consistent with the median voter and maximum worker surplus models of union wage determination. The median voter model, for instance, states that the preferences of the average worker drive wages in union settings, whereas the preferences of the marginal worker set wages in competitive labor markets. The implications of the median voter and competitive models lead to two predictions. First, since the marginal worker has less of an aversion to risk than does the average worker, union members should receive larger compensating differentials for job risks. Second, since the preferences of the marginal worker define the largest acceptable wage-benefit tradeoff, workers' compensation benefits should decrease wages less for union workers. Both of these results hold in all four columns of Table 8.3. In particular, the more plausible results of columns 3 and 4 indicate that risk differentials are between 10 and 40 percent higher and benefit tradeoffs are at least 30 percent smaller in absolute value for union members.

A final perspective on the role of unions in altering wage-risk and wage-benefit tradeoffs can be gained by comparing the relative efficiency of the wage-benefit tradeoffs for union and nonunion workers. If we use the result derived in Chapter 3, if workers' compensation benefit levels are set optimally, the rate of tradeoff between wages and workers' compensation benefits is given by the expression

$$\frac{\partial w}{\partial b} = \frac{-p(1+a)}{(1-p)}.$$

If the estimated wage-benefit tradeoff is less than the optimal tradeoff, benefits are too low. Reasons for the observed inefficiency of benefits, which is documented for the year 1976 in Chapter 3, include moral hazard problems associated with monitoring both worker care and the filing of spurious claims.[13]

A number of authors, most notably Freeman and Medoff (1984), have suggested recently that in many instances unions increase the overall efficiency of the firm through a variety of practices. Whether this increased efficiency is reflected in wage-benefit tradeoffs is an empirical question, which can easily be answered by using the results in Table 8.3. Assuming a loading factor of 0.2, which is approximately the national average for this period, and using the average job risk in the sample of approximately 0.6 fatalities per 10,000 workers, the optimal rate of tradeoff between wages and benefits for the sample used here is $-7.2E-5$.

If we now use the estimated tradeoffs in the last two columns of Table 8.3, and divide by 40 to reflect the fact that the model is estimated from the hourly wage, while the optimal rate of tradeoff is expressed in terms of the weekly wage, the observed tradeoffs range between $-8.0 \times E-5$ and $-10.0 \times E-5$ for nonunion workers, and between $-2.3 \times E-3$ and $-5.5 \times E-3$ for union workers. This result suggests that unions decrease the amount of wage-benefit substitution beyond the level that is suggested by the theory as optimal. In fact, unions appear to capture rents for workers beyond those due simply to wage increases, by preventing wage reductions in the face of exogenously mandated benefit increases. Thus, the incidence of the workers' compensation premiums appears to fall more heavily on unionized firms.

Conclusions

Unions play an important role in altering market-determined tradeoffs between wages and job risks and between wages and workers' compensation insurance. Union workers receive higher compensating differentials for exposure to job risks, and their wages fall by less in response to increases in workers' compensation benefits. Furthermore, the wage-benefit tradeoff estimated for union workers indicates that the wage reduction generated in unionized firms by benefit increases is not large enough to allow firms to break even on the increase, so that the net cost of benefit hikes is greater for union than for nonunion firms.

The finding that benefit increases cause wage decreases for unionized workers when risk is treated as an endogenous variable explains a heretofore counterintuitive result in the literature. Instrumental variable estimates of the wage-benefit tradeoff for unionized workers were negative and statistically significant, which is in accord with a priori expectations. The estimated effects of risks and of benefits on wages were both larger in absolute value for union members, which is consistent with the predictions of the surplus maximization and median voter models.

Nine

The Effects of Workers' Compensation on Job Safety

A KEY economic and regulatory issue pertains to the efficacy of different compensation mechanisms in promoting safety. The primary market mechanism of compensating differentials creates substantial incentives for safety. The Occupational Safety and Health Administration (OSHA) provides an additional institutional mechanism for direct regulation of risks. OSHA policies have failed to fulfill their initial promise, however, as observed safety effects are statistically significant, but of small magnitude.[1]

As a substitute for regulatory policies, some economists advocate an injury tax approach, not unlike the funding mechanism for workers' compensation.[2] This approach could potentially enhance safety levels, but most formal statistical evidence documenting the workers' compensation–safety linkage indicates the opposite—that moral hazard effects dominate and, therefore, that increased benefits lead to greater injury rates.[3]

In the case of compensating differentials, we have a dollar price tag in terms of risk premiums paid. This is also true of workers' compensation. However, we do not as yet have a definitive estimate of the ultimate safety effect of workers' compensation. Since premiums are not always fully experience rated, particularly for small firms, and because of potential moral hazard problems, the extent of the safety incentive effect of workers' compensation is not clear-cut.

One key to understanding the observed workers' compensation–accident relationship lies in the severity of the accidents considered. The majority of existing studies (Chelius 1982; Chelius and Smith 1987; Butler and Worral 1983; Worral and Butler 1985; Ruser 1985a; and Krueger 1988) use a risk measure based largely on nonfatal accident rates, on some composite of fatal and nonfatal rates, or on measures of claims filed for nonfatal and fatal accidents. These studies reach a unanimous conclusion—increased insurance benefits cause injury and claim rates to rise significantly.

This result reflects an obvious limitation of injury rate and claim data—risk measures, such as total injury rates or lost workday case rates, include claims for injuries that may not, in fact, have occurred. This fact leads most researchers to conclude that moral hazard effects dominate the safety effects of injury insurance. Furthermore, it is impossible to distinguish whether there is any safety effect at all.

Evidence contrary to this finding is limited. However, it appears that when the risk measure captures more accurately the severity of accidents, benefit increases have a negative effect on risk levels for more severe risks. For example, Chelius (1976) finds that the introduction of workers' compensation in the United States led to a decrease in fatality rates over the period 1900–1940. Also, Chelius (1982) finds a significant negative relationship between benefit levels and lost workdays per case, a risk measure that varies with the severity of the injury.

This general result—that benefit increases increase the incidence of less severe accidents, but decrease their severity—is examined in this chapter. The most severe accident—death—should reflect very little moral hazard. Deaths cannot be falsely claimed, of course, and the high values that workers implicitly attach to lives saved suggest that workers would not be willing to substitute fatality benefits for their own lives. Therefore, if workers' compensation provides any safety incentives to firms, these will be reflected most strongly in fatality rate data.

The first objective of this chapter is therefore to assess the performance of workers' compensation in reducing fatality rates. Our estimates indicate a dramatic safety effect, particularly when compared with evidence regarding the impact of OSHA and previous evidence regarding the effect of workers' compensation on nonfatal injuries. The second issue we consider is the net dollar cost to firms of responding to these safety incentives.[4] Examination of dollar premiums for workers' compensation provides a useful starting point for such analyses, but does not give a complete measure of the financial incentives, since workers will accept a wage reduction in return for the insurance coverage. Furthermore, if greater safety is promoted through workers' compensation, the required compensating wage differential for risk and the level of injury costs to the firm will both be reduced. Thus, there are both direct and indirect effects of workers' compensation on worker wages that act to offset both the cost of the insurance premiums and the employer's expenditures on safety.

This chapter extends research on the labor market effects of workers' compensation in two ways. It analyses the joint determination of wages and risks in a structural hedonic model, and it computes the total effect of benefits on wages by taking the indirect effect into account. Our focus on fatality rates to minimize moral hazard problems is also new.

Our findings in this chapter are as follows. Increases in fatality rates increase wages, while increases in workers' compensation benefits lower both wages and fatality rates. The risk reduction is most pronounced in large firms. This risk reduction, in turn, has an additional wage effect, equal to about one-fifth of the direct benefit effect.

These results, in general, document the constructive economic function served by workers' compensation. The consensus in the literature is correctly summarized in the 1987 *Economic Report of the President*: "A growing body of research has found that workers' compensation benefits have unfavorable effects on safety. Higher benefits appear to increase both the frequency of work injuries and the number of compensation claims filed" (p. 197). In contrast, our results indicate that workers' compensation generates truly dramatic reductions in workplace fatalities. This finding does not cast doubt on the moral hazard issue. It does, however, establish a function of workers' compensation that yields considerable benefits in the form of reduced workplace fatalities.

Overview of the Economic Relationships

The empirical analysis focuses on two equations—a risk equation and a wage equation. Neither of these equations is unprecedented in the literature, although they have heretofore been analyzed separately.[5] Here we will discuss the economic forces reflected in the main variables.

All of the key variables in the fatality rate equation are related to workers' compensation. The funding mechanism for workers' compensation creates safety incentives for firms that should increase the safety level provided. Even for relatively small firms that are not perfectly experience rated, the insurance underwriting procedures lead to some link between workplace conditions and insurance premiums.

Moral hazard provides two potentially offsetting influences. More generous benefit levels will lead workers to decrease their level of care, an aspect of worker behavior just as unambiguous theoretically as the opposite safety incentive effect for employers. A number of studies also indicate that more generous benefits lead to more extended periods of recovery and possible overreporting of injuries.[6] These abuses are likely to be more responsive to the benefit level than is the fatality rate, which is the subject of this chapter. Although one cannot rule out the possibility of a dominant moral hazard effect in fatalities on theoretical grounds, the high estimated value of life that workers imply by their wage-risk tradeoffs suggests that workers would not endanger their lives to any substantial degree because of more generous ex post compensation for their surviving heirs. Furthermore, a worker's ability to report a fatality when one has not occurred is obviously quite limited. Our working hypothesis is therefore that higher benefits will lower fatality risk levels so that the workers' compensation variable will have a negative sign in the fatality rate equation.

The second variable of interest—the square of the workers' compensation variable—pertains to the nonlinearity of the effect of workers' compensation on fatality rates. This relationship is highly complex once all feedback effects, such as moral hazard, are taken into account. Given these complex counteracting effects, the relationship is likely to be highly nonlinear. We therefore include a quadratic term to capture the nonlinearities.

The third workers' compensation variable interacts workers' compensation and firm size. The cost of an accident to a firm in terms of increased insurance premiums depends crucially on the degree to which firms are experience rated.[7] Large firms, particularly those that self-insure, will be rated according to their own accident experience and feel the full impact of accidents on their insurance premiums. Thus, the safety incentives should be greater in larger firms.

The variables included in the wage equation represent less complex influences. Wages should increase with the risk level. For economically similar reasons, higher levels of workers' compensation should lead to a wage reduction; ex post compensation for job risks should decrease the level of ex ante compensation required. The extent of the offset depends on the attractiveness of the insurance provided. As shown in Chapter 3, increases in such factors as the degree of insurance loading and the risk level increase the value of benefits to the worker.

The Sample and the Variables

Our primary data source in this study is the 1982 PSID data utilized in the previous chapters. Our PSID subsample in this chapter contains 1,173 observations after exclusion of farmers and farm managers, workers who are not household heads, government employees (for whom no risk data are available), and cases with missing data. The sample is broadly representative of the working population, considering these exclusions.

The key variables used in the empirical analysis are defined in earlier chapters. Our primary measure of pecuniary compensation is the worker's weekly wage (WAGE) for 1981, the year covered by the 1982 PSID. As in the previous chapter, use of the weekly wage rather than its natural logarithm is required in order to estimate the model developed below.

The primary focus of our analysis is on the interrelationships among wages, hazardous working conditions, firm size, and insurance for job-related injuries. Because the PSID did not include information on job risks, workers' compensation benefits, or firm size, we collected these measures from published sources and matched the information to workers in the PSID. The death risk data come from the NTOF census.[8]

The second key variable used below is the measure of workers' compensation benefits. Previous analyses have utilized a range of measures that include the weekly wage replacement rate (Chapters 3–7; Chelius 1982; Arnould and Nichols 1983), weekly benefits (Chapter 8; Ruser 1985a), annual payments by industry (Butler 1983), and workers' compensation premium rates (Dorsey and Walzer 1983). In most cases benefits for the most frequent type of claim—temporary total disabilities—are used as a proxy for all types of benefits, including those for temporary total, permanent total, and permanent partial disabilities, and for fatality benefits, although Butler attempts, with some success, to identify the effects of each type of benefit separately and also constructs a benefit index using principal components analysis. Chapter 3 documents the high correlations among the various benefit categories that make separation of their effects difficult. We base our benefit measure on the temporary total disability category, and define weekly benefits using equation 7.3. We report results below, using the most common benefit measure, the wage replacement rate, and contrast these with results using other benefit measures to determine the robustness of our findings.

The third variable collected externally is the firm size variable. Since the PSID does not include such a measure, we matched average firm size data from the U.S. Department of Commerce (1984) to workers in the sample by state and one-digit industry. Workers in the transportation, utilities and sanitary services, and finance, insurance, and real estate industries were excluded from our sample in the matching process, because firm size data are not available for these industries. This exclusion accounts for the difference in size between the PSID subsample in this Chapter and those in previous chapters, where these groups were included.

Empirical Framework

Our empirical analysis estimates two equations describing the determination of risk and wage levels. The first of these, an industry death risk equation, estimates the effects of workers' compensation on death risk levels. This equation is of the form

$$(9.1) \quad \text{Death risk}_i = \alpha_0 + \delta_f \text{Firm size}_i + \delta_b \text{Weekly benefits}_i + \delta_{bb} \text{Weekly benefits}_i^2 + \delta_{bs} \text{Weekly benefits}_i \times \text{Firm size}_i + \sum_{j=1}^{6} \alpha_j \text{Industry}_{ij} + \varepsilon_{Ri}.$$

In equation 9.1, the key explanatory variables are as defined above. In addition to the benefit variables, we include a measure of firm size and dummy variables for industry-specific unobservables.[9] We estimate an identical equation using the natural log of death risk as the dependent variable.

A number of statistical issues arise in the estimation of equation 9.1. Most important, it is possible that the three benefit measures are endogenous, since they equal the worker's wage in those cases in which the benefit cap is not binding. Using the state maximum benefit amount, its square, its interaction with the firm size variable, state dummy variables, and the exogenous variables in equation 2 as instruments, we therefore estimate the risk equations using two-stage least squares.

A second issue concerns the exclusion of state dummy variables as regressors from the risk equation. State dummies were used by Ruser (1985a) and Krueger (1988) to control for interstate differences in the types of injuries that firms are required to report. The inclusion of state dummies makes it difficult to estimate the workers' compensation effects, however, since these vary primarily by state for workers whose wage exceeds the benefit cap. Fortunately, this problem does not arise for the risk variable considered here. Firms in all states must report on-the-job fatalities and the definition of what constitutes a fatality is certainly clear-cut. State dummy variables are therefore excluded, and aid in the identification of the weekly benefit variables.

The final specification issue concerns the inclusion of a wage variable in the risk equation. In a structural risk equation, the correct wage variable would be the implicit price of risk, that is, the compensating differential. Rather than take this approach, we utilize the fact that in hedonic systems the characteristics—in this case, the risk—can be expressed as a function of either firm characteristics, worker characteristics, or the wage.

As discussed earlier, our hypothesized effects of workers' compensation on death risk are $\delta_b < 0$, $\delta_{bb} > 0$, and $\delta_{bs} < 0$. If moral hazard offsets the safety incentive effect the net effect of workers' compensation will be to raise the fatality risk.

Death Risk Equation Estimates

Table 9.1 presents two-stage least squares estimates of the death risk equations described by equation 9.1. The total effects of the key explanatory variables are presented at the bottom of Table 9.1.

The results indicate that workers' compensation, on balance, serves as a fatality reduction mechanism. The weekly benefit variable has a

TABLE 9.1

Death Risk Equation Estimates: Coefficients and Standard Deviations

Coefficient Variable[a]	Dependent Variable	
	ln Death Risk	*Death Risk*
$\alpha_f(s)$	0.34E − 3	0.024
	(1.80E − 3)	(0.015)
$\delta_b(b)$	−6.07E − 3[b]	−0.031[b]
	(1.15E − 3)	(0.010)
$\delta_{bb}(b^2)$	8.31E − 6[b]	4.43E − 5[b]
	(1.85E − 6)	(1.59E − 5)
$\delta_{bs}(bs)$	−8.04E − 6[b]	−8.33E − 5[b]
	(4.58E − 6)	(3.94E − 5)
R-squared	0.612	0.663
Total effects of explanatory variables[c]		
Weekly benefits	−2.88E − 3	−1.53E − 2
F (Benefits)[d]	13.04[b]	5.09[b]
Firm size	1.68E − 3	2.03E − 2
F (Size)[e]	51.93[b]	6.30[b]

[a] Also included as control variables are seven industry dummy variables.

[b] Statistically significant at the 0.05 confidence level, one-tailed test.

[c] Evaluated at sample means.

[d] Test of joint significance of the three benefit variables.

[e] Test of joint significance of the two size variables.

negative sign and very strong statistical significance in both equations, indicating a large positive benefit impact on safety levels. The nonlinearity of the benefit effect is also very strong, as evidenced by the significant positive coefficients for the squared benefit term. The negative effect of the benefit x size interaction, which is statistically significant in both equations, indicates that rating firms more in line with their experience serves to reinforce the dampening effect of workers' compensation on risks.

The finding that workers' compensation has a significant negative effect on fatality rates is unprecedented in the literature. Of the major studies that have identified statistically significant effects, Chelius (1982) finds a positive relationship between benefits and injury frequencies, and Ruser (1985a) finds the same relationship between benefits and injuries that resulted in lost workday cases. Butler and Worral (1983) likewise find a positive effect of benefits on the claims rate for temporary total disabilities. Most recently, Krueger (1989) finds a positive relationship between benefits and participation rates for workers' compensation programs, except for female workers. On the other hand, Chelius (1982) also finds a negative relationship between benefits and injury severity, measured by total lost workdays.

The most likely reason why our results run counter to those in the literature appears to lie in the nature of the risk variable. There are two aspects of moral hazard reflected in the injury rate studies—reduced care and the filing of spurious claims. Available evidence indicates that the latter effect can be substantial. Butler and Worrall (1983, 1985) document a positive effect of benefits on both the filing of claims and their duration, and Smith (1988) finds that a large number of claims for sprains and strains occur on Monday mornings, suggesting that workers might postpone treatment for some injuries suffered while out of work in order to qualify for benefits. For two reasons, it is not likely that reduced care or the filing of false claims will be reflected in our data. Evidence on workers' implicit valuations of life suggests that increases in the risk of death will not be adequately compensated by increased survivor benefits. More important, the ability to file a false claim is severely limited for fatalities.

Another important difference in our risk variable is the process by which the NTOF data were collected. Since the NTOF data represent a census of fatalities on the job, they are not subject to the sampling error that is inherent in the risk data collected by the Bureau of Labor Statistics and other agencies. Evidence presented in Chapter 4 indicates that this error is not entirely random, which may also help explain the differences in our results.

Wage Equation Estimates

The main result of the preceding section, that is, that workers' compensation benefits exert strong downward pressure on death rates, identifies a third linkage in the wage-risk-benefit model. The majority of the empirical research on wage-risk and wage-benefit tradeoffs indicates that increases in fatality risks cause wages to rise, while increases in workers' compensation benefits generate wage reductions. To the extent that benefit increases cause fatality risks to fall, these previous analyses have understated the estimates of the wage-benefit tradeoff by ignoring the indirect effect of benefits on wages through fatality risks.

To explore the complete wage-risk-benefit model, we can use the estimated risk-benefit tradeoffs from Table 9.1 in conjunction with a standard compensating differential wage equation,

(9.2)   Wage$_i$ = $X_i\beta$ + γ_wDeath risk$_i$ + δ_wDeath risk$_i$ ×
              Weekly benefits$_i$ + ε_{wi},

where X_i includes measures of firm size, education, job tenure and its
square, experience and its square, and race, sex, blue-collar, health impairment, union, and state of residence dummy variables. Combining
equation 8.3 and equation 9.2 yields

(9.3)   Wage = ($X\beta$ + γ_wDeath risk + δ_wDeath risk ×
              Benefit maximum)/[$1 - \delta_w$Death risk ×
              $(1 - d)(2/3)$] + ε_w^*.

Note that the error term ε_w^* is heteroskedastic, since

$$\varepsilon_{wi}^* = \varepsilon_{wi}/[1 - \delta_w\text{Death risk}_i(1 - d_i) \times (2/3)],$$

and

$$\sigma_{wi}^{*2} = E[\varepsilon_{wi}^{*2}] = \sigma_w^2/[1 - \delta_w\text{Death risk}_i(1 - d_i) \times (2/3)]^2 = \sigma_w^2/\omega_i^2.$$

Differentiating equation 9.2 gives the total effect of benefits on
wages,

$$\frac{\partial w}{\partial b} = \gamma_w\frac{\partial p}{\partial b} + \delta_w p + \delta_w b\frac{\partial p}{\partial b},$$

where w, b, and p are defined as in Chapter 8, and where we now allow
for an effect of benefits on risk levels. The more interesting policy implications concern the effect of an increase in the benefit ceiling, c, on
wages, since the ceiling represents the main workers' compensation
parameter that varies across states. Replacing b and p in equation 9.2,
using the expressions in equations 8.3 and 9.1, and then totally differentiating equations 9.1 and 9.2 yields

$$\frac{\partial p}{\partial c} = \delta_b d + 2\delta_{bb}cd + \delta_{bs}sd,$$

and

$$\frac{\partial w}{\partial c} = \frac{\gamma_w + \delta_w c}{1 - \delta_w p(1 - d)(2/3)} \times \frac{\partial p}{\partial c} + \frac{\delta_w pd}{1 - \delta_w p(1 - d)\times(2/3)} =$$

$$\frac{\gamma_w + \delta_w c}{1 - \delta_w p(1 - d)(2/3)}(\delta_b d + 2\delta_{bb}cd + \delta_{bs}sd) +$$

$$\frac{\delta_w pd}{1 - \delta_w p(1 - d)\times(2/3)}.$$

When the ceiling is binding, so that d = 1, the latter expression reduces to

$$(9.4) \quad \frac{\partial w}{\partial c} = (\gamma_w + \delta_w c)(\delta_b + 2\delta_{bb}c + \delta_{bs}s) + \delta_w p.$$

Thus, increases in the benefit maximum have two wage effects for workers at whose wage the maximum is binding: a direct effect due to the increase in benefits ($\delta_w p$) and an indirect effect due to the change in risk level that alters both the compensation for risk (γ_w) and the benefit ceiling effect ($\delta_w c$). The sign of this indirect effect, although theoretically ambiguous, is negative in all existing empirical studies.[10] When the ceiling is not binding ($d = 0$) the wage-benefit tradeoff equals zero, since changes in the maximum have no effect on risk or benefit levels.

Estimates of $\partial p/\partial c$ can be computed by using the coefficients presented in Table 9.1. Using the column 2 estimates, a one dollar increase in c causes p to fall by −0.013, when measured at the mean values of c ($239) and s (44.0). To determine the total wage offset, we need only to estimate the parameters γ_w and δ_w.

Three issues must be addressed in the estimation of equation 9.3. First, the presence of the parameter δ_w in both the numerator and denominator of equation 9.4 requires nonlinear estimation. Second, the dummy variable d is a function of the worker's weekly wage and must be treated as an endogenous variable in the estimation of the model. Third, the heteroskedasticity, if significant, must be taken into account.

To correct for the endogeneity of d in equation 9.3, we use the expected value of d as an instrumental variable, following Duncan and Leigh's (1984) analysis of the union wage differential. The expected values $E[d_i]$ are unknown so we estimate them in a first-stage regression using nonlinear least squares. In particular, we estimate the parameter vector ϕ in the model

$$d = 1/[1 + \exp(-Z\phi)] + \varepsilon,$$

where Z is a vector of variables that cause variation in the benefit maximum. These variables include measures of the demographic and industrial composition of each state. The demographic variables include the percentages of residents who are poor, black, female, and less than sixty-five years old and the percentages with more than twelve and more than sixteen years of education. Industrial composition measures include the percentages of workers in each of the seven single-digit industries included in our sample and the percentage of small firms (less than twenty employees) and large firms (more than a hundred employees) in the state. We also include variables for number of children and marital status. Although these latter two variables might be related to the wage, they are also important determinants of the benefit maximum. To determine the sensitivity of our estimates to the use of the family status variables as excluded instruments, we estimated equation 9.3 with and without them. There was virtually no change in the estimate of δ_w when they were included, while there was a reduction in the estimated standard errors. On the basis of this result, we include the family status variables as identifying instruments. A similar experiment led us to add a dummy indicator of residence in the Southeastern United States as an instrument. Thus, we secure identification through two sources: the nonlinearity of the predicted value, d, and the exclusion of the variables in Z from the wage equation.[11]

We then estimate equation 9.3 using nonlinear two-stage least squares. We tested for the heteroskedasticity indicated earlier using the test suggested by Amemiya (1977). The results of this test reject the heteroskedasticity hypothesis. We therefore report unweighted estimates only. Table 9.2 presents estimates of the parameters γ_w and δ_w in equation 9.3, and of analogous parameters from a number of competing specifications, including those that have appeared previously in the literature and in the preceding chapters. The estimates in the columns 1–3 treat the variable d as endogenous, and thus represent structural estimates of the wage–workers' compensation tradeoff. The estimates in columns 3 and 4 represent more conventional specifications. The column 3 estimates report the results from a wage equation with benefits captured by the after-tax weekly wage replacement ratio used in the previous chapters. Column 4 presents results from estimation of a reduced form wage equation, where each worker's wage is regressed on the personal characteristics described above and on the benefit ceiling variable.

The results in column 1 present estimates of the model we use for answering the policy questions posed above. The column 1 estimates reflect use of the instrument set described in the preceding section. We also experimented with a number of other instrumental variables in addition to those in the vector Z. None of these provided any diminution of the estimated standard error without substantially altering the magnitude of the estimated coefficient, and therefore did not appear to be valid instruments in this equation.

The estimated coefficient on the workers' compensation variable in column 1, δ_w, is negative as expected and marginally significant at the 0.10 confidence level. The relatively large standard error around this estimate reflects in part the effects of the instrumental variables procedures. The coefficient on the risk variable, γ_w, is positive and significant, and the risk and workers' compensation variables are jointly significant.

TABLE 9.2
Wage Equation Estimates: Coefficients and Standard Errors

Coefficient (Variable)[a]	Estimate for Equation:			
	(1)	(2)	(3)	(4)
$\delta_w(p)$	3.136[b]	5.165[b]	3.497[b]	5.604[b]
	(1.586)	(2.655)	(0.749)	(1.937)
$\delta_w(pcd)$	−8.75E − 3	—	—	—
	(6.73E − 3)			
$\delta_{w0}\ (pb/w) \times (1-d)$	—	−8.047[b]	—	—
		(2.822)		
$\delta_{w1}\ (pb/w) \times d$	—	−5.600	—	—
		(5.119)		
$\delta_w(pb/w)$	—	—	−9.416[b]	—
			(2.301)	
$\delta_w\ (c)$	—	—	—	−0.016[b]
				(0.008)
R-squared	0.642	0.483	0.482	0.449

[a] Also included as explanatory variables are measures of the worker's sex, race, marital status, number of dependent children, health status, education, experience, job tenure, union status, firm size, and state dummy variables.
[b] Statistically significant at the 0.05 confidence level, one-tailed test.

The results in column 2 present the more traditional formulation of the risk-benefit relationship by using the replacement rate variable as the benefit measure. Unlike these previous studies, however, we interact the replacement rate with the variable d and estimate the benefit effect separately for workers below (δ_{w0}) and above γ_{w1}) the benefit maximum, which amounts to estimating a switching equation for workers above and below the maximum, with the remaining coefficients restricted to be equal across equations.[12] Both coefficients are negative, and the two taken together are jointly significant. Furthermore, the coefficient on the replacement rate variable for workers below the maximum (γ_{w0}) is highly significant. Since the coefficient estimates are not significantly different from each other, we next estimated a wage equation with a single replacement rate variable. To control for the presence of the wage in the denominator of the replacement rate, we again used the instrumental variables described above. Thus, the main factors identifying the replacement rate coefficient in column 3 are the variables in Z, which cause variation through their effect on the benefit maximum. The estimated coefficient (γ_w) is again negative and significant.

The final results reported in Table 9.2 present reduced form estimates of a wage equation, where the wage is regressed on worker characteristics and on the exogenous benefit maximum. The estimated effects are in the expected direction and are statistically significant. However, since they do not account for the endogeneity of benefits, their use for policy purposes is limited. The column 4 results are best used as a benchmark by which to evaluate the more ambitious estimates in columns 1–3, and also those that have appeared elsewhere.

Implications for Market Behavior

The most important implication of the results reported in Tables 9.1 and 9.2 is the perspective they give on those market effects of workers' compensation that extend beyond the payment of premiums and compensation. Consider first the safety incentive effect. Although the net impact of insurance benefits on the fatality rate is theoretically indeterminate, the estimates of the risk equations indicate empirically that benefit increases exert considerable pressure on firms to improve safety levels, thus reducing fatality risk levels. Indeed, using the estimates from Table 9.1, if benefits were nonexistent, the average fatality rate would rise by approximately 3.2 deaths per 100,000 workers, or an increase of 48 percent.[13] The Table 9.1 results also indicate that benefits exert downward pressure on injury rates, which diminishes as benefits rise. The estimates in column 2 of Table 9.1 indicate that the safety effect continues to dominate up to a weekly benefit maximum of $391, or $450 in 1988 prices.[14] The second notable result concerns the wage-risk feedback effects of workers' compensation. For a worker at or above the maximum, a $10 increase in c reduces the weekly wage by approximately 70 cents.[15]

If benefit increases cause fatalities to fall, as our results indicate, the net wage savings generated by the wage-benefit tradeoff include an indirect effect resulting from the positive relationship between wages and risks. On the basis of the estimates in column 2 of Table 9.1, which indicate that a $1 increase in the weekly maximum benefit results in 0.013 fewer deaths per 100,000 workers, we can compute the portion of the 70 cents per week wage savings generated by risk reductions. The structural weekly wage equation estimates (Table 9.2, column 1) indicate that 1 additional death per 100,000 workers results in a weekly wage increase of $1.04. Thus, a $10 increase in benefits, which lowers the death rate by 0.13, causes weekly wages to fall by 14 cents ($1.04 × 0.13), or about $8.08 per worker annually in 1988 prices. This effect equals about one-fifth of the direct effect.

One implication of these results is that safety expenditures induced by the benefit hikes are self-financed at least in part through wage reductions. To get an idea of the magnitude of the savings generated by risk reductions in 1982, the year covered by our sample, consider the effect of a 10 percent increase in the benefit maximum, which corresponds roughly to annual growth rates in workers' compensation premiums for the years 1977–1983.[16] At the mean value of c in our sample of $240, the implied increase of $24 would lower the death rate by 0.31, with a resulting decline in weekly wages of 32 cents ($1.04 × 0.31), or about $17 annually ($20 in 1988 prices). This figure, which measures the safety incentive effects of workers' compensation acting as an injury tax, dwarfs OSHA fines per worker for the period of about 50 cents per year. The $20 per worker wage reduction also equals approximately one-third of the reported per-worker expenditures on health and safety for the year 1981 of $57, expressed in 1988 prices.[17]

In addition to the self-financing aspect of the risk reductions caused by workers' compensation increases, there is also a substantial direct wage saving generated by the benefit increases. The direct effect of an increase in the benefit maximum equals approximately 5.8 cents in weekly wages per dollar of benefits. Thus, if a worker is earning $486 per week (the mean in our sample) and is above the maximum, which equals, say, $240, a 10 percent increase in c of $24 will cause weekly wages to fall by about $1.40 (5.8 × $24), or about $83 per year in 1988 prices, as a result of the direct benefit effect.

We do not have information on the changes in fatality insurance premiums per worker that would result from a 10 percent increase in the benefit maximum. Therefore, we cannot determine what portion of this increase is paid for out of wage reductions. The $83 annual wage decrease due to workers' compensation is nonetheless substantial. In the absence of benefits, annual wages would be $890 higher (in 1988 prices).[18] By way of comparison, total compensation per year for fatality risks, assuming a mean death rate of 6.6 deaths per 100,000 workers, equals about $1,000 in our results.

Conclusion

The workers' compensation program has not enjoyed the most favorable reputation. In the past critics charged that benefit levels were not high enough to provide for full income replacement. States increased benefits beginning in the 1970s, but this improvement evoked cries of alarm regarding spiraling premium costs and abuses with respect to moral hazard problems, such as false claims and overextended periods of recovery from illnesses.[19]

Although moral hazard problems are important, workers' compensation also plays a constructive role. The results in this chapter indicate that workplace fatalities could double in the absence of this program. Worker's compensation thus represents by far the most influential governmental program for reducing workplace fatalities. This effectiveness suggests that if the current level of safety is considered too low, one might wish to assess the degree to which some responsibilities of OSHA could be shifted to an injury tax approach. Complaints voiced by firms with respect to escalating workers' compensation premiums may be overstated, even beyond the extent indicated in the earlier chapters, since they also neglect the substantial wage offset resulting from the fatality risk reduction induced by workers' compensation.

The favorable evidence presented here with respect to the performance of workers' compensation is not intended to lead observers to dismiss as unimportant the difficult causality problems raised by health risks, litigation problems raised by permanent disabilities, and continuing moral hazard problems with respect to nonfatal injury claims and their duration.[20] Nevertheless, our results do suggest that workers' compensation is more successful in promoting its intended objectives than previously believed.

Ten

Tort Liability Remedies for Job Injuries: Product Liability and Its Interaction with Workers' Compensation

RECENT ATTENTION devoted to the emerging product liability crisis has highlighted the increased role played by tort remedies for individual accidents. Before the advent of workers' compensation, workers pursued legal remedies for individual accidents in much the same manner as they did in litigation for product-related injuries.[1] Tort liability remedies were replaced by administrative compensation systems in most states, but in recent years tort liability suits have reemerged as a prominent source of compensation for job injuries (Weiler, 1986).

The significance of the role of the different institutions that address job injuries is suggested by a review of the economic rationale for adoption of workers' compensation systems earlier in this century. Reliance on product liability for ex post compensation was generally viewed as an unsatisfactory solution, and as a consequence states established workers' compensation systems as the exclusive remedy. The sources of the dissatisfaction with tort remedies can be traced to legitimate economic concerns. Employers exert substantial control and monitoring over workplace conditions, and from a safety incentives standpoint, they should be given financial inducements to provide safe capital equipment and to ensure safe work practices. Tort liability remedies can establish such incentives, but this is a cumbersome process that imposes substantial costs on both sides. Workers' compensation offers an administrative compensation remedy that imposes lower transaction costs on claimants and avoids the confrontational aspects of a product liability case, which might damage the employment relationship after recovery from the injury. Workers' compensation also provides for more certain and rapid compensation, thus promoting society's objectives of insuring workers against drops in income. In return for the greater certainty of compensation, injured workers receive lower levels of compensation under workers' compensation than they would in a tort judgment.

The advent of workers' compensation marked a shift in the basis for determining whether compensation would be paid.[2] Under tort remedies, fault is the key issue. Is the employer responsible for the accident, for example, through negligence in the provision of safety equipment? Under workers' compensation, the focal point is not on fault but on causation. In particular, was the accident or illness one that "arose out of and in the course of employment?" Thus, there must be evidence of an adverse health outcome that passes a job-relatedness test. The worker's contribution to the accident is not an issue.[3] Although there may be a resulting moral hazard problem, employers have at least some capacity to dampen it through their control and supervision of workplace operations.

It should be noted, however, that the job-relatedness test imposed by workers' compensation is not innocuous. In cases of occupational disease, it has led to denial of many claims.[4] Overall, the requirements that must be met under workers' compensation are much more stringent than under general social insurance programs, such as the disability insurance program of social security, for which the existence of an adverse health effect and economic loss is a sufficient basis for compensation.

Although workers' compensation is the most prominent ex post remedy for job risks, product liability continues to play an important role. Workers generally cannot sue their employer, but they can file third-party suits. A worker driving a lift truck that tips over and disables him or her can, for example, sue the lift truck manufacturer. Similarly, the workers' compensation insurance company that pays off the claim for the injured lift truck driver could file a subrogation action to obtain compensation from the firm that manufactured the defective lift truck.

Overall, however, workers' compensation is the more prominent remedy. Because of the lower probability of showing that a third party should be liable, the cases that do tend to be involved in third-party suits involve larger stakes than in the typical product liability suit. The total share of job-related claims is a minority of all product liability claims—about 13 percent—but since the dollar losses involved are greater, their relative role is somewhat higher. Cases with small losses are unattractive targets for litigation because of the transaction costs involved.

From the worker's standpoint, there is little incentive to pursue a third-party suit unless those stakes are substantial. Collateral source rules prevent the courts from lowering a tort award because the injured worker has received workers' compensation benefits. However, the worker cannot obtain a double recovery, since in such contexts the employer or the insurer who paid the claim is generally subrogated to the worker's tort claim, up to the amount of the workers' compensation benefit.[5] There are a few exceptions, however, as some jurisdictions (Georgia, Ohio, and West Virginia) do not have subrogation rights.

Thus, the injured party's financial incentive to file a product liability claim will be diminished by the extent of the workers' compensation benefits that have been already received. As a result, the cases for which litigation is worthwhile will tend to be only those with larger losses.

In this chapter, we will provide the first detailed analysis of product liability claims for job-related injuries, using a data set that includes 1,447 closed claims for job-related injuries. Since the focus of this chapter is on a litigation process, the empirical analysis will be structured similarly. In particular, the types of concerns will be the following. What factors lead to cases' being dropped or lead to successful attempts to receive compensation? How do aspects of the injury, such as the size of the loss, affect this outcome? Do subrogation actions by insurers follow the same litigation pattern as do workers' third-party lawsuits?

Many of the variables of influence will be similar to those for product liability cases overall. For example, as was found in Viscusi (1986a, 1988c), cases involving large losses are less likely to be dropped because of their high expected payoff. Other legal influences, such as the stronger performance of cases based on strict liability, will also parallel the performance of all product liability claims. Of particular interest is the set of factors that are specific to job-related claims. The survey data that will be used include an extensive set of variables pertaining to such interactions, such as whether the claim was the result of a subrogation action. A large number of variables capturing various dimensions of the workers' compensation system will be shown to have a pivotal effect on all aspects of the litigation process.

A particularly striking aspect of these results is that the law matters, both with respect to the main product liability doctrines and the interactions between workers' compensation and tort liability. There are a number of alternative hypotheses that can clearly be rejected. One might have hypothesized that the law would not matter because it is unclear or imprecise, or that the law would not matter in the long run because either litigants or the courts would adjust to it so that no effects would be observed. The results here are quite different in that they show a strong influence of these legal variables in the expected direction.

The Sample and the Variables

The sample that will be used in the analysis is the Insurance Services Office's (ISO) Product Liability Closed Claims Survey (Insurance Services Office 1977). This data set represents an extensive national survey of over 10,000 product liability claims that were closed between mid-1976 and mid-1977. Of the 10,784 observations with complete data for the major variables, 1,447 pertained to on-the-job injuries. This job-related subsample will be the focal point of the analysis.

Although the data pertain to claims a decade ago, this data base remains the most recent and most detailed data set available on the litigation of product liability claims. In addition, since the time period represented by the data postdates the emergence of the strict liability doctrine and expansion in the concept of a product defect, the current features of modern product liability law were in place. In short, it is the best and only available data set of its kind.

The ISO data set is quite comprehensive in that it provides extensive information regarding the nature of each claim and its dispositon. The information included represents the judgment of insurance company officials based on their retrospective assessment of each product liability claim.

Figure 10.1 provides an overview of the dispositon of the job-related claims. Almost one-fourth of all claims were dropped without ever going to court or receiving an out-of-court settlement. Of the claims that were not dropped, the great majority (89 percent) were settled out of court. The small portion of litigated claims consists largely of cases in which the plaintiff lost (69 percent), as most of the successful claims were resolved at the settlement stage.

Table 10.1 summarizes the variable definitions, and Table 10.2 provides the corresponding means and standard deviations. In each situation, statistics are provided for the full sample as well as for the subsample at each stage of disposition. The three case dispositon vari-

FIGURE 10.1
Disposition of job-related product liability claims

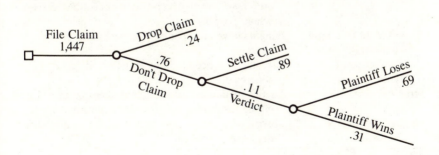

TABLE 10.1
Variable Definitions

Variable	Definition
Case dropped	Case disposition 0-1 dummy variable (d.v.) for cases that were dropped
Case settled	Case disposition d.v. for cases settled out of court
Case won	Case disposition d.v. for cases that resulted in a successful verdict for the plaintiff
Bodily injury losses	Bodily injury loss, in dollars: the sum of wage loss, medical costs, and other bodily losses
Bodily injury payments	Bodily injury payments, in dollars
Age	Injured party's age at time of injury
Sex	Injured party's sex d.v.
Experience	Years of experience that injured party had on the job he or she was performing at the time of the injury occurrence
Death	Accident led to victim's death, that is, fatality d.v.
Regulatory violation	Regulatory violation d.v. for alleged violations of Consumer Product Safety Commission (CPSC) regulations or standards of federal, state, or local governmental bodies other than OSHA
OSHA	Regulatory violation d.v. for alleged violations of OSHA regulations
Subrogation actions	Subrogation d.v. for cases in which subrogation by a workers' compensation carrier of employer instigated the claim
Amount of lien	Dollar amount of lien against insured by workers' compensation carrier or employer
Indemnification	Indemnification or contribution or subrogation has been sought by the insurer against other parties, for example, the employer
Cross-complaints	Cross-complaints involved in this case d.v.
Sole remedy rule	Legal context d.v. for case where applicable state law has the sole remedy rule, and insured would most likely have sought compensation from the employer or workers' compensation carrier where possible
Government collateral payments	Benefits have been paid by governmental collateral sources d.v.
Private collateral payments	Benefits have heen paid by private collateral sources d.v.
Strict liability rule	Theory of liability used in settlement of award is either absolute liability or strict liability d.v.
Negligence rule	Theory of liability used in settlement or award is negligence d.v.

TABLE 10.2

Sample Characteristics: Means and Standard Deviations

Variable	Full Job Sample	Case Dropped Subsample	Case Settled Subsample	Court Verdict Subsample
Case dropped	0.24	1.00	0.00	0.00
	(0.43)	(0.00)	(0.00)	(0.00)
Case settled	0.68	0.00	1.00	0.00
	(0.47)	(0.00)	(0.00)	(0.00)
Case won	0.02	0.00	0.00	0.31
	(0.15)	(0.00)	(0.00)	(0.46)
Bodily injury losses	51,800.43	27,755.38	53,815.04	109,165.73
	(232,961.11)	(83,882.06)	(269,588.61)	(195,729.09)
Bodily injury payments	25,644.90	0.00	32,726.22	44,466.66
	(75,770.78)	(0.00)	(78,215.54)	(132,918.91)
Age	36.00	35.62	36.28	34.72
	(12.68)	(11.46)	(13.24)	(11.25)
Sex	0.83	0.82	0.83	0.90
	(0.37)	(0.38)	(0.38)	(0.30)
Experience	5.95	5.94	5.92	6.29
	(5.66)	(5.52)	(5.73)	(5.51)
Death	0.11	0.10	0.09	0.25
	(0.31)	(0.30)	(0.29)	(0.43)
Regulatory violation	0.26	0.15	0.29	0.32
	(0.44)	(0.36)	(0.45)	(0.47)
OSHA	0.17	0.10	0.19	0.18
	(0.37)	(0.31)	(0.39)	(0.38)
Subrogation actions	0.23	0.34	0.20	0.15
	(0.42)	(0.48)	(0.40)	(0.36)
Amount of lien	9795.83	4508.55	10,615.48	15,310.69
	(29,881.70)	(18,918.96)	(33,034.20)	(17,747.82)
Indemnification	0.24	0.05	0.31	0.24
	(0.43)	(0.22)	(0.46)	(0.43)
Cross-complaints	0.24	0.01	0.31	0.36
	(0.43)	(0.12)	(0.46)	(0.48)
Sole remedy rule	0.46	0.47	0.45	0.53
	(0.50)	(0.50)	(0.50)	(0.50)
Government collateral payments	0.10	0.08	0.11	0.15
	(0.31)	(0.27)	(0.31)	(0.36)
Private collateral payments	0.59	0.69	0.55	0.66
	(0.49)	(0.46)	(0.50)	(0.48)
Strict liability rule	0.36	0.24	0.41	0.32
	(0.48)	(0.43)	(0.49)	(0.47)
Negligence rule	0.32	0.25	0.36	0.17
	(0.47)	(0.43)	(0.48)	(0.37)
	(N= 1447)	(N = 354)	(N = 979)	(N = 114)

ables are for whether the case was dropped, settled out of court, or resolved in court through a verdict for the plaintiff.

The dollar magnitudes involved are quite impressive. The average bodily injury loss is $91,400 and the average bodily injury payment, including cases with zero award, is $45,200, where each of these figures is in 1988 dollars. The loss figures represent the reports by the insurance companies of the combined total medical expenses, wage losses, and other financial losses associated with the claim. The direction of bias with respect to the true losses is unclear since it is not known to what extent to which the insurer filling out the questionnaire relied on the claims amount stated by the plaintiff.

The profile of job-related claims is quite different from that of product claims that did not involve a job injury. The principal characterization of the differences is that job-related claims are less likely to be dropped and more likely to be litigated, both of which are expected effects since the stakes involved in job-related claims are much greater. In terms of claims disposition, the drop rate for job-related claims is 6 percent higher than for other products claims, and the settlement rate is 10 percent lower. Whereas 4 percent of other products claims are litigated, 8 percent of job-related claims go to a court verdict.

This high litigation rate may be due to the substantially greater stakes involved in job-related claims, as compared with other products claims. Claims involving injuries not on the job have an average loss value of $13,800 and an average payment value of $13,400, each of which is considerably below the comparable values for claims involving on-the-job injuries. The greater stakes of job-related claims decrease the propensity to drop a case by boosting the expected payoff from litigation. A number of litigation models predict that there will be such a greater propensity to litigate high stakes-claims, as is borne out in the comparison of job-related and other products claims.[6]

The tendency for job-related claims to be the subject of a product liability suit more often than smaller loss claims is not unexpected, given the factors that affect the loss levels in the claims that are filed. The general presumption in the law is that workers' compensation is the exclusive remedy for seeking redress from one's employer for job-related claims. Third-party product liability suits will consequently exclude a group of potential defendants (that is, employers). The prospects of plaintiff success will consequently be lower and the litigation costs will be higher than for product liability claims in general. Victims of job injuries will be less likely to pursue job-related claims than to pursue comparable product claims since the inability to sue one's employer reduces the likelihood that the claim will be successful. The substantial costs involved in subrogation actions also will tend to limit these suits to the larger claims, and workers will be reluctant to press product liability claims unless they can receive more than their workers' compensation benefits.

The fraction of injuries involving fatal injuries is 0.11, which is almost four times the average fatality rate for all product liability cases. Once again, it appears that the mix of job-related cases that are the object of product liability claims tend to be more severe than the typical product claim.

The demographic profile of the accident victims follows the expected pattern, given the nature of the accidents involved. Claimants tend to be largely males, with an average age of thirty-six. The worker's average experience at his or her current job is almost six years. The experience variable is relevant to a claimant's case, since a more experienced worker is more likely to have mastered the job operations. As a result, one might expect such a worker to be less likely to be found to be contributorily negligent.

The ISO data also include a wide range of variables pertaining to the legal character of the cases.[7] The first pair of variables concern regulatory violations. The regulatory violation variable captures whether the claimant alleged that there were violations of regulations other than the standards of the Occupational Safety and Health Administration, and the variable denoted by "OSHA" captures whether there were alleged violations of OSHA standards. These variables pertain only to alleged or claimed violations, and the survey included no information to ascertain whether there actually were regulatory violations. Regulatory violations should enhance the plaintiff's prospects, since in many courts the showing of statutory violations is tantamount to demonstrating the existence of a product defect.

The next set of four variables characterizes the nature of the claim. Almost one-fourth of all job-related product liability claims are the result of subrogation actions, in which an employer or insurer is seeking reimbursement for its payment of worker losses.[8] The dollar amount of the liens against the insured average just under $10,000. Since only 23 percent of all claims are the subject of subrogation actions, this average includes three-fourths of the observations in which the value of the lien variable is zero. The resulting average figure is in keeping with the sample's average loss levels.

The defendant counterpart of the subrogation variable is indemnification. Whereas the subrogation variable captures claims in which the defendant insurer is the target of a claim by an employer or other insurer, the indemnification variable pertains to claims in which the insurer who is or was the defendant in a suit brought by the insured or a would-be subrogator is seeking indemnification, contribution, or subrogation from another party. Almost one-fourth of plaintiffs' actions are subrogation actions, and almost an equal number of the defendants have initiated indemnification or subrogation actions of their own. Similarly, in 24 percent of the cases, there are cross-complaints involved. The extent of overlapping and multiple lawsuits for job-related product liability claims is quite substantial.

Slightly less than half of the tort claims by workers are in states that have adopted the sole remedy rule (the rule that if a worker is eligible for workers' compensation benefits, workers' compensation is the exclusive remedy against the employer). Such claimants most likely would have sought compensation from workers' compensation or the employer. As expected, a higher percentage (69 percent) of cases that were dropped were covered by the sole remedy rule.

The extent of the overlaps among these workers' compensation variables and the relationship among the five workers' compensation variables are summarized by the cross-tabulations appearing in Table 10.3. Column 1 indicates the sample group for which the conditional values were obtained. For each of the variables, information is given on the conditional fraction of other workers' compensation variables that are pertinent. For example, for 69 percent of the claims for which the subrogation variable takes on a value of 1.0, indemnification also has a value of 1.0. Since the lien variable is a continuous rather than a dichotomous variable, for the sake of comparability a new variable has been created that takes on a value of 1 where the lien amounts are positive and 0 otherwise.

All of the variables overlap, but there are no perfect correlations. Some of the most prominent linkages are the following. About half of all claims in which the defendant is seeking indemnification, contribution, or subrogation from some other party are also situations in which the defendant is a target of other claims by an employer or other insurer. The reverse linkage is even stronger, as 69 percent of the cases in which the defendant is the target of claims by an employer or insurer also involve a suit by the defendant against some other party. In some, but not all, cases, these suits involve the same pair of parties, as the frequency of cross-complaints reaches a high value of 34 percent in the case of claims involving indemnification actions. The presence of a subrogation action by the workers' compensation carrier or employer greatly increases the likelihood that there is a reported value of the workers' compensation lien against the insured, since the variable represents the magnitude of the subrogation action when this dollar value is known. The relative invariance of the data in the last column indicates that the applicability of a sole remedy rule has little effect on the presence of the various other interactions between workers' compensa-

TABLE 10.3
Overlaps of the Workers' Compensation Doctrine Variables

Conditional Group	Mean Value of Variable for Group (Fraction Equal to 1)				
	Subrogation	Nonzero Lien	Indemnification	Cross-Complaint	Sole Remedy Rule
Full sample	0.23	0.57	0.33	0.24	0.46
Subrogation	1.00	0.87	0.69	0.15	0.48
Nonzero lien	0.35	1.00	0.44	0.26	0.50
Indemnification	0.47	0.77	1.00	0.34	0.48
Cross-complaints	0.14	0.63	0.47	1.00	0.56
Sole remedy rule	0.24	0.62	0.35	0.29	1.00

tion and tort liability. The primary interactions appear to be among cross-complaints, indemnification and subrogation actions, and the scaled variant of the subrogation variable, nonzero lien.

These institutional overlaps are of substantial consequence for legal policy reform. Some observers, such as Weiler (1986), have recommended the abolition of subrogation actions for job-related injuries. Policy proposals such as this do not represent minor tinkerings with arcane legal doctrines but instead will engender a fundamental transformation in the functioning of the tort liability and workers' compensation systems. In the subsequent empirical analysis, we will trace through our model the different ways in which such policy variables affect litigation behavior.

It is noteworthy that in many cases workers have already obtained some other type of compensation. In 10 percent of the cases, collateral governmental benefits have been received, and in 59 percent of the cases, workers have received private collateral payments. Such benefits do not necessarily imply that there will be multiple recoveries, since some of the claims in the sample are the result of subrogation actions by insurers and employers.

The final two variables pertain to whether the claim was based on strict liability grounds or negligence. The omitted legal argument variable is for claims based on breach of warranty grounds. The coding of the liability theory variable permitted the listing of only one doctrine; consequently, in circumstances where more than one doctrine was used (for example, strict liability and negligence), the variable may be capturing a mixture of the influences at work, thus dampening the empirical differences that will be observed. This compounding of variable effects should not be a major problem if the data coders identified the most important doctrine.

It is generally believed that the strict liability doctrine strengthens the legal basis for the claim by facilitating the claimant's task of demonstrating fault.[9] In particular, the plaintiff need not show that a product defect was the result of producer negligence. Strict liability is not tantamount to absolute liability, so defendants are not liable for all accidents irrespective of their cause. However, the task of demonstrating fault is facilitated by applying such criteria as the risk-utility test for product safety, rather than requiring that producer negligence be shown.

The legal doctrine relied upon in the claims is somewhat different for job-related claims. Whereas other products claims are evenly divided among breach of warranty, negligence, and strict liability arguments, in the case of job-related claims, the role of the strict liability and negligence doctrines is much more prominent. These are generally viewed as a stronger basis for a liability case. A breach of product warranty is less likely to be pertinent in employment contexts, as this legal basis for liability is relied upon more than twice as often in nonjob products cases as in job-related ones.

Litigation Outcomes for Job-Related Claims

The influence of the various variables on the prospects of an individual claim can be investigated in more detail if we impose some structure on the litigation process. Here, we outline a fairly standard risk-neutral model of litigation, which represents a simplified variant of that in Viscusi (1988c). Since many of the predicted outcomes hinge on the interaction of the effects of different variables on both plaintiffs and defendants, some structure of this type is needed to organize one's thinking concerning the nature of the effects.

Let subscript 1 denote the plaintiff and subscript 2 denote the defendant. At this stage of court verdicts, the expected court award is A, and each party has an assessed probability p_i (where $i = 1,2$) that the plaintiff will win. These perceptions of the likelihood of plaintiff success may differ. The plaintiff and defendant have an associated litigation cost LC_i. The plaintiff's expected payoff, V_1, from going to court is

(10.1) $V_1 = p_1 A - LC_1,$

and the defendant's expected loss is given by

(10.2) $V_2 = -p_2 A - LC_2.$

The empirical formulation adopts the usual assumption that the plaintiff will drop the claim if V_1 is negative. This type of naive behavior is possible if both parties are aware of the stakes and probabilities facing each of them, since a claimant could never obtain a positive settlement for a claim with a negative V_1 value. If, however, such information is not shared, a claimant conceivably could extract a positive settlement value, even though the minimum V_1 amount was negative. The actual regressions estimated do not impose any restrictions requiring cases with negative V_1 values to be dropped, and the empirical structure given below is intended to provide a general backdrop for interpreting the results.

Let V^* be the true expected payoff and u_1 be the error with which this payoff is measured by the plaintiff. In terms of the estimation, we have the formulation

(10.3) $V_1 = V^* + u_1,$

so that

$$pr \text{ [Case dropped]} = pr \: (-u_1 > V^*).$$

Variables that enhance the probability of winning the court case, increase the size of the award, or reduce the level of litigation costs will reduce the probability of the case's being dropped. Since we do not observe such variables as the expected size of the award directly, various variables must be used as proxies for such influences. These are discussed below.

Out-of-court settlements will be driven by the Ask and Offer amounts of the plaintiff and defendant, and these influences also depend on the parties' prospects in court. The plaintiff's minimum Ask value is given by

(10.4) $\text{Ask} = \text{Max } (0,V_1) = V^* + u_1,$

if we assume that the case has not been dropped. Similarly, the defendant's maximum Offer amount is given by

(10.5) $\text{Offer} = -V_2 = V^* + u_2.$

A potentially feasible bargaining range exists if

(10.6) $\text{Offer} - \text{Ask} = u_2 - u_1 > 0,$

or the

(10.7) $pr \text{ [Case settled]} = pr \: (u_2 - u_1 > 0),$

so that equation 10.7 can be written

(10.8) pr [Case settled] = $\{1 + \exp[-(p_2 - p_1)A - (LC_1 + LC_2)]\}^{-1}$,

assuming that u_2 and u_1 have the Weibull distribution.

The likelihood of a settlement is enhanced by variables that increase the defendant's perceived loss probability more than they increase the plaintiff's so that there is a differential effect on the parties' perceived prospects. Variables with symmetric effects on p_1 and p_2 will not be consequential. In addition, factors that raise the litigation costs of either party make settlement more likely.

Factors that influence the expected settlement level are more straightforward. If we let λ be the bargaining weight on the plaintiff's Ask amount and $1 - \lambda$ be the bargaining weight on the maximum Offer, then the predicted settlement is given by

(10.9)   Settlement = λ Ask + $(1 - \lambda)$ Offer,

if Ask < Offer. As λ increases, the plaintiff reaps a greater share of the bargaining rents. Variables that boost the expected court award (that is, raise p_1, p_2, or A) will increase the settlement amount, as will variables that raise defendants' litigation costs and lower plaintiffs' litigation costs.

The empirical analysis will follow two different approaches. The first is the conditional formulation shown in Figure 10.1. For example, we will assess the probability that a case will be settled out of court if it is not dropped. This conditional formulation does not address such issues as what the court award would have been for cases settled out of court, which are considered elsewhere in the product claims study by Lillard and Viscusi (1988). The main reason for excluding such selectivity issues is that estimation of such a specification requires that only the most salient variables be included. As a result, refined workers' compensation variables cannot be analyzed.

An alternative perspective will be provided by analyzing the multinomial logit formulation, where the three possible outcomes are that the case is dropped, is settled out of court, or goes to a court verdict. The rationale for this approach is based on a model in which the plaintiff and defendant develop their Ask and Offer amounts, after which they are committed to play out the legal bargaining process according to the model specified above. Given any combination of Ask and Offer amounts, one can predict which of the three outcome categories will prevail (case dropped, case settled out of court, or case goes to verdict), subject to possible random errors that may distort this process. The empirical issue is which of the three modes of disposition will result, given the relationship between the Ask and Offer amounts.

TABLE 10.4
Disposition of Product Liability Claims Groups

	Offer < Ask	*Offer ≥ Ask*
Ask ≤ 0	Drop claim	Drop claim
Ask > 0	Litigate claim	Settle out of court

Table 10.4 summarizes the different categories into which a claim outcome could fall, if we rule out bargaining impasses in situations in which there is a feasible bargaining range and if we exclude the role of random errors in case disposition. Both situations in Table 10.4 with negative Ask value lead to the case's being dropped. For claims with a positive Ask amount, there will be litigation if Offer < Ask and an out-of-court settlement if Offer > Ask. For concreteness, I have assigned the cases with Ask = 0 to the category in which claims are dropped and claims where Offer = Ask to the settlement category.

Empirical Results

To assess the different influences on the litigation process, two sets of estimates are provided. Table 10.5 presents the conditional estimates of the three sequential aspects of claims distribution—whether a claim is dropped, whether a claim is settled out of court given that it was not dropped, and whether a claim that goes to a court verdict leads to a claimant's victory. Table 10.6 presents the multivariate logit estimates of the model for three disposition outcomes. Unlike the results in Table 10.5, these estimates are not conditional upon the claim's reaching a particular stage. The dropped claims category serves as the reference point (no loss of generality) and is the omitted disposition outcome for the multivariate logit model. The focus of these estimates is consequently somewhat different. For example, the Table 10.5 settlement equation pertains to the probability of an out-of-court settlement given that the claim was not dropped, where the other possible outcome in this binary logit is a court verdict. The multivariate logit estimates of settlement probabilities in Table 10.6 address the three disposition outcome situations using the entire sample of product liability claims, rather than only those that have not been dropped.

Since the operative economic mechanisms in the different equations are similar, let us focus on the role of each of the variables across the

TABLE 10.5
Logit Estimates of Disposition Probability Equation

Independent Variables	Coefficient and Asymptotic SE		
	Case Dropped	Case Settled	Case Won
Intercept	−0.689[a]	1.642[a]	0.696
	(0.303)	(0.470)	(1.305)
Bodily injury losses	$-1.77E-6$[a]	$-2.00E-7$	$-6.00E-5$[a]
	$(0.92E-6)$	$(3.11E-7)$	$(3.02E-5)$
Age	$3.11E-2$	0.020[a]	−0.088[a]
	$(6.56E-2)$	(0.010)	(0.033)
Sex	0.202	−0.411	0.542
	(0.191)	(0.351)	(0.924)
Experience	−0.012	−0.030	0.143[a]
	(0.015)	(0.022)	(0.057)
Death	0.801[a]	−1.180[a]	1.433[a]
	(0.296)	(0.276)	(0.854)
Regulatory violation	−0.937[a]	−0.391	1.616[a]
	(0.303)	(0.312)	(0.899)
OSHA	0.084	0.586	−0.374
	(0.355)	(0.379)	(0.939)
Subrogation actions	0.734[a]	0.178	1.266
	(0.161)	(0.291)	(0.817)
Amount of lien	$-5.56E-4$[a]	$-5.38E-7$	$9.84E-6$
	$(1.14E-4)$	$(25.33E-7)$	$(17.18E-6)$
Indemnification	−1.293[a]	0.803[a]	−0.918
	(0.276)	(0.279)	(0.795)
Cross-complaints	−2.807[a]	−0.559[a]	0.925
	(0.468)	(0.249)	(0.641)
Sole remedy rule	0.271[a]	−0.417[a]	−1.593[a]
	(0.147)	(0.218)	(0.631)
Government collateral payments	−0.428	−0.114	1.527[a]
	(0.264)	(0.317)	(0.808)
Private collateral payments	0.929[a]	−0.440[a]	0.163
	(0.156)	(0.233)	(0.657)
Strict liability rule	−1.124[a]	1.259[a]	2.115[a]
	(0.174)	(0.242)	(0.674)
Negligence rule	−0.983	1.838[a]	2.421[a]
	(0.174)	(0.294)	(0.844)
Log—likelihood	−603.8	−318.7	−48.2
	(N = 1447)	(N = 1093)	(N = 114)

[a] Statistically significant at the 0.05 percent confidence level, one-tailed test.

TABLE 10.6
Multinomial Logit Estimates of Disposition Probability Equation
(N = 1,447)

Independent Variable	Coefficients and Asymptotic SE	
	Outcome = Verdict	Outcome = Settle
Intercept	0.593[a]	−1.091[a]
	(0.304)	(0.511)
Bodily injury losses	$0.17E - 5$[a]	$0.19E - 5$[a]
	$(0.09E - 5)$	$(0.09E - 5)$
Age	$-0.20E - 2$	−0.022[a]
	$(0.66E - 2)$	(0.011)
Sex	−0.254	0.184
	(0.192)	(0.367)
Experience	0.011	0.039
	(0.015)	(0.025)
Death	−0.961[a]	0.147
	(0.295)	(0.365)
Regulatory violation	0.547[a]	0.766[a]
	(0.230)	(0.328)
OSHA	0.576[a]	0.143
	(0.237)	(0.363)
Subrogation actions	−0.778[a]	−1.035[a]
	(0.187)	(0.337)
Amount of lien	$0.58E - 4$[a]	$0.58E - 4$[a]
	$(0.11E - 4)$	$(0.12E - 4)$
Indemnification	0.185	0.251
	(0.185)	(0.289)
Cross-complaints	3.173[a]	3.349[a]
	(0.465)	(0.506)
Sole remedy rule	−0.332[a]	0.079
	(0.147)	(0.237)
Government collateral	−0.168	0.105
payments	(0.263)	(0.364)
Private collateral payments	−0.954[a]	−0.471[a]
	(0.150)	(0.241)
Strict liability rule	1.348[a]	−0.017
	(0.177)	(0.272)
Negligence rule	1.195[a]	−0.632[a]
	(0.176)	(0.317)
Log—likelihood	−940.11	

[a] Statistically significant at the 0.05 confidence level, one-tailed test.

five equations in Tables 10.5 and 10.6. A key variable is the magnitude of the financial loss, since this variable defines the stakes of the litigation. Claims with large financial losses are less likely to be dropped, since the size of the anticipated court award is greater. This result is a direct implication of the litigation model. In addition, in some litigation models, there is a greater incentive to litigate large loss claims. Our findings that large bodily injury loss claims are less likely to be dropped (Table 10.5) and more likely to be settled or litigated (Table 10.6) provide mutually consistent evidence of the impact of higher stakes.

A particularly intriguing finding is the negative loss coefficient in the equation for the plaintiff's propensity to win a favorable verdict. This result reflects the selection of cases that goes to court. Small stakes cases that are litigated must offer a substantial probability of obtaining an award for the plaintiff to find it desirable to incur the litigation costs. In contrast, it will be financially worthwhile to pursue a case with a very substantial reward even if the chance of a successful court verdict is slim. This inverse relationship between the level and the cutoff level of the required probability of success is consequently quite consistent with a rational case selection process.[10] This selection process in turn will generate an observed inverse relationship between bodily injury losses and the propensity to win in court.

The three victim characteristic variables capture a variety of factors relating to differing accident propensities and variations in litigation costs with personal characteristics. Older claimants are less likely to win a court case, perhaps because of the greater role of contributory negligence among older claimants. On-the-job experience has the opposite effect on the claimant's prospects in court, perhaps because familiarity with job tasks enhances safety-related behavior. The claimant's sex plays no role whatsoever, in part because the loss variable already captures sex-related differences in last earnings.

Claims resulting from fatal injuries are more likely to be dropped. This increase in the frequency of cases that are dropped in turn reduces the overall rate of out-of-court settlements for fatal accident victims, since the increased drop rate necessarily reduces the frequency of other dispositions. Although severe injuries tend to be associated with greater financial losses, the loss effect is already taken into account through the loss variable. Litigation costs may be greater in the case of fatal accident victims, since the most immediate witness to the circumstances of the accident cannot testify on the factors causing the accident. Differences in compensation rules for fatal and nonfatal accident victims in terms of the treatment of pain and suffering and loss of consortium are also potentially instrumental.

Regulatory violations have a twofold effect in that they increase the probability of plaintiff success and they reduce the litigation costs by simplifying the task of demonstrating that the product is defective. These influences should have a negative effect on the rate of dropping claims (Table 10.5), coupled with an increase in the rate of out-of-court settlements and court verdicts (Table 10.6). Although the OSHA variable is only statistically significant in one instance—the positive effect on settlements shown in Table 10.6—the regulatory violations variable does have consistently significant effects in the expected direction. The weak effect of the OSHA variable is not surprising. The accidents captured in the sample occurred in the early and mid-1970s. At the time of the injury occurrences, OSHA regulations had been in place for only a brief period, and compliance with these standards was not widespread. The violations of the regulatory standards of other governmental bodies consequently played a more instrumental role in litigation contexts, which is not unexpected since these standards are more likely to have been in place at the time of the accidents and to have constituted a well-defined and accepted benchmark for performance.

The group of variables pertaining to workers' compensation and interactions with tort liability play an instrumental role in several instances. Consider first an interrelated pair of variables—subrogation actions and the amount of lien. The subrogation variable is the dummy variable for all subrogation actions by the employer or workers' compensation carrier against the defendant listed in the ISO claims data, and the lien variable represents the scale of this claim. When viewed together, these variables suggest that the magnitude of the stakes is a critical factor, since subrogation and amount of lien have opposite signs. Cases involving subrogation actions are more likely to be dropped (Table 10.5) and less likely to be settled or taken to a court verdict (Table 10.6), but the opposite is observed for amount of lien. These results simply reflect the magnitude of the claims captured by each variable. Claims become increasingly worthwhile to pursue once the stakes become sufficiently large. For the decision to drop a claim, the critical lien amount is $1,320, which is just over one-tenth of the average amount for the sample. For all subrogation actions above this threshold, the dominant influence of the lien and subrogation variables is to increase the incentive to pursue a claim. Below this threshold, there is a reduced incentive to pursue the claim, since the stakes are too small.

Situations in which the insurance company defendants have launched indemnification actions of their own with respect to the claim are less likely to be dropped, since such actions reflect recognition of a potentially legitimate claim, where the main issue is which party should be held liable. For indemnification actions to be successful, the worker's initial claim must be valid, and there must be a legitimate reason for the insurer to be filing a claim as well. A significant negative coefficient is observed if the insurer defending the claim is seeking indemnification, contribution, or subrogation against other parties. This variable also raises the settlement probability, conditional upon not dropping the case, which would occur if the insurance company defendant raised the amount that it was willing to offer a claimant if it had the prospect of obtaining compensation from the employer or another insurer. For such a positive effect to occur, this increase must exceed the magnitude of any increase in the Ask amount on the part of claimants who might be influenced by the defendant's ability to pay.

If there are cross-complaints involved between the defendant and another party, the claim is less likely to be dropped and more likely to be litigated. Because of the high drop rate, such claims are more likely to be settled out of court (Table 10.6), but those that are not dropped are less likely to be settled and more likely to be litigated (Table 10.5). The cross-complaint variable seems primarily to reflect a complex legal dispute that is difficult to resolve without litigation. On balance, plaintiffs have no particular advantage or disadvantage once these claims go to court—the cross-complaint coefficient in the case-won column in Table 10.5 is not statistically significant, so there seems to be no evident bias in the mix of cases that is litigated.

An additional variable reflecting the interaction of workers' compensation and product liability is whether the jurisdiction had adopted a sole remedy rule, under which workers' compensation is the worker's exclusive remedy against the employer when the worker is eligible for benefits. Subrogation rules and other rights may also be restricted in sole remedy states, where the extent of such restrictions vary from state to state. The sole remedy rule variable has the expected positive effect on the rate of dropping claims in the unconditional results (Table 10.5), which in turn is associated with a reduced settlement rate in the multivariate logit results (Table 10.6).

For much the same reason, the collateral payment variables are also of interest, since they may be a signal that other institutional mechanisms may have been a more appropriate source of compensation than a tort liability suit. The receipt of privately provided compensation, such as employer-provided sick leave or disability pay, increases the likelihood that the claim will be dropped and decreases both the settlement and litigation rates, but governmental benefits have no significant effect. Publicly provided social insurance does not imply the same degree of private responsibility for the accident, which may account for the different results for the collateral government payment variable.

The final set of variables pertains to the liability doctrine that was pertinent to the claim. The omitted legal doctrine variable is that of warranty-based claims, which is not a particularly relevant doctrine for product injuries that occur on the job, rather than subsequent to a consumer purchase. Of the two other doctrines, strict liability appears to provide the stronger basis for such claims, since strict liability claims are less likely to be dropped, which is consistent with a higher perceived chance of plaintiff success. Both strict liability and negligence have positive effects on settlement rates. These effects are quite powerful, in terms of both their magnitude and statistical significance. The role of these stronger liability criteria implies either that they raise the litigation costs or else that they boost the defendant's expected court award more than they do the plaintiff's. The asymmetry in the expected court award could arise, for example, if firms believed that a successful claim would establish a precedent for future claims.

The effect of the liability doctrine variables on the propensity to win in court is of particular interest. Although the expected directions of influence of the variables would be clear-cut if all cases were litigated, if some cases are settled out of court, then this selection process affects the mix of cases taken to court and their litigation prospects. In the litigation context in which parties' payoffs are symmetrical and the bargaining weights are equal, Priest and Klein (1984) hypothesize that differences in liability standards will not be consequential in affecting plaintiff success rates, as the parties will fully take into account the expected court performance at the earlier settlement stage. Priest and Klein also show that if the bargaining structure is asymmetrical, these legal variables will influence the case-won equation.

The results in Table 10.5 should be treated with some caution because of the small sample of litigated claims (114). Nevertheless, these results are consistent with a lack of symmetry, as many of the variables have statistically significant effects that have not been fully taken into account at an earlier stage. Most pertinent is that cases based on strict liability and negligence arguments have a significantly higher probability of being won in court. The stronger liability doctrines do give plaintiffs the expected advantage. Although one might have expected a larger effect of strict liability on the probability of winning the case, there is no statistically significant difference between the strict liability and negligence coefficients. The main implication of the results is that warranty-based claims are comparatively weak. Two other legal doctrine variables—regulatory violation and sole remedy rule—also have significant effects on the probability of winning the case. These results are also in line with the theory if there is an asymmetry in payoffs.

The Determinants of Compensation Levels

Loss and Payment Levels by Injury Type

The character of the compensation for job injuries is reflected in the loss and payment levels by injury type reported in Table 10.7. There are nineteen injury diagnoses reported. The most frequent injury groups for job claims are fractures, amputations, lacerations, and burns, which together account for over half of all claims. Nonjob product injuries have a similar relative frequency in many cases, but appear to be less heavily concentrated in the injury groups with large losses, such as brain damage and paraplegia. The third and fourth columns of data report the average values of bodily injury losses and payments for all claims (including both claims that resulted in compensation and those that did not). Although payment levels are below loss levels for almost all injuries, in many cases the payment variable takes on a zero value because the claim was dropped or lost in court.

The most meaningful statistics are those reported in the final two columns, which give the average payment levels and the loss replacement rates (that is, payments/losses) for the subgroup of claims resulting in some positive amount of compensation. The seriousness of the claimed financial losses varies widely. For several injury groups—bruise-abrasion, dermatitis, and poisoning—the loss levels are under $3,000. At the high end of the spectrum, there are several injury groups with losses in excess of $100,000: asphyxiation, brain damage, and paraplegia. The large loss claims typically involve substantial medical expenses.

The general pattern displayed in the summary statistics in Table 10.7 is that the loss replacement rates are generally about 1.0, with an average of 0.794. Overall, there is less than full replacement for finanacial losses. Diseases are the greatest exception, as they have a replacement rate in excess of 10.0, but this injury group is very small, so this result may not be reliable.

The existence of loss replacement levels in excess of 1.0 in ten of the instances does not indicates an irrational outcome. Compensation for pain and suffering and nonmonetary losses, such as loss of consortium for the surviving spouse, are legitimate and important concerns.

The considerable degree of replacement for job-related claims is similar to the average performance of product liability claims. The evidence presented in Viscusi (1986a) for the pooled sample of job and nonjob claims indicates an average loss replacement rate of 1.0 for cases settled out of court and 1.7 for favorable court verdicts. The frequency of overcompensation of losses is somewhat lower for job-related claims.

TABLE 10.7
Compensation Amounts by Injury Type

Injury Diagnosis	Frequency for Job Claims (%)	Frequency for Job Claims/ Frequency for Nonjob Claims	All Claims		Claims Resulting in Payments > 0	
			Average Bodily Injury Losses	Average Bodily Injury Payments	Average Bodily Injury Payments	Average Payments/ Losses
Amputation	16.0	14.5	44,932	35,714	55,000	1.016
Asphyxiation	1.2	1.2	117,862	45,517	110,543	0.598
Brain damage	2.1	3.0	280,982	123,695	161,341	0.496
Bruise/abrasion	5.0	1.1	8,984	1,336	2,829	1.448
Burn	11.4	1.4	44,015	16,002	26,404	1.451
Cancer	1.2	12.0	54,225	48,944	64,003	2.417
Concussion	2.4	3.0	49,971	26,672	40,588	0.652
Dermatitis	1.2	0.5	1,736	1,132	1,750	1.515
Dislocation	0.8	2.0	23,521	23,667	47,333	2.638
Disease	0.4	0.4	87,968	13,428	20,142	10.596
Electrical shock	0.9	3.0	175,551	16,991	27,610	0.148
Fracture	20.5	1.2	32,181	22,488	33,064	1.041
Laceration	11.7	1.2	42,337	7,270	11,999	0.179
Paraplegia	0.5	5.0	769,545	35,935	125,773	0.371
Poison	2.4	0.2	9,520	833	1,535	0.771
Quadraplegia	0.2	1.0	360,000	0	—	—
Respiratory	2.6	5.2	53,394	37,062	50,788	1.045
Sprain/Strain	7.0	1.7	10,586	29,056	39,516	3.211
Other	8.8	0.3	84,901	40,898	67,454	0.886

[a] $N = 641$.

Bodily Injury Payment Regressions

The theoretical basis for assessing the influence of factors affecting compensation levels is relatively straightforward. Court awards are based on financial and nonfinancial components. The financial loss consists of medical costs, wage loss, and other financial expenses, which have been summed in the bodily injury loss variable. Compensation for nonfinancial loss covers pain and suffering experienced by the accident victim, as well as loss of consortium for the spouse. Court awards may be diminished if there is evidence of contributory negligence on the part of the accident victim. As indicated in equation 10.8, the expected out-of-court settlement amount is the weighted average of the expected court award plus a weighted average of the parties' litiga-

TABLE 10.8
Regression Analysis of Determinants of Amount of Compensation
(*ln* Bodily Injury Payments)

	Coefficients and SE		
Variable	All Cases with Payments > 0	Settled Cases with Payments > 0	Court Verdicts with Payments > 0
Intercept	−0.468	−0.380	38.564[a]
	(0.675)	(0.677)	(22.988)
ln Bodily injury losses	1.649[a]	1.636[a]	−6.920
	(0.163)	(0.164)	(4.829)
(*ln* Bodily injury losses)^2	−0.062[a]	−0.062[a]	0.339
	(0.009)	(0.009)	(0.233)
Age	−0.009[a]	−0.010[a]	0.070[a]
	(0.005)	(0.005)	(0.029)
Sex	0.015	−0.012	—[b]
	(0.143)	(0.142)	—[b]
Experience	0.022[a]	0.021[a]	0.010
	(0.012)	(0.012)	(0.076)
Death	0.407[a]	0.397[a]	−0.190
	(0.181)	(0.187)	(0.899)
Regulatory violation	0.436[a]	0.444[a]	3.156[a]
	(0.135)	(0.138)	(1.571)
OSHA	−0.200	−0.206	2.967[a]
	(0.140)	(0.144)	(1.352)
Subrogation actions	−0.432[a]	−0.474[a]	3.363[a]
	(0.137)	(0.138)	(1.371)

tion costs. Out-of-court settlements rise with the magnitude of the court award, the probability of plaintiff success, and the size of the litigation costs.

Table 10.8 presents the regression results for the determinants of the size of the bodily injury payment. The dependent variable is the natural logarithm of bodily injury payments, and results are presented for all cases receiving compensation, cases settled out of court, and successful plaintiff verdicts. Since most of the cases receiving compensation were settled out of court, the full sample and the settlement subsample results are very similar.

Consider first the cases settled out of court. Increases in the level of bodily injury losses raise the compensation amount, but not on a one-for-one basis. In particular, the elasticity of payments with respect to

TABLE 10.8, *cont.*

	Coefficients and SE		
	All Cases with	Settled Cases with	Court Verdicts with
Variable	Payments > 0	Payments > 0	Payments > 0
ln (1 + Amount of lien)	0.068[a]	0.069[a]	0.011
	(0.016)	(0.016)	(0.132)
Indemnification	−0.175	−0.180	−0.494
	(0.116)	(0.118)	(1.199)
Cross-complaints	0.337[a]	0.363[a]	−1.181
	(0.115)	(0.117)	(1.259)
Sole remedy rule	−0.072	−0.045	1.474
	(0.105)	(0.106)	(1.116)
Government collateral	0.151	0.106	−0.072
payments	(0.170)	(0.174)	(1.152)
Private collateral payments	0.018	−0.021	0.828
	(0.105)	(0.107)	(0.865)
Strict liability rule	0.122	0.158	3.662[a]
	(0.139)	(0.142)	(1.552)
Negligence rule	−0.165	−0.115	1.176
	(0.142)	(0.145)	(1.764)
Adjusted *R*-squared	0.57	0.57	0.29
	(N = 641)	(N = 619)	(N = 21)

[a] Statistically significant at the 0.05 confidence level, one-tailed test.
[b] Coefficient could not be estimated because there were too few females in the subsample used.

losses evaluated at the mean values of the variables is not significantly different from 1.0. The roughly proportional linkage between payments and losses is similar to the pattern of all product liability claims for which the elasticity is below 1.0 (see Viscusi 1986a). The somewhat higher elasticity for job-related claims may be due to the mix of claims that are picked up in the sample. Because of the presence of workers' compensation, the job-related claims include only losses that pass a minimal threshold; consequently, the very small losses with the highest replacement rates overall are screened out of the sample. It is the high replacement rates for these low loss claims that contribute to the large dropoff in the replacement rate for all product liability claims as claim size increases. Since these claims do not appear in the job-related claims sample, the estimated elasticity is a bit greater.

A variety of workers' compensation variables play an instrumental role. The opposite signs of the subrogation and lien variables follow the earlier pattern. Claims that are the result of subrogation actions with a low claims amount are associated with low payments, but if the dollar amount of the claim is substantial, then the bodily injury payment amount is increased.

Although the presence of an indemnification action by the defendant does not influence the payment level, cross-complaints do have a signficant positive effect in two of three instances. Given the fact that a payment has been made, the existence of cross-complaints may indicate that the potential stakes were sufficiently large so that both parties were willing to incur substantial costs in an effort to shift the liability burden. This variable consequently may be a proxy for influences related to claims size.

A variety of workers' compensation variables play an instrumental role. The opposite signs for subrogation and indemnification are particularly striking. Cases that are the result of subrogation actions against the insured tend to be settled for lower amounts, presumably since the insurer or employer who initially assumed the claim bears some of the liability. Thus, both the Ask and Offer amounts will be less. In contrast, if defendant is an insurer that has initiated a subrogation or indemnification action against another party, then its Offer amount will be greater because of the prospect of recouping some of its losses in subsequent actions. Since the plaintiff's Ask amount will not be reduced, the expected amount of the out-of-court settlement will rise.

The amount of lien variable is more straightforward in its interpretation since its role is similar to that of bodily injury losses in that it serves as a damages measure. Claims in which the dollar amount of the lien against the insured by the workers' compensation carrier are greater correspond to cases that will receive awards relatively larger than expected in court and as a consequence will settle for a larger amount.

Two of the legal foundation variables also are of consequence. Claims in which there are regulatory violations or in which the plaintiff's case is based on strict liability grounds are likely to settle for larger amounts. In each instance the relationship arises because these variables should enhance plaintiffs' probability of winning in court, thus increasing the Ask and Offer amounts.

The determinants of the court awards shown in the last column of Table 10.8 are also quite diverse, which is of interest, since one might have expected court damages to be a simple function of loss levels and claimant characteristics.

Conclusion

In general, these results indicate that for the increasing number of situations in which a product liability claim is filed for job-related injuries, both workers' compensation and tort liability play important roles. These social institutions do not operate in parallel, but instead have overlapping responsibilities and effects.

The extent of the overlap suggests that there is a dual compensation mechanism for which the coordination problems are fundamental. Roughly one-fourth of all claims are the result of subrogation actions against the insured; in almost an equal number of cases, the insurer defending the case has initiated an action against the employer or some third-party insurer. In many other cases, workers have received compensation through private or governmental sources.

These interrelationships also operate out in the litigation process. The effects of the variables follow the expected patterns based on the structure of liability law and rational economic responses by claimants and defendants within the legal bargaining process. The decisions to settle a case out of court or to drop a case, as well as the settlement amounts, all accord with one's expectations. Although the size of the loss and the operative liability doctrine are influential, as one would expect, it is particularly striking that a quite broad range of variables capturing differing facets of the operation of the workers' compensation system plays a fundamental role.

It is clear that any discussion of tort liability reform for job-related accidents must take into account the role of workers' compensation. Moreover, since job-related claims are an important component of the total product liability burden, in terms both of the number of claims and their magnitude, any comprehensive program for tort liability reform must examine the workers' compensation–product liability linkage.

Perhaps the main open research issue is the reverse linkage. In particular, for a sample of workers' compensation claims, how prominent is the reliance on product liability remedies by workers, by their employees, and by the workers' compensation carriers? These linkages may also prove to be substantial, and an understanding of the relationships may be essential to formulation of a sound workers' compensation policy.

Eleven

Conclusion

THE GENERALLY ACCEPTED economic analysis of the role of compensating differentials does not go far enough in terms of capturing the complexity of the systematic operation of labor market forces in the job safety area. Workers receive some wage rewards in return for facing greater risks of injury and death, and we presented new evidence that suggests the labor market value of life is much greater than previously believed. In addition, we broke down the implicit value of job injuries into monetary and nonmonetary components. Our analysis was also consistent with the dynamic aspects of the labor market relationship between worker learning about job risks and worker quitting explored in the literature over the past decade.

Our analysis does not focus on the wage-risk relationship, but rather on the role of a diverse set of labor market institutions that affect the compensation package and, in turn, have far-reaching effects on labor market performance. The workers' compensation system, which is comparable in size to the unemployment insurance system but which has received far less attention in the literature, generates a wide array of important labor market effects. The wage offsets resulting from workers' compensation benefits exceed the premium cost to firms so that the system is self-financing and does not place a financial burden on firms. In addition, through the linking of premiums for workers' compensation with the injury performance of firms, powerful risk reduction incentives are created in the case of workplace fatalities. Fatal injuries are consequently much lower than they would have been in the absence of this program. The workers' compensation system also interacts in complicated ways with third-party product liability suits brought on behalf of workers injured on the job.

An additional labor market function of workers' compensation benefits is their role in reducing worker turnover. Workers who experience adverse job conditions are most likely to quit, and value the social insurance provided by this program most highly. Increased benefits reduce their expected injury costs and, consequently, the effects of expected injuries on turnover.

Unions act as an institution that alters the manner in which the wage-risk and wage–workers' compensation mechanisms operate. In each case, the unions advance the interests of their members, as unions boost the wage-risk tradeoff and diminish the wage reduction that workers receive in return for higher workers' compensation benefits.

In terms of our analysis, the role of product liability suits for job injuries parallels workers' compensation in its function more than do unions, which operate through the various compensation mechanism tradeoffs. Workers' compensation programs were established in large part to serve as an alternative remedy for workers injured on the job and to substitute for product liability suits. The emergence of product liability suits for job injuries in the past decade suggests that in many cases product liability serves as an additional mechanism for compensation of workers injured on the job. An often highly complex set of legal rules relates the workers' compensation system and the tort liability system, and these rules are particularly instrumental in determining the outcome of worker claims.

The diverse nature of these labor market effects as well as their interconnected nature suggests that those considering policy reform should be cognizant of the entire set of policies and institutions that affect labor market behavior. In the past, most analyses have been highly myopic. Those wishing to decrease risk levels sought to tinker with OSHA regulations to alter workplace technologies. Proponents of higher levels of social insurance viewed the workers' compensation mechanism solely as a means for boosting benefit levels for injured workers. Similarly, cries of alarm evoked with respect to the emerging product liability crisis led to calls for a massive overhaul of the linkages between workers' compensation and tort liability so as to dampen the burden on the courts.

In each of these cases, these policies were considered on a piecemeal basis. Such an approach is certainly not appropriate given the diverse and interconnected roles that these various institutional and economic mechanisms play. For example, individuals concerned with promoting safety in the workplace might wish to consider whether an injury tax approach similar to the role of workers' compensation premiums provides a more effective alternative than direct control of workplace conditions. Our results for workplace fatalities suggest that the effects of the workers' compensation program on death risks dwarf any estimates of OSHA's impact that have appeared in the literature.

The main result that we have sought to demonstrate is that the labor market implications of job risks and, in particular, the compensation mechanisms for job risks are both far reaching and highly complex. The survey data we have analyzed suggest that one need not restrict the analysis to a simple relationship between wages and risk. Rather, one can push the implications of economic models of job risks and individual responses to these risks much farther. When the standard models are extended they shed additional light on the nature of the labor market response to risk. Indeed, many of the mechanisms identified in our study imply enormous economic effects. What is at stake is not a debate over minor economic influences that are theoretical curiosities. Rather, these influences are fundamental to the operation of the market for hazardous work.

Appendix A

Estimation of the Value of Life Using
Flexible Functional Forms

AN UNRESOLVED PROBLEM in estimating the value of life is the selection of a functional form of the dependent variable in the compensating differential model.[1] Typically, empirical studies present results for wage equations that enter either the wage or its natural logarithm as the dependent variable. Neither one of these measures is theoretically superior to the other, however, so there is a degree of uncertainty introduced into the estimates of the value of life that is derived from these regressions.

In this appendix, we embed the wage and *ln* wage models in the flexible functional form given by the Box-Cox transformation. This formulation will enable us to ascertain which transformation of the wage variable is most consistent with the data. This technique has previously been applied in the job risk context in a study using different data.[2] It is shown there and below that neither the linear nor the semilogarithmic model is ideal. Evidence does indicate that the *ln* wage regression is more compatible with the functional form that best fits the data.

The Box-Cox transformation assumes that there is a value of λ such that the regression model

(A.1) $$\frac{\text{Wage}^\lambda - 1}{\lambda} = X\beta + \varepsilon$$

is normally distributed, homoskedastic, and linear in β.[3] Various functional forms are special cases of this model. For instance,

$$\lim_{\lambda \to 0} \frac{\text{Wage}^\lambda - 1}{\lambda} = ln \text{ Wage},$$

while $\lambda = 1$ implies the linear wage regression, $\lambda = 0.5$ implies the regression of the square root of the wage on X, and so forth. It is therefore possible to test the restrictions implied by the linear, semilogarithmic, and square root transformations as special cases of the model given by equation A.1.

The curvature coefficient λ and the vector β, which includes the risk and insurance coefficients necessary to estimate the value of life, are estimated using the maximum likelihood method. The likelihood function is

(A.2) $L(\lambda) = \dfrac{-N}{2} \ln \hat{\sigma}^2(\lambda) + (\lambda - 1) \sum\limits_{i=1}^{N} \ln \text{Wage}_i,$

where

$$\hat{\sigma}^2(\lambda) = \frac{1}{N} \left[\frac{\text{Wage}^\lambda - 1}{\lambda} - X\hat{\beta}(\lambda) \right]' \left[\frac{\text{Wage}^\lambda - 1}{\lambda} - X\hat{\beta}(\lambda) \right],$$

and X includes all of the variables listed in the Table 5.4 regressions.

Choosing λ and β to maximize equation A.2 yields a value of λ that equals approximately 0.3. The test statistic for the restrictions $\lambda_R = 1.0$, which implies that the wage is the appropriate dependent variable, and $\lambda_R = 0.0$, which implies the use of $\ln$ wage, against the unrestricted value $\lambda_U = 0.3$ is

(A.3) $\Omega = -2 \left[L(\lambda_R) - L(\lambda_U) \right],$

which has an asymptotic chi-square distribution with degrees of freedom equal to the number of restrictions tested (in this case, one). The values of $L(\lambda)$ corresponding to λ_U, $\lambda = 0$, and $\lambda = 1$ are 887.0, 904.2, and 932.7, respectively. Substituting these values into equation A.3 yields values of the test statistic equal to 34.4 for the test of $\lambda_R = 0$, and 91.4 for the test of $\lambda_R = 1$. Since the value of $\chi^2(0.05, 1)$ is 3.84, we reject both the linear and semilogarithmic models as admissible specifications.

The 90 percent confidence interval for λ contains those values of λ for which

$$\left[L(\lambda) > L(\lambda_U) - \chi^2(0.10, 1) \right],$$

or all values of λ such that

$$L(\lambda) > -888.36.$$

This interval includes values of λ that fall approximately between 0.25 and 0.45. It is noteworthy that this result exactly replicates earlier results that used a different data set and a different measure of risk.[4]

We can compute the value of life based on the Box-Cox regressions as follows. Rewrite the regression model of equation A.1 as

(A.4) $\dfrac{w^{\lambda - 1}}{\lambda} = X_O \beta_O + \gamma_w p + \delta_w pR + \varepsilon,$

where β_O and X_O are the coefficients and individual characteristics listed in Table 5.4, p is the NIOSH death risk variable, and R is the replacement rate. The wage-risk tradeoff is found by totally differentiating equation A.4 with respect to w and p:

$$w^{\lambda-1}dw = (\gamma_w + \delta_w R)dp,$$

which upon rearrangement of terms simplifies to

$$\frac{dw}{dp} = (\gamma_w + \gamma_w R)/w^{\lambda-1}.$$

Thus, computation of the wage-risk tradeoff requires estimates of γ_w, δ_w, and λ.[5] The maximum likelihood estimates of these parameters are $\hat{\gamma}_w = 0.016$, $\hat{\delta}_w = 0.017$, and $\hat{\lambda} = 0.3$. Evaluated at the sample mean values of the wage ($7.01) and the replacement rate (0.544), the wage-risk tradeoff is 0.0225. With use of the technique described above, this yields a value of life of $5.617 million, which is bounded from below by the *ln* wage equation estimate and from above by the wage equation estimate. The 90 percent confidence interval for the value of life lies approximately between $5.5 million and $5.7 million. Thus, the *ln* wage equation estimates, although different from the unrestricted estimates in a statistical sense, yield a comparable estimate of the value of life.

Appendix B

A Conceptual Model of Worker and
Firm Responses to Insurance Benefits

THE DISCUSSION in chapter 9 suggested that a complex array of influences operates among workers' compensation benefits, wages, and safety levels. Increases in accident insurance theoretically should induce two opposing effects. Increased benefits will impose additional injury costs on firms, leading them to devote more resources to providing safety. The extent of the safety incentive effect hinges on the extent to which additional accidents cause an increase in a firm's insurance premium through the experience-rating procedure. The incentive effect should be particularly strong for large firms, which either self-insure or are rated according to their own experience and thus pay most or all of the costs of the accident in terms of increased premiums. Higher benefits also may produce an opposite influence on safety through moral hazard problems for covered workers. If the higher benefit levels on balance reduce injury risks, workers' compensation insurance could provide an effective means of regulating safety by acting as an injury tax.

The empirical analysis considered a number of influences. Benefit increases were shown to increase safety levels at a decreasing rate. Benefit-induced increases in safety levels were shown empirically to reduce wages indirectly through the effect of the wage-risk tradeoff. Benefit increases also reduce wages directly through the wage-benefit tradeoff. The experience-rating effect was indicated by the strong interactive effect of benefits and firm size on the level of safety.

To illustrate the direct effect of benefits on safety levels conceptually, consider a simple model in which firms choose the level of safety through the safety cost function $c(s)$, where $c_s > 0$ and $c_{ss} > 0$, and through the expected value of output, sv. The safety level also affects profits through its effect on expected wages, sw, and on expected benefits, $(1 - s)b$.

In this simplified variant of the model, we abstract from the dependence of w on s and b. The unit profit function is

$$\pi = sv - c(s) - sw - (1 - s)b,$$

where v is the unit of output. First-order conditions for a maximum with respect to s are

$$\pi_s = v - c_s - w + b = 0.$$

Thus, the costs of safety improvements to the firm include the increased wage bill and the safety expenditures, while the benefits depend on the insurance level, b, and on the value of output, v. Totally differentiating the first-order condition yields

$$\frac{ds}{db} = \frac{1}{c_{ss}} > 0,$$

which is positive given the assumption $c_{ss} > 0$. The curvature of the safety-benefit relationship is theoretically ambiguous, since the second-order effect

$$\frac{d^2s}{db^2} = \frac{1}{c^2_{ss}} c_{sss}$$

depends upon the sign of the third derivative of the safety cost function.

Extensions of this simple model that are explored in the empirical analysis include recognition of moral hazard and the feedback effects of benefits and risks on wages. If there are feedback effects of benefits and risks on wages, the benefit-induced safety expenditures are partially financed by wage reductions on two margins—wages will fall in response to both lower risks and higher benefits. In the empirical analysis, we estimate these financing effects. More important, we estimate the effect of benefits on fatality risk levels and find that moral hazard does not play a dominant role. Workers' compensation benefits exert significant downward pressure on fatality risk levels. This effect decreases with benefit increases, as predicted by the conceptual model.

To analyze the effects of the two types of moral hazard, introduce the worker reaction function

$$e = e(s,b),$$

where $e_s > 0$ and $e_b > 0$. The safety level now depends on firm expenditures on safety, s, benefit levels, b, and the worker's reaction to s and b, $e(s,b)$, which firms will take into account in determining expenditures on safety.

Let

$$p^*(s,b) = p[s,e(s,b)] \ \varepsilon \ (0,1)$$

indicate the probability that a worker remains "uninjured," net of moral hazard effects. The assumptions concerning p are $p_s > 0$ and $p_e < 0$. Let

$$p_s^* = p_s + p_e e_s > 0$$

denote the situation in which the moral hazard effect described in Viscusi (1979a) is not dominant, while

$$p_s^* < 0$$

indicates a serious moral hazard problem. Furthermore,

$$p_s^* = p_e e_b < 0,$$

so that the effect of benefit increases on the frequency and duration of claims decreases the probability that a worker works.

The dependence of wages on risks and benefits is captured by the wage function

$$w = w(s,b),$$

where

$$w_s, w_b < 0$$

reflect the desirability of both insurance and safety to workers. The profit function for the most general version of the model is

$$\pi = p^*(s,b)v - c(s) - p^*(s,b)w(s,b) - [1 - p^*(s,b)]b.$$

The first-order condition is

(B.1) $\pi_s = -c_s + (b + v - w)p_s^* - p^*w_s = 0.$

Equation B.1 consists of three terms: the marginal cost of safety, $-c_s$, the marginal profitability of safety expenditures, $(b + v - w)p_s^*$, and worker expenditures on safety, p^*w_s. The last two terms in equation B.1 are critical for interpreting the comparative static result to follow. The first of these, $(b + v - w)p_s^*$, represents the net change in profits that results from changes in accident rates. The remaining term, p^*w_s, equals the wage savings due to increased safety, since w_s is the implicit price of safety to the worker, and p^* is the quantity of safety. In other words, p^*w_s are expenditures by the worker on safety.

Totally differentiating equation B.1, the effect of an increase in benefits on the level of safety is

(B.2) $\dfrac{ds}{db} = H^{-1} [(w - v)p_{sb}^* - p_s^*(1 + \eta)] + H^{-1}p_s^*w_b + H^{-1}(w_s p_b^* + p^*w_{sb}),$

where η is the benefit elasticity of p_s^*, and H is the Hessian matrix for the problem.

It seems plausible that marginal changes in the safety level will induce a greater shirking reaction on the part of workers, the higher the benefit level, so that $e_{sb} > 0$. Since $p_e < 0$, p^*_{sb} is <0, and the first term in equation B.2, $H^{-1}(w - v)p^*_{sb}$ is negative, assuming $w < v$.

The second term depends on η, the elasticity of p^*_s with respect to benefits. If p^*_s and the elasticity are both positive, then $-H^{-1}p^*_s(1 + \eta)$ is positive. If p^*_s is greater than zero, and η is negative, then $-H^{-1}p^*_s(1 + \eta)$ is still positive if the elasticity is less than one in absolute value. If significant shirking results from the firm's provision of safety ($p^*_s < 0$), the term $-H^{-1}p^*_s(1 + \eta)$ is negative, and benefit increases may decrease safety levels.

The third term in equation B.2, $H^{-1}p^*_s w_b$ is also positive if there is not a substantial moral hazard problem ($p^*_s > 0$). The final term, which represents the effect of a benefit increase on worker expenditures on safety, is negative. Thus, the total impact of benefit changes on risk levels is indeterminate when moral hazard is considered.

The importance of moral hazard is illustrated most clearly by analyzing the solution to the problem when there are no wage-risk or wage-benefit feedbacks (that is, when $w_s = w_b = w_{sb} = 0$). In this case, profits are

$$\pi = p^*(s,b)v - c(s) - p^*(s,b)w - [1 - p^*(s, b)]b,$$

and the optimal level of s is given by the first-order condition

(B.3) $\pi_s = -c_s + p^*_s(v - w) + p^*_s b = 0,$

or

$$-c_s + (b + v - w)p^*_s = 0.$$

The effect of a benefit increase on safety in equation B.3 is

$$\frac{ds}{db} = H^{-1}[(w - v - b)p^*_{sb} - p^*_s].$$

The sign of this term thus depends on both p^*_{sb} and p^*_s. Rearranging terms,

(B.4) $\dfrac{ds}{db} = H^{-1}(w - v)p^*_{sb} - H^{-1}p^*_s(1 + \eta).$

As discussed above regarding equation B.2, equation B.4 is ambiguous in sign.

Notes _____

Chapter 2
The Research Context of the Analysis

1. See Smith ([1776] 1937), book 10.
2. See Moore (1988a) for an analysis of the impact of measurement error on estimates of compensating differentials.
3. See Arthur (1981) and Rosen (1988) for theoretical analyses of the life cycle job risk problem.
4. See Viscusi (1983) and Smith (1976) for reviews of the performance of OSHA.
5. Fishback (1987) also uses fatality rates as the risk variable. However, his results are not directly comparable to those discussed here, as Fishback's empirical analysis focuses on the effects of liability rules on risk, rather than on the effects of the benefit levels themselves.

Chapter 3
The Performance of Workers' Compensation as a
Social Insurance Program

1. See, for example, the studies by Brown (1980), Duncan and Holmlund (1983), Olson (1981), Smith (1976), Thaler and Rosen (1976), and Viscusi (1978, 1983). Also see the reviews by Bailey (1980), Rosen (1986), Smith (1979), and Viscusi (1983). The literature began with Adam Smith ([1776] 1937).
2. Recent empirical work includes studies by Arnould and Nichols (1983), Butler (1983), and Dorsey and Walzer (1983). Also see the broader perspectives by Chelius (1977), Darling-Hammond and Kniesner (1980), Ehrenberg (1988), and Oi (1973) as well as the volumes edited by Worrall (1983) and by Worrall and Appel (1985).
3. This theme of inadequate benefits has continued to be emphasized in the more recent work by the former Chairman of the National Commission on State Workmen's Compensation Laws, John Burton. See particularly Burton (1978).
4. See Viscusi (1979a, 1980b). Risk aversion and moral hazard also yield this result.
5. See Worrall and Butler (1985).
6. This discussion addresses a homogeneous class of injuries. If social security benefits vary by injury severity, the net effect is to raise the level of $U^2(x)$ for these more heavily compensated injuries. The empirical analysis will address whether there is any remaining benefits gap, where in effect the higher social security benefits can be viewed as making classes of injuries less severe.

7. This result is derived in Viscusi (1979a), who also cites related formulations in the medical insurance literature. It should be noted that this result only pertains to earnings replacement. Medical expenditures that may enhance the chance of returning to good health are an entirely different issue.

8. Although their paper focuses on 1983, similar calculations by Burton for other years suggest that the ratio of losses incurred to the net cost to policy holders has been in the 0.80 range in recent years.

9. There were major changes in the workers' compensation benefit formulas in the 1970s so that, to the extent that there is a lag in the wage adjustment, the full equilibrium effects of the revisions may not be apparent. The results consequently may understate the equilibrium wage response to higher benefits.

10. U.S. Chamber of Commerce (1976).

11. See Price (1984).

12. These correlations are reported in unpublished work by John Burton and Alan Krueger. Using a sample of thirty-one states, Burton and Krueger have found that the logarithm of temporary total disability benefits has a correlation coefficient of 0.58 with the logarithm of permanent total disability benefits, 0.64 with the logarithm of fatality benefits, and 0.38 with permanent partial benefits. Their research effort takes into account benefit maximums, minimums, replacement rates, and durations. In contrast, our measure abstracts from duration but is otherwise an accurate measure of both temporary total disability and permanent total disability.

13. Tax rates are from Commerce Clearing House, Inc. (1977a, 1977b).

14. Z_i includes the number of dependents, a marital status dummy variable, and all exogenous variables in the wage equation. Thus, differences across states in average benefits provide the primary source of variation, augmented by individual differences in family size and marital status.

15. In subsequent research, we have examined the bias in the estimated standard errors introduced by using the predicted value as a regressor in lieu of true two-stage least squares estimation. The replacement rate variable is always negative and highly significant.

16. In only a few cases was it necessary to use two-digit risk measures.

17. Our specifications are similar to those of Butler (1983). Butler's findings also indicate a negative effect that is quite robust with respect to specification.

18. Table 3.1 describes the variables in X_i.

19. Dorsey and Walzer (1983) adopted a similar formulation, using BLS injury rate data, and found a substantial positive effect on the job premium for non-union workers and a negative effect for union workers. Another approach that has appeared in papers by Ruser (1985b) and Butler (1983) is to include both a separate workers' compensation variable and one that has been interacted with the risk level, but their results usually are not statistically significant or have unexpected signs.

20. All estimates are in 1988 dollars.

Chapter 4
Net Workers' Compensation Costs

1. See Viscusi (1983, 1986b), Smith (1976), and Bartel and Thomas (1982, 1985), for reviews of the performance of OSHA.

2. Viscusi (1984) discusses these and related issues.

3. Notable exceptions include Butler (1983), Worrall (1983), Worrall and Appel (1985), Worrall and Butler (1985), Viscusi (1980b), Darling-Hammond and Kniesner (1980), and the references cited below.

4. See Watkins and Burton (1973).

5. Estimates of this substitution are found in Chapters 3 and 4, and in Arnould and Nichols (1983), Dorsey and Walzer (1983), Butler (1983), and Ruser (1985b). This prediction is an implication of the equalizing difference model (Smith 1979; Rosen 1986; Viscusi 1978). Ehrenberg (1989) provides a survey of evidence on this and related issues.

6. Data on payments and premiums are taken from Price (1986) and from prior issues of the *Social Security Bulletin*.

7. The average tax rate faced by workers in the data sets is about 30 percent. Thus, the wage savings to firms before taxes are 30 percent higher than those calculated by using our estimated wage reduction rates, which are estimated on an after-tax basis. Since wage savings to firms must also be calculated on an after-tax basis, we assume for simplicity that firms face the same marginal tax rate, on average, as workers.

8. Similar findings are discussed in Bartel and Thomas (1985), Chelius (1974, 1982) and Worrall and Appel (1985).

Chapter 5
Workers' Implicit Value of Life

1. See Viscusi (1983). Also see Smith (1979), Mishan (1971), and Shelling (1968).

2. A discussion of the willingness to pay principle can be found in any standard policy analysis text, such as the widely used text by Stokey and Zeckhauser (1978).

3. The main notable exception is the study using Society of Actuaries data for very hazardous occupations by Thaler and Rosen (1976).

4. Because benefits are only paid to decedents with surviving dependents, the benefit variable is set equal to zero if the worker is single.

5. For an analysis of workers' risk perceptions, see Viscusi (1979a) and Viscusi and O'Connor (1984).

6. A nonfatal risk variable was not included, since it was not statistically significant and did not substantially alter the death risk coefficients. Excluding the nonfatal risk variable is a common practice in the literature. In addition, mixing the NTOF fatality variable with a BLS nonfatal risk variable creates comparability problems.

7. See Chapters 3, 5, and 7.

8. Indeed, using the BLS data on the 1976 PSID, the estimated value of life estimate is $8 million to $12 million in 1986 dollars (the year for which our nominal life values are calculated). See Viscusi (1979a).

Chapter 6
The Value of Life

1. Theoretical analyses of life cycle job risk models have appeared in the literature. See, for example, Conley (1976), Viscusi (1979a), and Arthur (1981).

2. Zeckhauser and Shepard (1976) provide an extensive policy discussion of their concept of quality-adjusted life years. Arthur (1981), Shepard and Zeckhauser (1984), Rosen (1988), and Cropper and Sussman (1986) have developed elaborate life cycle models. Arthur and Rosen explicitly treat the quantity of life effects that are our principal focus here.

3. The following studies include measures of workers' compensation benefits for nonfatal injuries: Arnould and Nichols (1983), Butler (1983), Dorsey and Walzer (1983), and Chapters 3 and 4.

4. Since the study that forms the basis of this chapter (Moore and Viscusi 1988a) was completed prior to the release of the NTOF data described in Chapter 5, BLS data on risk levels and U.S. Census data on remaining life were used. The sample is smaller than in Chapter 3 because of the lack of fatality risk data for some industries.

5. Tax rates for 1976 are from Commerce Clearing House, Inc. (1977a, 1977b).

6. This level of detail in terms of industry aggregation is greater than is available from published sources. Death risk measures were obtained by copying death statistics manually from the death statistic files at the BLS office in Washington.

7. Life expectancies are taken from U.S. Department of Health and Human Services (1980).

8. Of the two, it seems likely that increased participation will be compensated, while increased fertility will not. However, Arthur's (1981) results indicate that the participation effect is small relative to the life year effect (about 10 percent), so failure to include participation should not bias the results significantly.

9. See U.S. Chamber of Commerce (1976).

10. See Arnould and Nichols (1983) and Butler (1983) for aggregate studies that include a fatality risk measure. As noted above, our weighted replacement rate variable offers several additional refinements over those appearing in the literature, including recognition of their favorable tax status, the appropriateness of the interaction with the lost workday accident rate, and detailed calculation of the worker-specific benefit levels. See Viscusi and Moore (1987) for detailed comparisons with other benefits approaches.

11. For purposes of estimation, the categorical variables indicating a high school degree and residence in the Northeast are excluded.

12. The most extensive analyses of the Survey of Working Conditions are Viscusi (1979a) and Duncan (1976). Moore (1984) utilizes the 1973 survey.

13. The home mortgage interest rate is the Federal Home Loan Bank Board rate on new-home mortgage yields, from Council of Economic Advisers (1980), 278.

14. The results from a poll by Lawrence Summers suggest that the rate of interest companies use to discount investments is on the order of 15 percent or more for a majority of firms. See *Washington Post*, National Weekly Edition, July 16, 1986, 22.

Chapter 7
Worker Learning and the Valuation of the Compensation Package

1. See, for example, Smith (1979) and Viscusi (1979a) for analyses of wage-risk tradeoffs. Table 2.4 summarizes the estimates of wage–workers' compensation tradeoffs that appear in Arnould and Nichols (1983), Butler (1983), and Dorsey and Walzer (1983) and in Chapters 3, 4, 6, 7, and 8.

2. See Table 2.2.

3. A variant of this analysis without learning appears in Diamond (1977).

4. One could adopt the assumption that the alternative job poses a known risk of injury without altering the model structure, even in the n-period case. If both jobs are uncertain and there are more than two periods, the model structure becomes more complex.

5. See Viscusi (1980a, 1980b, 1980c).

6. Detailed exploration of the differences in disability benefits and their interrelationship are provided by Burton and Krueger (1986) and Krueger and Burton (1983). An analysis of the important permanent partial disability component is provided by Burton (1983). More generally, see Berkowitz and Burton (1987) for an analysis of permanent disability benefits

7. These results parallel those in Viscusi (1980c).

8. These losses consist of pain and suffering and both work disability and nonwork disability. See Burton (1983) and the discussion in Chapter 3.

Chapter 8
The Role of Unions in Altering the Structure of Risk Compensation

1. See Freeman (1981) for an analysis of the effect of unions on fringe benefits.

2. See Farber (1986) for a review of competing models of trade union behavior.

3. This result is counterintuitive in the median voter and surplus maximization models. However, as shown by Dickens (1984), the opposite prediction is possible under the Nash bargaining model.

4. In this and in subsequent chapters, workers below the minimum, who consttitute about 1 percent of the sample, are treated as if their wages fell between the upper and lower benefit limits. Separating these workers for estimation purposes is not feasible.

5. Tests for heteroskedasticity along the lines suggested by Amemiya (1985) indicate that weighting is not necessary.

6. These restrictions are tested and found not to be binding. The intercepts of each equation are allowed to differ.

7. See Ruser (1985a) for a discussion. The benefit maximum essentially acts like a set of state dummy variables.

8. For an early test, see Lee (1978). In a recent paper, Duncan and Leigh (1985) test and reject the hypothesis that union status is exogenous.

9. See Rosen (1986), Butler (1983), Biddle and Zarkin (1988), Garen (1988), and Kahn and Lang (1988). For a dissenting view on this aspect of model specification, see Smith (1978).

10. State dummy variables are still included, however, to control for unobservable state-specific determinants of the wage.

11. Estimates for the remaining variables are not reported, as they are not the focus of this chapter, and do not differ from those reported throughout the literature.

12. See Freeman (1984) for a discussion of measurement error problems in estimating union wage effects.

13. Evidence presented in Chapter 4 suggests that, following the large benefit increases of the 1976–1985 period, the rate of tradeoff has declined to the point that benefit levels are now adequate.

Chapter 9
The Effects of Workers' Compensation on Job Safety

1. See Viscusi (1985, 1986c) and the references contained therein for assessments of OSHA's safety impact.

2. See, in particular, Smith (1976), Diamond (1977), and Viscusi (1983). Chelius (1976) and Fishback (1987) examine the effects of changing from a negligence standard to a strict liability standard for workplace injuries such as the standard imposed by Workers' Compensation. Larson (1953) is the seminal work on Workers' Compensation Law.

3. See, for example, Chelius (1977, 1982), Butler (1983), and Ruser (1985a).

4. Chelius and Smith (1987) analyze the combined role of compliance costs and premiums, and find that costs per dollar of loss are U-shaped with respect to size. Our analysis provides empirical evidence on the total size-safety cost relationship below.

5. Two important exceptions are Butler (1983) and Garen (1988).

6. See Butler and Worral (1983, 1985), Kniesner and Leeth (1987), and Krueger (1988).

7. Chelius and Smith (1987) and Ruser (1985a) explore the role of experience rating in determining costs and safety levels.

8. In those studies that have analyzed the impact of workers' compensation on injury rates, Butler (1983) uses time series data on risks and benefits within a single state (South Carolina) to circumvent this problem. Chelius (1982) uses unpublished data on two-digit (SIC) manufacturing industries for thirty-six states, and Ruser (1985b) uses BLS injury data for twenty-five three-digit manufacturing industries across forty-one states. Of the three studies, only Butler analyzes the combined impact of benefits on both injury rates and wages.

9. The industry categories include mining, construction, manufacturing, communication, wholesale trade, retail trade, and services. The services dummy was excluded for estimation purposes.

10. See Table 2.3.

11. In the earlier chapters, where the endogenous right-hand variable in the wage equation was the wage replacement rate, identification arose primarily through the nonlinearity of the wage variable and from variation across states in benefit levels. For an analysis along the lines of this chapter using the same instruments as in the earlier chapters, see Viscusi and Moore (forthcoming b). The results reported there are quite similar to those in this chapter.

12. There were no significant differences between these coefficients when the models were estimated separately.

13. Using the risk-benefit tradeoff in column 2 of Table 2, the total effect of b on the fatality rate is $-0.0153 \times 213 = -3.2$ deaths per 100,000 workers. This result assumes that the point estimates are valid over the entire range of b, which may not be the case.

14. Setting $\partial p/\partial b$ equal to zero and solving for b at the mean firm size of 44.0 yields this result. The price inflator used is 1.15.

15. Using the estimates in column 2 of Table 2,

$$\partial p/\partial c = -0.01296$$

so that, using equation 5,

$$\partial w/\partial c = [3.136 - (0.00875 \times 239.6)] \times (-0.01296) - 0.0087 \times 6.61 = -0.071$$

Thus, a \$10 increase in c reduces the weekly wage by about 70 cents.

16. See Price (1984).

17. Actual expenditures on employee safety and health in 1981 for all businesses, reported by McGraw-Hill (1986), were \$5.1204 billion. The total civilian labor force in 1981 included 107 million workers, as reported by the Council of Economic Advisers (1987). Safety expenditure data are taken from the *14th Annual McGraw-Hill Survey of Investment in Employee Safety and Health* (New York: McGraw-Hill Economics, 1986).

18. The weekly wage effect equals seven cents per dollar of benefits. Multiplying by b (\$213) and by fifty-two weeks yields \$775 per year, or \$890 in 1988 prices.

19. See, for example, Smith (1987), Butler and Worral (1985), Kniesner and Leeth (1987), and Krueger (1988) for analyses of moral hazard.

20. For an excellent discussion of the agenda for workers' compensation reform, see Weiler (1986).

Chapter 10
Tort Liability Remedies for Job Injuries

1. For reviews of the history of workers' compensation, see Darling-Hammond and Kniesner (1980) and Weiler (1986).

2. See Weiler (1986) for a discussion of the legal issues raised in this paragraph as well as the general characterization of the different compensation systems.

3. This shift from a negligence to a strict liability test is discussed in Chelius (1976).

4. See Viscusi (1986a, 1988a). Weiler (1986) cites statistics showing that workers' compensation compensates only 250 cancer cases per year, as compared with the expected job contribution of thousands of cancer fatalities annually.

5. See Weiler (1986).

6. See, for example, the discussions in Posner (1973) and Danzon and Lillard (1983).

7. These variables are discussed in greater detail in Viscusi (1986a). Stewart (1987) provides an excellent discussion of the interaction between regulation and tort liability. See also Viscusi (1988b).

8. See Weiler (1986), Abraham (1986), and Keeton (1971) for a discussion of subrogation provisions.

9. In Viscusi (1986a, 1988c) the relative performance of the strict liability and negligence views is consistent with this view.

10. For discussion of this particular selection issue see Viscusi (1986a).

Appendix A
Estimation of the Value of Life Using
Flexible Functional Forms

1. This problem was first noted in the seminal article in the literature by Rosen (1974) and in the review by Smith (1979).

2. See Moore (1984).

3. It has been shown elsewhere that Box-Cox estimates are sensitive to the problem of heteroskedasticity when cross-section data, such as ours, are used. See Amemiya and Powell (1981), who analyze the sensitivity of Box-Cox estimates to the normality assumption, which only holds when $\lambda = 0$. In our earlier runs with the 1982 PSID data, these problems were not apparent.

4. See Moore (1984).

5. By ignoring the effect of wage changes on the replacement rate, we are assuming implicitly that wages (w) and benefits (b), change identically. This essentially amounts to the assumption that all workers' wages put them below the benefit ceiling. Although a large portion of the workers are above the maximum, in practice, the effect is negligible.

Bibliography

Abraham, Kenneth. 1986. *Distributing Risk: Insurance, Legal Theory, and Public Policy*. New Haven: Yale University Press.

Adamache, Killard W., and Frank A. Sloan. 1982. "Unions and Hospitals: Some Unresolved Issues." *Journal of Health Economics* 1:81–108.

Amemiya, Takeshi. 1985. *Advanced Econometrics*. Cambridge, Mass.: Harvard University Press.

———. 1977. "A Note on a Heteroskedastic Model." *Journal of Econometrics* 6:365–70.

Amemiya, Takeshi, and James L. Powell. 1981. "A Comparison of the Box-Cox Maximum Likelihood Estimator and the Non-Linear Two-Stage Least Squares Estimator." *Journal of Econometrics* 17:351–81.

Arnould, Richard J., and Len M. Nichols. 1983. "Wage-Risk Premiums and Workers' Compensation: A Refinement of Estimates of Compensating Wage Differential." *Journal of Political Economy* 91:332–40.

Arthur, W. B. 1981. "The Economics of Risks to Life." *American Economic Review* 71:54–64.

Bailey, Martin J. 1980. *Reducing Risks to Life: Measurement of the Benefits*. Washington, D.C.: American Enterprise Institute.

Bartel, Ann P., and Lacy Glenn Thomas. 1985. "Direct and Indirect Effects of Regulation: A New Look at OSHA's Impact." *Journal of Law and Economics* 28:1–26.

———. 1982. "OSHA Enforcement, Industrial Compliance, and Workplace Injuries." NBER Working Paper No. 953.

Berkowitz, Monroe, and John F. Burton, Jr. 1987. *Permanent Disability Benefits in Workers' Compensation*. Kalamazoo, Mich.: Upjohn Institute.

Biddle, Jeff E., and Gary Zarkin. 1988. "Worker Preferences and Market Compensation for Job Risk." *Review of Economics and Statistics* 70:660–67.

Brown, Charles. 1980. "Equalizing Differences in the Labor Market." *Quarterly Journal of Economics* 94:113–34.

Burton, John F., Jr. 1983. "Compensation for Permanent Partial Disabilities," in John D. Worrall, ed., *Safety and the Work Force: Incentives and Disincentives in Compensation*. Ithaca, N.Y.: Cornell Industrial and Labor Relations Press, 18–60.

———. 1978. "Wage Losses from Work Injuries and Workers' Compensation Benefits: Shall the Twain Never Meet?" in *1978 Convention Proceedings of IAIABC*. Quebec City: International Association of Industrial Accident Boards and Commissions, 74-83.

Burton, John F., Jr., and Alan B. Krueger. 1986. "Interstate Variations in the Employees' Cost of Workers' Compensation, with Particular Reference to Connecticut, New Jersey, and New York," in James R. Chelius, ed., *Current Issues in Workers' Compensation*. Kalamazoo, Mich.: Upjohn Institute.

Butler, Richard J. 1983. "Wage and Injury Rate Response to Shifting Levels of Workers' Compensation," in John D. Worrall, ed., *Safety and the Work Force: Incentives and Disincentives in Compensation.* Ithaca, N.Y.: Cornell Industrial and Labor Relations Press, 61–86.

Butler, Richard J., and John D. Worrall. 1985. "Work Injury Compensation and the Duration of Nonwork Spells." *Economic Journal* 95:714–24.

———. 1983. "Workers' Compensation: Benefit and Injury Claims Rates in the Seventies." *Review of Economics and Statistics* 65:580–99.

Cain, Glen G., Brian E. Becker, Catherine G. McLaughlin, and Albert E. Schwenk. 1981. "The Effect of Unions on Wages in Hospitals." *Research in Labor Economics* 4:191–320.

Chelius, James R., ed. 1986. *Current Issues in Workers' Compensation.* Kalamazoo, Mich.: Upjohn Institute.

———. 1982. "The Influence of Workers' Compensation on Safety Incentives." *Industrial and Labor Relations Review* 35:235–42.

———. 1977. *Workplace Safety and Health: The Role of Workers' Compensation.* Washington, D.C.: American Enterprise Institute.

———. 1976. "Liability for Industrial Accidents: A Comparison of Negligence and Strict Liability Systems." *Journal of Legal Studies* 5:293–309.

———. 1974. "The Control of Industrial Accidents: Economic Theory and Empirical Evidence." *Law and Contemporary Problems* 38:700–29.

Chelius, James R., and Robert S. Smith. 1987. "Firm Size and Regulatory Compliance Costs: The Case of Workers' Compensation Insurance." *Journal of Policy Analysis and Management* 6:193–206.

———. 1983. "Workers' Compensation and the Incentive to Prevent Injuries," in John D. Worrall, ed., *Safety and the Workforce: Incentives and Disincentives in Workers' Compensation.* Ithaca, N.Y.: Cornell Industrial and Labor Relations Press.

Commerce Clearing House, Inc. 1977a. *1977 U.S. Master Tax Guide.* New York: Commerce Clearing House.

———. 1977b. *1977 State Tax Handbook.* New York: Commerce Clearing House.

Conley, Bryan C. 1976. "The Value of Human Life and the Demand for Safety." *American Economic Review* 66:45–55.

Council of Economic Advisers. 1987. *Economic Report of the President.* Washington: U.S. Government Printing Office.

Cropper, M. L., and F. G. Sussman. 1986. "Valuing Future Risks to Life." University of Maryland Bureau of Business and Economics Research. Working Paper.

Danzon, Patricia Munch, and Lee Lillard. 1983. "Settlement Out of Court: The Dispositon of Medical Malpractice Claims." *Journal of Legal Studies* 12:345–77.

Darling-Hammond, Linda, and Thomas J. Kniesner. 1980. *The Law and Economics of Workers' Compensation.* Rand Institute for Civil Justice Report R-2716-ICJ.

DeGroot, Morris H. 1970. *Optimal Statistical Decisions.* New York: McGraw-Hill.

Diamond, Peter. 1977. "Insurance Theoretic Aspects of Workers' Compensation," in Alan S. Blinder and Philip Friedman, eds., *Natural Resources, Uncertainty, and General Equilibrium Systems.* Essays in honor of Rafael Lusky. New York: Academic Press, 67–89.

Dickens, William T. 1984. "Differences Between Risk Premiums in Union and Nonunion Wages and the Case for Occupational Safety Regulation." *American Economic Review Papers and Proceedings* 74:320–23.

Dillingham, Alan E. 1985. "The Influence of Risk Variable Definition on Value of Life Estimates." *Economic Inquiry* 24:277–94.

Dorsey, Stuart. 1983. "Employment Hazards and Fringe Benefits: Further Tests for Compensating Differentials," in John D. Worrall, ed., *Safety and the Work Force: Incentives and Disincentives in Compensation.* Ithaca, N.Y.: Cornell Industrial and Labor Relations Press, 18–60.

Dorsey, Stuart, and Norman Walzer. 1983. "Workers' Compensation, Job Hazards, and Wages." *Industrial and Labor Relations Review* 36:642–54.

Duncan, Greg J. 1976. "Earnings Functions and Nonpecuniary Benefits." *Journal of Human Resources* 11:462–83.

Duncan, Greg J., and Bertil Holmlund. 1983. "Was Adam Smith Right After All? Another Test of the Theory of Compensating Wage Differentials." *Journal of Labor Economics* 1:366–79.

Duncan, Gregory M., and Duane E. Leigh. 1985. "The Endogeneity of Union Status: An Empirical Test." *Journal of Labor Economics* 3:385–402.

Ehrenberg, Ronald G. 1988. "Workers' Compensation, Wages, and the Risk of Injury," in John F. Burton, Jr., ed., *New Perspectives in Workers' Compensation.* Ithaca, N.Y.: Cornell Industrial and Labor Relations Press.

Farber, Henry S. 1986. "The Analysis of Union Behavior," in Orley Ashenfelter and Richard Layard eds., *Handbook of Labor Economics.* Amsterdam: North-Holland.

Fishback, Price V. 1987. "Liability Rules and Accident Prevention in the Workplace: Empirical Evidence from the Early Twentieth Century." *Journal of Legal Studies* 16:305–28.

Freeman, Richard. 1984. "Longitudinal Analyses of the Effects of Trade Unions." *Journal of Labor Economics* 2:1–26.

———. 1981. "The Effect of Unionism on Fringe Benefits." *Industrial and Labor Relations Review* 34:489–509.

———. 1980. "The Exit-Voice Tradeoff in the Labor Market: Unionism, Job Tenure, Quits, and Separations." *Quarterly Journal of Economics* 94:643–73.

———. 1976. "Individual Mobility and Union Voice in the Labor Market." *American Economic Review* 66:361–68.

Freeman, Richard, and Medoff, James. 1984. *What Do Unions Do?* New York: Basic Books.

Fuchs, Victor R. 1982. "Time Preference and Health: An Exploratory Study," in Fuchs, Victor, ed., *Economic Aspects of Health,* Chicago: University of Chicago Press.

Garen, John. 1988. "Compensating Differentials and the Endogeneity of Job Riskiness." *Review of Economics and Statistics* 70:9–16.

Gately, Dermot. 1980. "Individual Discount Rates and the Purchase and Utilization of Energy-Using Durables: Comment." *Bell Journal of Economics* 11: 373–76.

Gerking, Shelby, Menno de Haan, and William Shulze. 1988. "The Marginal Value of Job Safety: A Contingent Valuation Study." *Journal of Risk and Uncertainty* 1:185–200.

Hausman, Jerry. 1979. "Individual Discount Rates and the Purchase and Utilization of Energy-Using Durables." *Bell Journal of Economics* 10:33–54.

Hughes, James W. Forthcoming. "The Effect of Medical Malpractice Reform on Claim Disposition." *International Review of Law and Economics.*

Insurance Services Office. 1977. *Product Liability Closed Claims Survey: A Technical Analysis of Survey Results.* New York: Insurance Services Office.

Kahn, Shulamit, and Kevin Lang. 1988. "Efficient Estimation of Structural Hedonic Systems." *International Economic Review* 29:161–69.

Keeton, Robert E. 1971. *Basic Text on Insurance Law.* St. Paul: West Publishing.

Kniesner, Thomas J., and John D. Leeth. 1987. "Why Aren't OSHA and Workers' Compensation Insurance More Effective in Promoting Workplace Safety? A Numerical Analysis of Hedonic Labor Market Equilibrium." Center for the Study of Business Regulation Working Paper No. 87-8. Duke University.

Krueger, Alan B. 1988. "Moral Hazard in Workers' Compensation Insurance." Paper presented at Transatlantic Public Economics Seminar on the Future of the Welfare State.

Krueger, Alan B., and John F. Burton, Jr., 1988. "The Employers' Costs of Workers' Compensation Insurance: Magnitudes and Determinants." Working Paper.

————. 1983. "Interstate Differences in the Employers' Costs of Workers' Compensation: Magnitudes, Causes, and Cures." Working Paper. Cornell University.

Lang, Kevin, and Paul A. Ruud. 1986. "Returns to Schooling, Implicit Discount Rates, and Black-White Wage Differentials." *Review of Economics and Statistics* 48:41–47.

Larson, Arthur. 1988. *The Laws of Workmen's Compensation.* New York: Matthew Bender.

Lee, Lung-Fei. 1978. "Unionism and Wage Rates: A Simultaneous Equations Model with Qualitative and Limited Dependent Variables." *International Economic Review* 19:415–33.

Lillard, Lee, and W. Kip Viscusi. 1988. *A Structural Model of the Litigation Process.* Santa Monica, Cal.: Rand Co. Institute for Civil Justice.

McGraw-Hill. 1982. *Annual Survey of Investment in Employee Safety and Health.*

Mishan, E. J. 1971. "Evaluation of Life and Limb: A Theoretical Approach." *Journal of Political Economy* 79:687–705.

Moore, Michael J. 1988a. "The Impact of Measurement Error and Ability Bias on Estimates of Compensating Differentials." Center for the Study of Business Regulation Working Paper No. 87-5. Duke University.

————. 1988b. "Unions, Workers' Compensation, and Wages." Duke University Working Paper.

————. 1984. "Three Essays in Labor Economics." Ph.D. diss. University of Michigan.

Moore, Michael J., and W. Kip Viscusi. 1989. "Have Increases in Workers' Compensation Paid for Themselves?" in David Appel, ed., *Benefits, Costs, and Cycles in Workers' Compensation Insurance.* Norwood, Mass.: Kluwer Academic Publishers.

————. 1988a. "The Quantity Adjusted Value of Life." *Economic Inquiry.* 26: 369–88.

————. 1988b. "Doubling the Estimated Value of Life: Results Using New Occupational Fatality Data." *Journal of Policy Analysis and Management* 7: 476–90.

————. 1988c. "Promoting Safety Through Workers' Compensation: The Efficacy and Net Wage Costs of Injury Insurance." *Rand Journal of Economics,* forthcoming.

Oi, Walter. 1973. "Workmen's Compensation and Industrial Safety," in *Supplemental Studies for the National Commission on State Workmen's Compensation Laws,* 1. Washington, D.C.: U.S. Government Printing Office.

Olson, Craig A. 1981. "An Analysis of Wage Differentials Received by Workers on Dangerous Jobs." *Journal of Human Resources* 16:167–85.

Posner, Richard. 1973. "An Economic Approach to Legal Procedure and Judicial Administration." *Journal of Legal Studies* 2:399–458.

Price, Daniel N. 1984. "Workers' Compensation: 1976–80 Benchmark Revisions." *Social Security Bulletin* 47:3–23.

————. Annual report, 1976–1982 "Workers Compensation: Coverage, Benefits, and Costs." *Social Security Bulletin.*

Priest, George, and Benjamin Klein. 1984. "The Selection of Disputes for Litigation." *Journal of Legal Studies* 13:1–55.

Report of the National Commission on State Workmen's Compensation Laws. 1972. Washington, D.C.: U.S. Government Printing Office.

Rosen, Sherwin. 1988. "The Value of Changes in Life Expectancy." *Journal of Risk and Uncertainty* 1:285–304.

————. 1986. "The Theory of Equalizing Differences," in Orley Ashenfelter and Richard Layard eds., *Handbook of Labor Economics.* Amsterdam: North-Holland 1:641–92.

————. 1974. "Hedonic Prices and Implicit Markets: Product Differentiation in Pure Competition." *Journal of Political Economy* 82:34–55.

Rosenblum, Marcus, ed. 1973. *Compendium on Workmen's Compensation.* Washington, D.C.: U.S. Government Printing Office.

Ruser, John W. 1985a. "Workers' Compensation Insurance, Experience Rating, and Occupational Injuries." *Rand Journal of Economics* 16:487–503.

————. 1985b. "Workers' Compensation Benefits and Compensating Wage Differentials." Washington, D.C.: U.S. Bureau of Labor Statistics.

Shelling, Thomas. 1968. "The Life You Save May Be Your Own," in S. Chase, ed., *Problems in Public Expenditure Analysis*. Washington, D.C.: Brookings Institution.

Shepard, Donald, and Richard Zeckhauser. 1984. "Survival Versus Consumption." *Management Science* 30:423–39.

Smith, Adam. [1776] 1937. *The Wealth of Nations*. Reprint. New York: Modern Library.

Smith, Robert S. 1989. "Mostly on Monday: Is Workers' Compensation Covering Off-the-Job Injuries?" in David Appel, ed. *Benefits, Costs, and Cycles in Workers' Compensation Insurance*. Norwood, Mass.: Kluwer Academic Publishers.

———. 1979. "Compensating Wage Differentials and Public Policy: A Review." *Industrial and Labor Relations Review*. 32:339–52.

———. 1976. *The Occupational Safety and Health Act: Its Goals and Achievements*. Washington, D.C.: American Enterprise Institute.

Stokey, Edith, and Richard Zeckhauser. 1978. *A Primer for Policy Analysis*. New York: Norton.

Stewart, Richard. 1987. "The Role of Liability and Regulation in Controlling Enterprise Risks." Philadelphia: American Law Institute Project on Compensation and Liability for Product and Process Injuries.

Thaler, Richard, and Sherwin Rosen. 1976. "The Value of Saving a Life: Evidence from the Labor Market," in N. Terleckyj, ed., *Household Production and Consumption*. New York: Columbia University Press.

U.S. Bureau of Labor Statistics. 1979. *Occupational Injuries and Illness in the United States by Industry, 1976*. Bulletin 2019. Washington, D.C.: U.S. Dept. of Labor.

———. *Employment Compensation in the Private Nonfarm Economy, 1974 Summary 76-12*. Washington, D.C.: U.S. Government Printing Office, 3–4.

U.S. Chamber of Commerce. Various years. *Analysis of Workers' Compensation Laws*. Washington, D.C.: U.S. Chamber of Commerce.

U.S. Department of Commerce, Bureau of the Census. 1984. *State and Metropolitan Area Data Book*. Washington, D.C.: U.S. Government Printing Office.

U.S. Department of Health and Human Services. 1980. *Vital Statistics of the United States. 1978*, vol. II, sec. 5—Life Tables. DHHS Publication No. (PHS) 81-1104. Hyattsville, Md.: Public Health Service. National Center for Health Statistics.

Viscusi, W. Kip. 1989. "The Interaction between Product Liability and Workers' Compensation as Ex Post Remedies for Workplace Injuries." *Journal of Law, Economics, and Organization* 5:185–210.

———. 1988a. "Liability for Occupational Accidents and Illnesses," in R. Litan and C. Winston, eds., *Liability: Perspectives and Policy*. Washington, D.C.: Brookings Institution.

———. 1988b. "Product Liability and Regulation: Establishing an Appropriate Division of Labor." *American Economic Review Papers and Proceedings* 77:300–04.

———. 1988c. "Product Liability Litigation with Risk Aversion." *Journal of Legal Studies* 17:101–22.

———. 1986a. "The Determinants of the Disposition of Product Liability Claims and Compensation for Bodily Injury." *Journal of Legal Studies* 15:321–46.

———. 1986b. "The Valuation of Risks to Life and Health: Guidelines for Policy Analysis," in J.D. Bentkover, et al., eds., *Benefits Assessment: The State of the Art*. Proceedings of 1984 NSF Conference. Dordrecht, Holland: D. Reidel Publishing Co., 193–210.

———. 1986c. "The Impact of Occupational Safety and Health Regulation, 1973–1983." *Rand Journal of Economics* 17:567–80.

———. 1985. "Cotton Dust Regulation: An OSHA Success Story?" *Journal of Policy Analysis and Management* 4:325–43.

———. 1984. "Structuring an Effective Occupational Disease Policy: Victim Compensation and Risk Regulation." *Yale Journal on Regulation* 2:53–81.

———. 1983. *Risk by Choice: Regulating Health and Safety in the Workplace*. Cambridge, Mass.: Harvard University Press.

———. 1981. "Occupational Safety and Health Regulation: Its Impact and Policy Alternatives," in J. Crecine, ed. *Research in Public Policy Analysis and Management*, 2. Greenwich, Conn.: JAI Press.

———. 1980a. "A Theory of Job Shopping: A Bayesian Perspective." *Quarterly Journal of Economics* 94:609–14.

———. 1980b. "Imperfect Job Risk Information and Optimal Workmen's Compensation Benefits." *Journal of Public Economics* 14:319–37.

———. 1980c. "Self-Selection, Learning Induced Quits, and the Optimal Wage Structure." *International Economic Review* 21:529–46.

———. 1980d. "Sex Differences in Worker Quitting." *Review of Economics and Statistics* 62:388–98.

———. 1980e. "Unions, Labor Market Structure, and the Welfare Implications of the Quality of Work." *Journal of Labor Research* 1:175–92.

———. 1979a. *Employment Hazards: An Investigation of Market Performance*. Cambridge, Mass.: Harvard University Press.

———. 1979b. "Job Hazards and Worker Quit Rates: An Analysis of Adaptive Worker Behavior." *International Economic Review* 20:29–58.

———. 1978. "Wealth Effects and Earnings Premiums for Job Hazards." *Review of Economics and Statistics* 60:408–16.

Viscusi, W. Kip, and Michael J. Moore. Forthcoming a. "Rates of Time Preference and Valuations of the Duration of Life." *Journal of Public Economics*.

———. Forthcoming b. "Social Insurance in Market Contexts." in G. Dionne, ed., *Insurance Economics*.

———. 1988. "Differences in Wage-Workers' Compensation Tradeoffs as a Test of Worker Learning." Center for the Study of Business Regulation Working Paper No. 88-04. Duke University.

———. 1987. "Workers' Compensation: Wage Effects, Benefit Inadequacies, and the Value of Health Losses." *Review of Economics and Statistics* 69:249–61.

Viscusi, W. Kip, and Charles O'Connor. 1984. "Adaptive Responses to Chemical Labeling: Are Workers Bayesian Decision Makers?" *American Economic Review* 74:942–56.

Watkins, Nancy L., and John F. Burton, Jr. 1973. "Employers' Costs of Work-
men's Compensation," in *Supplemental Studies for the National Commission on
State Workmen's Compensation Laws*, 2. Washington, D.C.: U.S. Government
Printing Office, 217–40.

Weiler, Paul. 1986. *Compensation and Liability for Product and Process Injuries*.
American Law Institute, unpublished.

Weiss, Yoram. 1972. "The Risk Element in Occupational and Educational
Choices." *Journal of Political Economy* 80:1203–213.

Worrall, John D., ed. 1983. *Safety and the Work Force: Incentives and Disincentives
in Compensation*. Ithaca, N.Y.: Cornell Industrial and Labor Relations Press.

Worall, John D., and David Appel, eds. 1985. *Workers' Compensation Benefits:
Adequacy, Equity and Efficiency*. Ithaca, N.Y.: Cornell University Press.

Worrall, John D., and Richard J. Butler. 1985. "Some Lessons of Workers' Compensation." Paper presented at U.S. Department of Education Conference on
Disability.

Zeckhauser, Richard, and Donald Shepard. 1976. "Where Now for Saving
Lives?" *Law and Contemporary Problems* 40:5–45.

Index